EDUCATION AND SOCIAL CHANGE IN THE PEOPLE'S REPUBLIC OF CHINA

The Praeger Special Studies
Series in Comparative Education

Published in Cooperation with the Comparative
Education Center, State University of New York, Buffalo

General Editor: **Philip G. Altbach**

EDUCATION AND SOCIAL CHANGE IN THE PEOPLE'S REPUBLIC OF CHINA

John N. Hawkins

PRAEGER

PRAEGER SPECIAL STUDIES • PRAEGER SCIENTIFIC

Library of Congress Cataloging in Publication Data

Hawkins, John N.
    Education and social change in the People's
Republic of China.

    (Praeger special studies in comparative education)
    Bibliography: p.
    Includes index.
    1. Educational sociology—China.   2. Education and
state—China.   3. School management and organization—
China.   4. Education, Rural—China.   I. Title.
II. Series.
LC191.8.C5H38   1983   370.19′0951   83-6234
ISBN 0-03-059011-6

Published in 1983 by Praeger Publishers
CBS Educational and Professional Publishing
A Division of CBS, Inc.
521 Fifth Avenue, New York, New York 10175 U.S.A.

456789   052   98765432

Printed in the United States of America on acid-free paper

DEDICATED TO
MY WIFE, JUDI,
AND DAUGHTERS,
MARISA AND LARINA

PREFACE AND ACKNOWLEDGMENTS

Chinese educational policy and practice has captured the attention, admiration, criticism, and confusion of scholars of Chinese studies and education alike during the past three decades. Bold experiments have been contraposed with pragmatic conservatism. China's educational officials and leaders have sought to revolutionize education on the one hand, and institutionalize it on the other. Figures as diverse as Ivan Illich have praised China for "deschooling society" and contributing to progressive education everywhere, while others such as former Secretary of Health, Education and Welfare Joseph Califano were impressed with China's return to normalcy and convention in educational affairs. Egalitarians and elitists alike have found something to attract and repel them with respect to China's educational history since 1949, and we are left wondering how a society in the short span of less than 30 years, presumably espousing a common ideology, could draw such a wide-ranging base of support. The apparent contradictory interpretation of China's educational goals and objectives have inspired this study of the interaction of education and social change in China during the periods known as the Great Proletarian Cultural Revolution (1966-76) and the Four Modernizations Movement (1976-present).

Central to the wide-ranging educational policy shifts has been the Marxist concept of class struggle. During the Great Proletarian Cultural Revolution (hereafter referred as the GPCR), class struggle was treated as a key link as students, teachers, professors, and government officials were assessed according to a class stratification system worked out prior to the revolution (consisting of over 60 class designations). Critics of the GPCR revival of class struggle argue today that classes such as those that existed in prerevolutionary China have been eliminated, and therefore carrying out class struggle in the schools and other sectors of society is no longer necessary. This of course ignores the multigraded designations China's leaders have worked out for various professions (for example, a 12-grade system for professors, a 25-grade system for educational administrators, and so on), which effectively stratify Chinese society and will likely lead to more class conflict.*

---

*See Richard Curt Kraus, Class Conflict in Chinese Socialism (New York: Columbia University Press, 1981).

The political struggles that have characterized these two periods have been most intense in selected areas of education, not always the formal precollegiate and collegiate systems. The ten chapters of this study focus on these critical areas, including two background chapters and special interest chapters on administration and management, curricular reform, political socialization of China's youth, urban worker education, rural peasant education, education of national minorities, and teacher training. The study benefits greatly from the expertise of specialists in four of these areas, and I am fortunate to have been able to persuade them to contribute. The book as a whole was proposed to provide an introductory text to the field of comparative education with a focus on China. Many fine studies on Chinese education are available, and they are quoted throughout this study. This study fills a gap in the literature by comparing two important political periods through an analysis of broad educational issues. It is hoped that we have made a contribution to students of comparative education in general and education in China in particular.

This study has benefited from support given by both individuals and institutions. The UCLA Graduate School of Education has been very supportive by providing excellent manuscript preparation facilities through the Communications Processing Center; many thanks are due to Chris Carrillo and her staff. Margarette Lockwood, my assistant and secretary, has been with the manuscript since its beginnings — editing, proofing, typing, and assisting in rewriting portions — and her contributions have been essential to "getting the job done," always in good spirit. Financial support at UCLA was generously provided by the Spencer Foundation, administered through the dean's office in the Graduate School of Education, and through the Council on Comparative and International Studies. This support was utilized for travel to China, data collection, and research assistance. My thanks are extended to Dean John I. Goodlad of the Graduate School of Education and James S. Coleman, director of the Council on Comparative and International Studies. Portions of the study were supported by grants from the East-West Center in Honolulu, Hawaii. Particularly important were fellowships extended by the Resource Systems Institute through an Exxon education grant. Louis J. Goodman was responsible for administering the grant and provided me with both financial support and sage advice; I am very grateful for his continued colleagueship and encouragement. Bruce Koppel of the Resource Systems Institute took interest in my proposal for a study of human resource development and food for the city in Shanghai and was responsible for providing me with a fellowship to complete that study. I would like also to acknowledge John Dolfin and his staff at the University Service Centre in Hong Kong for providing access to library resources and other support facilities. Finally, at the University of Hawaii, Dean Andrew In, Chairman of Educational Foundations Shiro

Amioka, and Victor Kobeyashi and Edward Beauchamp of the Comparative Education department were most helpful in providing me with a visiting scholar appointment in the summer of 1982 to complete the first draft of the manuscript.

Graduate students have always provided one of the more critical sounding boards and sources of informed assistance for such studies. I would like to particularly thank my students in comparative and international education at UCLA who have listened to my arguments and opinions on developments in China over the years, sometimes agreeing and sometimes differing. I would especially like to thank Li Gebei, my research assistant over the past three years, for her help in locating, sorting, and displaying sources in Chinese and working with me on difficult translations and interpretations, and would also like to thank John Carroll and Mahmud Yahya for help in final editing and indexing.

I must also acknowledge the skill and fidelity with which Judith A. Takata prepared the graphics for the tables and figures in the text. And to Philip G. Altbach, general editor of the series of which this book is a part, I owe a debt for his constant support and encouragement throughout.

Finally, since my first visit to China in 1966 I have had the pleasure and honor of encountering many Chinese colleagues from both camps who have read my work, providing criticism and advice, who have consented to interviews and endless questions, and who in the end must be the ultimate judges of the appropriateness of my interpretations of educational events in China. Without their patience and openness, I and the other authors in this study would have been unable to participate in and learn about the many experiments and changes that have taken place during the past three decades in education in China.

NOTE ON EDUCATIONAL STATISTICS

Throughout this manuscript various educational statistics (numbers of schools, students, enrollment and dropout rates, etc.) are referred to either in the text or in tabular or graphic form. The gathering and interpretation of statistical data in China has always been a difficult task for Chinese officials and foreign scholars alike. The statistics used in this study have been garnered from many sources both official and unofficial. The Ministry of Education occasionally provides educational data, the World Bank recently conducted a study, and scholars from such prestigious institutions as Beijing Normal University have compiled their own data. With this in mind it should be noted that educational statistics have been used in this study to provide the reader with trends rather than precise figures. Efforts have been made to cross-check the various numbers released by the Chinese government with those gathered through independent studies.

CONTENTS

LIST OF TABLES, FIGURES, AND MAPS

xiii

ACRONYMS

BBC	British Broadcasting Company
BJRB	Beijing Ribao (Peking Daily)
CCP	Chinese Communist Party
CTN	China Trip Notes (notes and interviews from research trips in China during year indicated)
CYL	Chinese Youth League
FBIS	Foreign Broadcast Information Service
FYP	Five-Year Plan
GLF	Great Leap Forward
GPCR	Great Proletarian Cultural Revolution
JPRS	Joint Publications Research Service (U.S. Government Translation Service)
NCNA	New China News Agency (same as Xinhua)
NPC	National People's Conference
PLA	People's Liberation Army
PRC	People's Republic of China
SCMP	Survey China Mainland Press

PRONUNCIATION OF
CHINESE WORDS AND NAMES

The <u>pinyin</u> system of pronunciation is used throughout the text.

Initials

q	= <u>ch</u>eer	u	= r<u>u</u>de
x	= <u>sh</u>ip	u	= German ü
z	= rea<u>ds</u>	ai	= I
c	= tha<u>t's</u>	ao	= n<u>ow</u>
zh	= lar<u>ge</u>	eng	= s<u>ung</u>
r	= leisu<u>re</u>	ou	= <u>ol</u>d

Finals

o	= s<u>aw</u>
e	= French le
i	= mach<u>i</u>ne
ia	= <u>ya</u>h
ian	= <u>ye</u>n
iang	= young
uai	= <u>wif</u>e
ui	= way
uan	= one

The Praeger Special Studies
Series in Comparative Education

General Editor: *Philip G. Altbach*

ACADEMIC POWER: Patterns of Authority
in Seven National Systems of Higher Education
  John H. van de Graaff; Dietrich Goldschmidt; Burton R. Clark;
  Donald F. Wheeler; Dorotea Furth

ADAPTATION AND EDUCATION IN JAPAN
  Nobuo K. Shimahara

CHANGES IN THE JAPANESE UNIVERSITY:
A Comparative Perspective
  edited by: William K. Cummings; Ikuo Omano; Kazuyuki Kitamura

COMPARATIVE PERSPECTIVES
ON THE ACADEMIC PROFESSION
  edited by: Philip G. Altbach

FUNDING HIGHER EDUCATION: A Six-Nation Analysis
  edited by: Lyman A. Glenny

US AND UK EDUCATIONAL POLICY: A Decade of Reform
  Edgar Litt, Michael Parkinson

UNIVERSITY AND GOVERNMENT IN MEXICO:
Autonomy in an Authoritarian System
  Daniel C. Levy

PUBLISHING IN THE THIRD WORLD:
Trend Report and Bibliography
  Philip G. Altbach, Eva-Maria Rathgeber.

UNIVERSITIES AND THE INTERNATIONAL
DISTRIBUTION OF KNOWLEDGE
  edited by: Irving J. Spitzberg, Jr.

STUDYING TEACHING AND LEARNING:
Trends in Soviet and American Research
  edited by: Robert Tabachnick; Thomas S. Popkewitz;
  Beatrice Beach Szekely

INTERNATIONAL BIBLIOGRAPHY OF
COMPARATIVE EDUCATION
    Philip G. Altbach, Gail P. Kelly, David H. Kelly

SYSTEMS OF HIGHER EDUCATION IN TWELVE COUNTRIES:
A Comparative View
    Nell P. Eurich

ADULT EDUCATION AND TRAINING IN
INDUSTRIALIZED COUNTRIES
    Richard E. Peterson, John S. Helmick, John R. Valley,
    Sally Shake Gaff, Robert A. Feldmesser, H. Dean Nielsen

WOMEN'S EDUCATION IN DEVELOPING COUNTRIES:
Opportunities and Outcomes
    Audrey Chapman Smock

THE SCIENCE PROFESSION IN THE THIRD WORLD:
Studies from India and Kenya
    Thomas Owen Eisemon

NONFORMAL EDUCATION AND NATIONAL DEVELOPMENT:
A Critical Assessment of Policy, Research, and Practice
    John Charles Bock and George John Papagiannis

EDUCATION IN THE ARAB WORLD
    Byron G. Massialas and Samir Ahmed Jarrar

CHANGING SCHOOLS
International Lessons for Reform
    John Simmons

EDUCATION AND SOCIAL CHANGE
IN THE PEOPLE'S REPUBLIC OF CHINA
    John N. Hawkins

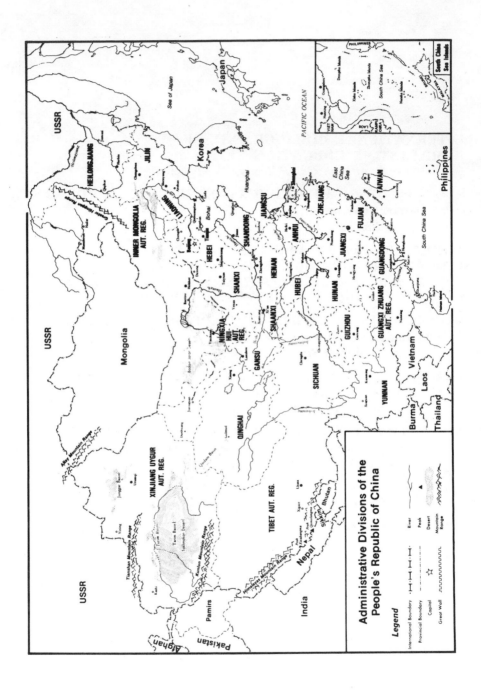

Administrative Divisions of the People's Republic of China

Legend

International Boundary

Provincial Boundary

Capital ☆

Great Wall ∿∿∿∿∿∿

River

Peak ▲

Desert

Mountain Range ∿∿∿∿∿

PART I
THE CONTEXT

1

EDUCATION AND SOCIAL CHANGE IN CHINA—AN INTRODUCTION

J.N. Hawkins

Historically, all cultures and societies have provided some form of education, whether formal or nonformal. These forms have ranged from traditional rites of passage to more formal and institutionalized educational systems that, in some cases, have become unnecessarily elaborate and bureaucratic in their goals, structure, and objectives. Whether we are discussing informal education, such as a rite of passage, or the highly formalized mechanisms of advanced degree programs, all systems of education operate implicitly or explicitly with a set of pedagogical objectives and orientation toward social change. In China the historical record is rather thorough regarding the role and function of education in society for the past 2,500 years. This chapter briefly establishes the context for education and social change in China by providing a short historical background, discusses current (post-1949) Chinese educational development against the more recent literature on education and social change, and finally sets the theme regarding education and social change for the chapters that follow through a brief discussion of the political, economic, and demographic context.

THE HISTORICAL CONTEXT

The Chinese word for education in many respects sums up historically how various Chinese governments and officials have defined the role of education in society. The first character of the compound jiao yu carries the literal meaning of "to teach,

3

educate, guide"; the second character (yu) means "to rear, nurture, nourish." Together, they form the concept of education that contains a cognitive aspect of imparting information, transmitting data, and acquiring skills, combined with the affective notion of moral and value education. Cognitive and affective education has been conducted in China in both formal and nonformal educational institutions. Formal educational institutions have consisted of village schools, academies, and institutes and, today, form a network of precollegiate, collegiate, and research institutions. Nonformal efforts in education have included tutoring programs, on-site educational efforts (in the family setting, at the work site), and currently refer to a widespread program of half-work, half-study schools, spare-time schools in factories and communes, and a variety of nonformal skill-transfer projects related to China's industrialization and development process. In all cases, however, there has been an explicit effort to link the acquisition of practical skills with correct value orientations in order to fulfill service to a larger cause. Whether the basic reason for studying was to become an official during the Confucian period, or to serve the people as during the past three decades, the sense of national service or mission was always present.

Four traditional (pre-1911 revolution) historical periods stand out as critically important in establishing the historical context of the role of education in society in China. The early period of the Zhou dynasty (500-200 B.C.) saw the emergence of a set of moral codes, later broadly termed Confucian, that focused on social relationships such as those between parents and children, brothers and sisters, and subject and emperor. Because the codes involved social behavior, they could be taught and Confucianism, in particular, emphasized the power of education to improve society and teach citizenship in both an intellectual and moral sense. By providing a model that people could emulate, education could transform society; to educate meant to change both the individual and the social system of which he was a part. The model had two main functions before the innate goodness (ren) of man could be brought forth: first, to provide peace and prosperity; and, second, to provide moral training and education."(1) Thus, the rationale was provided for considering education as a primary goal of the just society. Confucius suggested that, "in education there should be no class distinctions" (you jiao wu lei), thus laying the theoretical groundwork for a broadly based educational system designed to both maintain social stability and provide opportunities for individual achievement and change.(2) While social mobility was not widespread on a national scale, there were cases sufficient in number of merit that considered Chinese traditional education a system based on achievement value rather than ascription.

During the second major period of the Han dynasty (200 B.C.-220 A.D.), intellectuals and scholars assumed new roles as government advisers and officials. During this period, scholar officials grew to become the dominant social force in government. When Confucianism was decreed to be the official ideology, state universities or academies were established, along with a competitive civil service examination, which, in turn, served as a catalyst for whatever education existed at that time. The establishment of the examination system ensured the continual reproduction of the scholar elite, a segment of the ruling group.(3) The educational system thus established then became directly linked to national and local governmental activities; on the one hand, it was a creature of the official bureaucracy and, on the other hand, it provided the dynamic force for whatever social change occurred at that time.

The Song dynasty (A.D. 960-1279) represented, in some respects, a Confucian revival, as ideas formulated more than a thousand years previously were reaffirmed and discussed anew. Movable type was invented during this period, facilitating the widespread use of books and thus providing an impetus to educational development. Academies were established, and urbanization created the desire for new ideas.(4) With the new emphasis on learning and knowledge, an educational system was designed to prepare students for the more specialized civil service degrees. The idea of education as a social change agent and the belief that correct knowledge could transform human society firmly established the dynamic social change role perceived for formal education.(5) As a result of this pedagogical position held by the central government, proposals were formulated for the establishment of a national school system from the district level to the capital, in order to facilitate training of civil servants and other government personnel.(6)

The fourth major period of educational change and development occurred during the Qing dynasty (1644-1912). This period, which directly preceded the formation of the Republic of China and the subsequent "modernization" period, witnessed many scholars rejecting some of the idealism of the neo-Confucians, thus opening the way for a more scientific approach to the examination of questions of knowledge and learning. Against this background, education became more involved with problem solving, while retaining the philosophical idealism of Confucianism.(7) As the West and Japan began to threaten the centuries-old internal solidarity of the Chinese scholar class, it became apparent that to preserve some semblance of Confucian values and norms, concessions would have to be made to bring about a revitalized educational system more conducive to the needs of modernization and social change. From 1860 to 1905, the aim of education shifted from emphasis on the reproduction of a scholar class well versed in the classics to a new aim that subscribed some importance to Western learning. Modernization of the school system, however, took place primarily at the top, where some selected Western-style technical schools were established essentially for the purpose of training military personnel.(8)

The military defeat of the Chinese in the Sino-Japanese war (1894-95), the decline and fall of the Qing dynasty in 1911, and the establishment of the Republic of China in 1912 brought an abrupt end to an educational system that had endured for over 2,000 years. The examination system was abolished in 1905; increasing numbers of Chinese scholars traveled abroad and returned with new ideas regarding the role and function of education. For the next few decades Chinese educators and officials experimented with different forms of education borrowed primarily from Japan, the United States, and Germany. The Second World War, and the ongoing conflict between the Nationalist government and the Chinese Communists, created chaotic conditions during the period 1930-49; there was a distinct lack of any well-articulated policy regarding the role of education in society. However, the position that emerges historically clearly places education in a dynamic relationship with Chinese society by providing training functions, value orientation, and social change activities. Yet this system operated within boundaries and was never seen as an institution that could seriously challenge the status quo. The debates, as to the degree to which education should serve a systems maintenance function as opposed to promoting significant social change, became especially visible during the past three decades. Before discussing the modern period, it will be useful to briefly review some of the current literature on the relationship between education and social change to set the stage for analyzing China's recent efforts to reach a consensus on this issue.

EDUCATION AND SOCIAL CHANGE THEORIES: IMPLICATIONS FOR CHINESE EDUCATION

In recent years, important works have appeared that attempt to categorize typologically the relationship between education and social change. A classical typology of social change theory, which was used as the base for many of these efforts, is that of R. Applebaum.(9) In this scheme, four basic clusters of social change theory emerge. The first falls under the category of evolutionary theory (also termed Darwinian, or organismic, and modernization theory). According to this perception, all social change represents movement from the simple to the more complex. Thus societies change in a linear direction, becoming more complex along a scale of indicators reflecting industrialization factors. Societies then can be undeveloped, developing, and developed, as is reflected in much of the modernization literature.

The second major category of equilibrium theory incorporates the concept of homeostasis (also called functionalism, systems theory, cultural lag theory, and human exology theory). The emphasis here is on stability, harmony, and maintenance of balance in all societal affairs. Changes occur, but society must possess mechanisms to restore balance when disequilibrium is present. Any change that does occur, then, is "adaptive" change, which arises due to outside pressures.

The third category of conflict theory also falls under the heading of Marxist or neo-Marxist theories. Unlike the equilibrium model, conflict models hold to the basic premise that change is endemic to all societies due to internal irreconcilable contradictions. Those aspects of society that are in contradiction to one another often explode into violent conflict, the outcome being a new configuration containing its own internal contradictions and then the entire process begins anew.

The final category is termed "rise and fall" theories (theories of decay or cyclical theory). According to this model, societies indeed change, but both forward and backward in no particular direction. In the case of China, dynastic cycles have been a major theme in explaining China's traditional past, and cyclical theory applied to China in the modern era can also be found.(10)

These four basic theories of social change have been adapted and reapplied to the activity of education in order to place education in the context of larger social change concepts. The more significant works in this area are those of Rolland Paulston and of Thomas J. LaBelle and Robert E. Verhine.(11) The latter work perhaps best summarizes the voluminous literature on the subject of education and social change, and on a theoretical level develops two major categories. The first major category, termed "holistic" by the authors, includes various forms of systems theory (e.g., cybernetic, conflict, and functionalism). Under this scheme, the unit of analysis, whether it is macro (such as a society or culture) or micro (such as an educational system) is conceived of as a system having distinct boundaries and internal characteristics.

This holds true even for the conflict paradigm, which despite its name nevertheless presupposes stability and order. Systems theory has numerous implications for education, both formal and non-formal. The fundamental implication is that it serves an integrative function by providing the information, knowledge, and skills needed to facilitate a nation's political and economic development. Like-wise, if the conflict perspective is adopted, education can serve a dynamic function by expanding the boundaries of the system through the process of resolving contradictions. In both cases, education is seen as part of a larger system, change is viewed primarily in an institutional context, and the system is characterized by inter-dependence.

The second major category discussed by LaBelle and Verhine is called the "man-oriented" approach. Theories clustered under this scheme focus on the individual as the unit of analysis with an emphasis on psychological variables. The authors identify two major models: the psychodynamic (focusing on the individual's internal state) and the behavioral (an all-encompassing framework accounting for change through a variety of stimulus-response patterns). In both cases, however, the emphasis is on the individual and personality, and social change, political-economic development, and other forms of innovation will occur only after individuals change; thus, the schools have an important role to play in this personality change process.

In attempting to apply these various theories and their educational implications to China, it appears there are elements of several social change theories present in theoretical statements issued in China since 1949. The commitment to Marxist-Leninist ideology and to various interpretations of Mao Zedong's thought has meant that social change theory in China falls under the holistic category discussed above and, more specifically, an evolutionary form of that theory. All of China's leaders since 1949 have emphasized the goal of modernization and have suggested that this is the natural tendency among nations. They, of course, have disagreed on how to modernize most efficiently, but the goal has remained an important component of developmental planning for three decades. They have also expressed a tendency to view China's political-economic configuration in a systems perspective with all components interdependent and, ideally, functioning smoothly.

While the goal may have been development and change through a smoothly functioning social order, the process to achieve the goal has been the subject of radical and, at times, violent disagreement. The disagreement has been found among those groups who believed that the goals referred to above would best be reached through an ongoing conflict between differing social classes and/or their representatives and those groups who believed that the goals would be reached through an emphasis on cooperation, harmony, and equilibrium within the system.

During periods such as the Great Proletarian Cultural Revolution (GPCR), the former group focused on conflict and even tended to lean toward a psychodynamic approach with an emphasis on building the new socialist man as the focal point for continuing social change. During periods such as the current Four Modernizations Movement, the emphasis has been on balancing various elements of the system (including education) in order to achieve a conflict-free social order designed for rapid modernization. The focus, thus, must be on unity, harmony, and stability. A particular kind of person, such as the new socialist man, is not especially important; or, according to China's current leader Deng Xiaoping, the color of the cat does not matter — what matters is whether or not he catches mice.

Depending on which view prevailed, education occupied varying positions and was perceived as fulfilling different functions and roles. During the GPCR the fundamental premise regarding education was that the schools should become a large classroom for the study of Mao Zedong's thoughts. In practice, this meant that the class struggle being waged in the society as a whole would also be waged in the schools. Previous educational policies were criticized, the notion that education was above politics was reviled, and the institution of education was seen as an instrument of the dictatorship of the proletariat and an appropriate arena for promoting the interests of the urban industrial workers and the rural peasantry.(12)

In the context of the discussion above, the institution of education was viewed as one component of the social superstructure, thus reflecting the ongoing contradictions and conflicts of the economic base. For example, during the GPCR, a great deal of emphasis was placed on the need to continue the revolution against those who would "revise" Marxism-Leninism and Mao Zedong's thought (revisionists) on the one hand, and remnants of previous class enemies on the other. In short, the class struggle was not yet over despite the existence of a socialist political economy. Contradictions continued to exist in China's political economy and only through conflict could they be resolved. In this view, then, education was seen as a reflection of the tensions and conflicts that existed in the political-economic base, rather than an autonomous or semiautonomous social institution.

While much of this analysis has been recently rejected in China, the current leadership has not reached a clear conclusion on precisely what role education should play and what position the institution occupies with respect to China's political-economic base. Some Chinese writers continue to hold the view that education is basically a reflection of the political-economic base and, as such, can not be separated from political struggle.(13) But this view is being eclipsed by a more extended analysis on the possible alternative explanations of the role of education vis-a-vis the superstructure. Several writers have indicated that education is a complicated social phenomenon that does not fall neatly into any one theoretical category (conflict, systems, or psychodynamic). Education includes both ideological factors and material outcomes; it is involved not only with the transmission of ideological and intellectual values, but with the reproduction of labor power.

The debate thus far has centered on five competing views of the role of education with respect to the political-economic base. The first is a direct descendent of GPCR thinking and states flatly that education is an extension and reflection of the political-economic superstructure and is thus an instrument of class struggle.

The second opinion is that education plays a dual role, both a reflection of the political-economic base and, somehow, beyond or transcending it. Those aspects that transcend the base are knowledge content areas that have elements that are common to all social classes and thus are beyond class struggle (e.g., the natural sciences, objective truths of the social sciences, physical education, educational organization and management, and the psychological laws of child development). In this view, education as a whole is still part of the political-economic base, but has some aspects that transcend the base.

In the third view, it is stated that there are clearly two separate roles for education: the ideological role that clearly belongs to the superstructure and is a reflection of it, and the academic, intellectual role of skill and knowledge transmission that is completely separate and independent. This second aspect may be influenced by the political-economic base but, in turn, exerts an equal influence, and thus plays a role in transforming the base.

The fourth model suggests that the institution of education is analogous to the political-economic base and functions under its own laws and internal contradictions much in the same manner as does the political-economic system. Education in this view functions as a productive force in society, reproducing labor power and possessing its own dynamic forces. "Investment in education," then, becomes a priority in the same manner that investment in agriculture, industry, or commerce is a priority.

The fifth and final model presents a much more complex interpretation. In essence, it says that education contains elements of all of the above with the exception of the first view. Education is closely interwoven with all aspects of social life and is not primarily associated with any particular political-economic model. The fundamental purpose of education is to "train qualified personnel" for all aspects of social life. Education is not an instrument of the dictatorship of the proletariat, nor merely a reflection of the political-economic base; nor is it a separate and independent force. The best slogan to characterize the role of education under current conditions is "education must serve socialist modernization," which, in effect, means it is as complicated and, at times, as vague in purpose as that phenomenon called modernization.(14) Other writers have been more precise, stating simply that education during an intense modernization drive is essentially another important productive force transmitting the critical tools and skills to increase productivity and reproduce the labor force.(15) In any case, the dominant trend is toward viewing education from a systems approach clearly divorced from the conflict paradigm and focused on increasing productivity through stability and harmony. The notion that the schools are an instrument of class struggle is now flatly rejected.

We thus can identify two broad schools of thought regarding education and social change in China, each reflected in major political-economic movements. The first focuses on conflict as the primary means to assure the continued movement toward achieving the holistic goals of socialism and communism and was most evident during the GPCR. The second, while discussed in more complex language, nevertheless is clear on the need to view education and social change in a more functional way, that is, designed to fit together in such a manner as to proceed on an orderly, disciplined, and efficient track toward the goals of modernization. How these two views were operationalized during the past 15 years is the topic of the chapters that follow.

Although Chapter 2 will provide a more in-depth picture of the structure of the educational system and details regarding its various components, this section will briefly establish the main features of China's political economy as it relates to the educational system.

THE POLITICAL-ECONOMIC-DEMOGRAPHIC CONTEXT

The development of all aspects of education in China since 1949 has been embedded in the complex interactions of the political and economic system generally termed state socialism.(16) Structurally, the political system can be subdivided into two broad levels: the central government and local government. The central level consists of the National People's Congress (NPC), a standing committee of the NPC, the Supreme People's Court, the State Council and the various ministries under the State Council (see Figure 1.1).(17)

The NPC is an elected body with representatives from each province and autonomous region. Members stand for election every five years; however, the term of office has been extended during political crises. In 1978, the fifth NPC reportedly consisted of 26.7 percent workers, 20.6 percent peasants, 15 percent intellectuals, 14.4 percent People's Liberation Army (PLA), 13.4 percent revolutionary cadres, 10.9 percent national minorities, 9 percent other (e.g., overseas Chinese).(18)

The most politically significant administrative body at this level, however, is the State Council. The State Council has direct control over each of the various ministries, is headed by a premier and several vice-premiers, and generally provides direction for the day-to-day work of the ministries, offices, and commissions, in accordance with guidance and policies provided by the Chinese Communist Party. With respect to education, the Ministry of Education falls under the State Council and has overall responsibility for the national university system and general implementation of national educational policy for the precollegiate level (in Chapter 2 the role of the Ministry will be discussed in more detail). Nationally sponsored entrance examinations for key secondary schools and for universities and colleges are also a responsibility of the Ministry, as is overall coordination with other educational bodies such as research centers, curriculum development groups, and other ministries.

The second level of government consists of autonomous regions, provinces, and centrally administered cities. Below these divisions are a variety of rural urban division such as cities, prefectures, counties (xian), townships, communes (production brigades and teams), and urban districts (street offices, residents' committees).

Figure 1.1 PRC Government Organization Chart

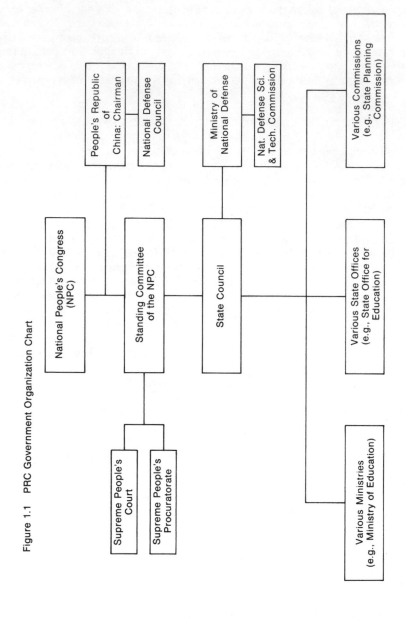

Responsibility for educational levels corresponds with the level of administration. For example, some colleges and universities are operated at the autonomous region, provincial and centrally governed city levels. Urban districts and street offices will have responsibility for secondary, primary, and day-care education as will communes and production brigades. The entire apparatus from the central level is designed to facilitate the implementation of national economic plans jointly designed by the Central Government and the Chinese Communist Party (CCP). The establishment of more efficient informational linkages, from the top to the bottom and back again, has been a major priority of the Chinese government since 1949, and the question of centralization versus decentralization has perhaps been at the forefront of policy debates between central government officials, CCP members, and local level representatives. The two political periods constituting the focus of this volume represent extremely divergent views on this question and in the following chapters the implications for education will emerge more clearly.

Mention has been made of the Chinese Communist Party. It should be noted that the CCP is the primary political organization in China, linking vertically and horizontally with both the central and local government levels discussed above. Decisions regarding all aspects of policy, including educational policy, are formulated in the CCP and communicated to each of the non-Party government offices where they are acted upon. CCP members and cadres permeate all aspects of Chinese society and, when in the form of small groups, can even extend into the individual classroom.(19) Structurally, the organization of the CCP can be seen in Figure 1.2. While the CCP has been of paramount importance in the past three decades, there have been periods, such as the GPCR, where its authority was severely eroded and alternative organizations emerged (e.g., the three-in-one committees of the GPCR). However, despite these anomalies, China's leaders have never suggested that the CCP should be abandoned and, indeed, the role of the Party today is of increasing importance.

A major role played by both the governmental apparatus and the CCP is to organize, design, and eventually transmit economic plans, plans which contain the general and specific goals and objectives for China's vast educational enterprise. China's economy is a subject of much controversy in terms of providing basic understanding, as is the interpretation of its performance over the past 30 years as well. Several studies are available that are useful for an introduction to this subject.(20) The purpose here is to illustrate historically the linkages between the economic system, the government, and the Party and to outline some of the main features of economic planning as related to education since 1949. The general model of planning as it relates to education will be discussed in Chapter 2.

Figure 1.2   Chinese Communist Party Organization Chart

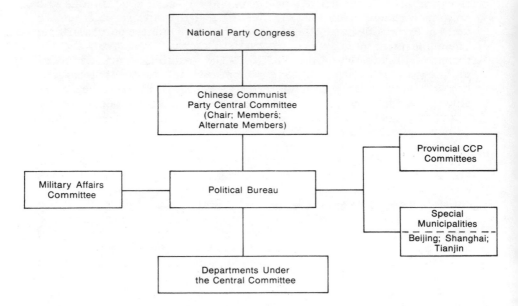

The first Five-Year Plan (FYP) was announced in 1953 and represented a development strategy borrowed primarily from the Soviet Union. It focused on heavy industry for the urban sector and a gradual transformation of agriculture based on large-scale farms for the rural sector. In addition, the plan rested on a highly centralized political-economic apparatus with low levels of participation at the local government level. In education, schools were reorganized along Soviet patterns, curricula uncritically translated from Russian, and the training of high level technical personnel the priority. This program was discredited in 1957 and the second FYP launched.

This plan was intended for the period 1958-62, but a mass political economic movement in 1958, known as the Great Leap Forward (GLF), interrupted the intended progress of the plan. The GLF continued to place an emphasis on heavy industry but was balanced with the large-scale mobilization of marginal resources and small-scale technology. Communes developed in the rural sector and a variety of nonformal worker and peasant educational programs were inaugurated. Following the decline of the GLF (1960), the plan continued but with more emphasis on tight financial and quality control of output.

The third FYP (1966-70) was totally eclipsed by the GPCR. Despite the chaos of this period, especially in the early stages, an economic position emerged that continues to influence planners today. Decentralization and self-reliance with support for appropriate technology became the leading economic goal of the late 1960s and early 1970s. The emphasis on local "self-reliance" meant, however, that there was a virtual total abandonment of long-range planning, including technical and scientific research and development (R & D) activities.

The emphasis on decentralization also had an enormous impact on the educational system. Economic dislocation, plus the political turmoil caused by the deaths of many of China's top leadership (Mao Zedong, Zhou Enlai, Zhu De), brought about the advent of a new political administration and economic policy currently called the Four Modernizations Movement. In 1978, a new Ten-Year Plan was announced, designed to hasten the development of agriculture, industry, national defense, and science and technology. Under this plan, an emphasis on order predominates, in contrast to the conflict of the previous ten years. Efforts are being made to rationalize all economic sectors and bring education into closer articulation with economic goals and objectives. Quality education has been stressed, high-achievement classes have been developed in special schools, and entrance examinations have been emphasized at both the secondary and tertiary levels.

The most current assessment of the relationship between education and the political-economic structure in China focuses on the need to raise the quality of China's human resources in such a way as to provide a closer fit between the output of the educational system and the technological needs of China's expanding economy. In a recent survey, it was noted that although quantitatively China's school-age cohort is large, only a fraction of this group continues on to higher educational levels and, in general, the skill and overall knowledge level of China's working population is low.(21) The survey showed that 40.2 percent of a sample of workers and staff from 26 provinces, autonomous regions, and municipalities have an educational achievement level below that of junior middle school (8.2 percent are illiterate or semiliterate). The survey continues to point out that a massive worker and staff educational program will be necessary to prepare the work force for the political and economic plan of the Four Modernizations. It is clear, in any case, that education is generally viewed as a mechanism to facilitate political-economic planning and the achievement of the goals and objectives articulated in the various plans. China's leadership has not always been in agreement on how this articulation should occur, although during both periods under investigation (GPCR and Four Modernizations), it was clear that education should follow the politics and economics of the leading group in power at the time. The disagreement, as we shall see, was on the emphasis placed on education, whether primarily serving politics or education, or primarily serving economics.

Perhaps the most striking feature of educational development in China, however, is the sheer numbers involved and the relationship between population and overall land resources and distribution. China's area is third in size after the USSR and Canada, and almost the same as the United States (9.6 million square kilometers for China, 9.5 for the United States). Spatially, China's population is clustered on about 45 percent of the land and only 12 percent of the land is cultivatable. Urban centers are overcrowded, yet over 80 percent of the population resides in rural areas. Although family planning programs have been an official component of China's overall development planning strategy, since 1954 the population has continued to grow at a rate ranging from 23 per thousand in 1971 to 12 per thousand in 1978.(22)

China's family planners are seeking a zero population-growth rate sometime near the year 2,000, but limiting fertility has been a continual problem. Since the early 1950s, the Chinese have utilized both educational alternatives and formal educational structures to introduce and transmit family planning messages. These efforts were found to be of limited utility until accompanied by significant structural reform in the health-care network. The expansion of the rural paramedic program in the 1960s and its continuation today (with an emphasis on upgrading the quality and training of rural health workers) has been a major factor in contributing to the declining birthrate.

Equally critical to China's efforts in fertility control have been the enormous social and economic reforms that have occurred since

1949 and have provided the base upon which an effective family planning program could be built. The reorganization of Chinese society, the increased efficiency of developmental planning, the rising level of literacy and general knowledge, changes in land tenure and economic activities, and the development of the commune structure have all contributed to changing attitudes toward receiving and implementing family planning information.

For educational planners, the relatively successful family planning program has not solved the immediate problem of the enormous school-age cohort. It is estimated that about 25 percent or 250,000,000 children are between the ages of 5-15. Another 20 percent or 200,000,000 young people between the ages of 15-25 bring the total elementary, secondary, and tertiary cohort to 450,000,000 people. The implications of this large number, in terms of teacher preparation, physical plant, curricular materials, classroom size, and so on, are such that the population question is at the forefront of all China's educational planning and policy discussions. The population size is a fundamental element in the context in which education is discussed and analyzed. It is clearly a major priority of China's leadership, regardless of which administration has been in power. Although family planning education has not been a major feature of the formal educational structure, there has been discussion that it might be included in future curricular reforms.(23)

Finally, another major demographic feature of considerable importance to China's educational planners is the ethnic composition of China's population. Although a thorough discussion of China's educational policy toward minorities is found in Chapter 7, it is worth noting in an introductory manner that 94 percent of the population can be classified as Han Chinese (ethnic Chinese), but the remaining 6 percent comprise a critical group located in strategic regions of the country. Their locations, cultures, languages, and social structure have presented China's leaders with a variety of sensitive educational, cultural, and linguistic dilemmas.

In general, China's leadership has attempted to grant a certain amount of autonomy to each of the groups while insisting they remain an integral part of China's overall political economy. At times special educational programs have been enacted for the minorities and at other times efforts have been made to pull them into the mainstream of Han educational policy and practice. Thus, although the numbers of minority members may appear small, the educational policy issue has loomed large, especially since the mid-1960s.

CONCLUSION

The discussion above has painted with broad strokes a picture of China's response to the dynamic linkage between schools and society. There exists a historical legacy that clearly establishes the importance of education to both social and individual change, and, since 1949, the precise nature of this relationship has been hotly debated. China's response to the education and social change relationship does not fall neatly into a particular theoretical category. However, the policies and practices that have characterized the past 30 years have not been random; for at least the past 15 years, policies can be closely identified with the conflict and functional paradigms discussed above.

The nature of the political-economic structure and the planning process have also contributed to the sharpness of the debates that have occurred since 1949, especially as they relate to a tendency toward conflict or harmony in seeking solutions in China's developmental problems. And all of this has been complicated by the enormity of the demographic problems facing China's leaders. Chapter 2 will focus more thoroughly on the educational structure, levels of authority, and school cohort characteristics. The remainder of the chapters in Part II will analyze eight critical educational issues as they have been identified and acted upon during two contrasting and conflicting periods.

The differing perceptions of education and social change held by China's leaders during these two periods are reflective of those discussed by leaders in many developing and industrialized countries. A close look at these debates, in one of the world's largest and most strategic nations, may place in clearer perspective the various costs and benefits of each approach.

NOTES

(1)   William Theodore de Bary, Wing-tsit Chan, and Burton Watson, eds., Sources of Chinese Tradition (New York: Columbia University Press, 1960), p. 147.

(2)   Ho Ping-ti, "Salient Aspects of China's Heritage," in China in Crisis: China's Heritage and the Communist Political Tradition, ed. Ho Ping-ti and Tang Tsou (Chicago: University of Chicago Press, 1968), p. 27. The phrase you jiao wu lei was more theoretical than real. It is questionable whether lei should be subscribed as the same meaning as the modern sociological term "class." As Derke Bodde comments (Ibid., p. 55), Ho perhaps overidealized the Confucian ideal of social equity with regard to education. Education was never seriously intended to reach a significantly broad section of the population.

(3)   de Bary, Chan, and Watson, Sources of Chinese Tradition, p. 148; Michael Loewe, Imperial China: The Historical Background to the Modern Age (New York: Praeger, 1965), p. 77.

(4)   Ibid., p. 481.

(5)   T.I. Dow, "Neo-Confucian Philosophical Systems and Mao's Theory of Multiple Contradictions" (paper delivered at the Tenth Annual Southwestern Regional Conference of the Association of Asian Studies, Rock Hill, South Carolina, January 1971), p. 2.

(6)   de Bary, Chan, and Watson, Sources of Chinese Tradition, p. 481.

(7)   Joseph R. Levenson, Modern China and Its Confucian Past (New York: Doubleday, Anchor Books, 1964), p. 64.

(8)   Cyrus H. Peake, Nationalism and Education in Modern China (New York: Columbia University Press, 1932), pp. 1-18; William Ayers, Chang Chih-tung and Educational Reform in China (Cambridge: Harvard University Press, 1971); and Knight Biggerstaff, The Earliest Modern Government Schools in China (Ithaca, N.Y.: Cornell University Press, 1961).

(9)   R. Applebaum, Theories of Social Change (Chicago: Markham, 1970).

(10)   G.W. Skinner and Edwin A. Winkler, "Compliance Succession in Rural Communist China: A Cyclical Theory," in A Sociological Reader on Complex Society, ed. Amitai Etzioni (New York: Holt, Rinehart and Winston, 1969), pp. 410-38.

(11)   Thomas J. LaBelle and Robert E. Verhine, "Education, Social Change and Social Stratification," Harvard Education Review 45 (1975): 3-71.

(12)   For an extended discussion of educational policy during this period see Stewart E. Fraser and John N. Hawkins, "Chinese Education: Revolution and Development," Phi Delta Kappa (April 1972): 487-500.

(13)   Ming Di, "Education is a Tool of the Ruling Classes," Jiaoyu Yanjiu 2 (1979): 14.

(14)   Li Kejing, "Is Education a Superstructure or a Productive Force?" Social Sciences in China 1, no. 3 (September 1980): 17-18.

(15)   Hong Fengzhang, "Modern Education is a New Factor of Modern Productive Forces," Jiaoyu Yanjiu 2 (1979): 22.

(16)   Frederic M. Kaplan, Julian M. Sobin, Stephen Andors, eds., Encyclopedia of China Today (New York: Harper and Row, 1980), p. 321.

(17)   A detailed description of China's political and administrative structure can be found in 1981/82 China Official Annual Report (Hong Kong: Kingsway International, 1981).

(18)   Kaplan, Sobin, and Andors, Encyclopedia of China Today, p. 70.

(19)   Martin K. Whyte, Small Groups and Political Rituals in China (Berkeley: University of California Press, 1978).

(20)   Christopher Howe, China's Economy: A Basic Guide (New York: Basic Books, 1978); Jan S. Prybla, The Chinese Economy: Problems and Policy (Columbia, S.C.: University of South Carolina Press, 1978); Evelyn S. Rawski, Agricultural Change and Peasant Economy of South China (Cambridge: Harvard University Press, 1972).

(21)   Based on a survey conducted by the World Bank, 1981; figures are approximations only. A more complete statistical break-down is available in Chapter 2.

(22)   Kaplan, Sobin, and Andors, Encyclopedia of China Today, p. 9.

(23)   Based on interviews conducted in Shanghai, 1981.

2

THE STRUCTURE OF THE
EDUCATIONAL SYSTEM

J.N. Hawkins

    This chapter outlines some structural features of China's educational system as it has evolved since the 1950s. More specifically, the pattern of the Great Proletarian Cultural Revolution (GPCR) and Four Modernizations periods will be highlighted. Chapter 3 discusses in a more analytical fashion the various conflicts and disputes that have arisen regarding the management and administration of education during these two periods.

    Administrative problems of all types faced China's leaders when the People's Republic was established in September 1949. Previous administrative experiences during the civil war period and the war of resistance against Japan had provided China's new leaders with valuable administrative experience, albeit on a microscale. With the establishment of the People's Republic of China (PRC), large numbers of administrators had to be recruited to staff the numerous governmental and public positions throughout China. Managers had to be found to fill administrative posts in the industrial sector, and a network had to be organized to administer a widespread educational system efficiently. The long-run result was that administration became more complex; it required the services of a bureaucracy and presented to China's leaders the specter of bureaucratic excesses and red tape, a specter that continues still to haunt China.

    Of the numerous governmental ministries established since 1949, at least four were directly related to education: Ministries of Culture, Education, Higher Education (no longer in existence), and Health. Below the higher level ministries, there existed several committees and commissions complete with line and staff relationships and a standard bureaucratic organization of a state socialist model.(1) Included in the subcentral government divisions were autonomous regions, provincial governments, and centrally administered cites, each with educational responsibilities; cities, prefectures, and urban districts; counties and street offices; townships (xiang), communes, and urban residents' committees; towns, production brigades; and finally, productions teams in the rural sector. The relationships between these various administrative levels can be seen in Figure 2.1.

The enormously complex bureaucratic structure of education at each of these levels has not been fully researched or documented. Each level, from the ministry to the production team, had some educational role to play, either of the formal or nonformal variety. In the chapters that follow, more detailed description and analysis of each of these will emerge in the context of the educational issue under exploration. For the purposes of this chapter, we will comment briefly on educational planning in general and the three basic educational structures that have emerged since the government consolidated political control in the late 1950s and early 1960s. Finally, we will present the current system in more detail supplemented by recently released educational statistics.

LEVELS OF AUTHORITY AND PLANNING

Despite changes in policy, political factions, and major political movements (such as the GPCR), a general authority and planning profile can be discerned with respect to education. Depending on the political period under discussion, shifts occurred in both form and content at all administrative levels, especially with regard to the detailed responsibilities of each division. However, none of China's various political interest groups have rejected totally, or even suggested, substantial changes in the state socialist planning model. The interpretation and implementation of this model, however, is an arena where a great deal of differentiation has occurred since 1949.(2)

The general planning model that has emerged since 1949 consists of national plans drawn up centrally with input from the various administrative levels attached to the different ministries (e.g., Ministry of Education). At different times the ministries have changed names and for a few years, at the outset of the GPCR, the Ministry of Education was abolished altogether and replaced by a special organization called the Scientific and Educational Leading Group. Major planning agencies in the PRC can be seen in Table 2.1. The commissions, banks, and ministries all fall under the State Council, which has final authority for approval of the national economic plan.

Figure 2.1 Relationships Between Governmental Levels

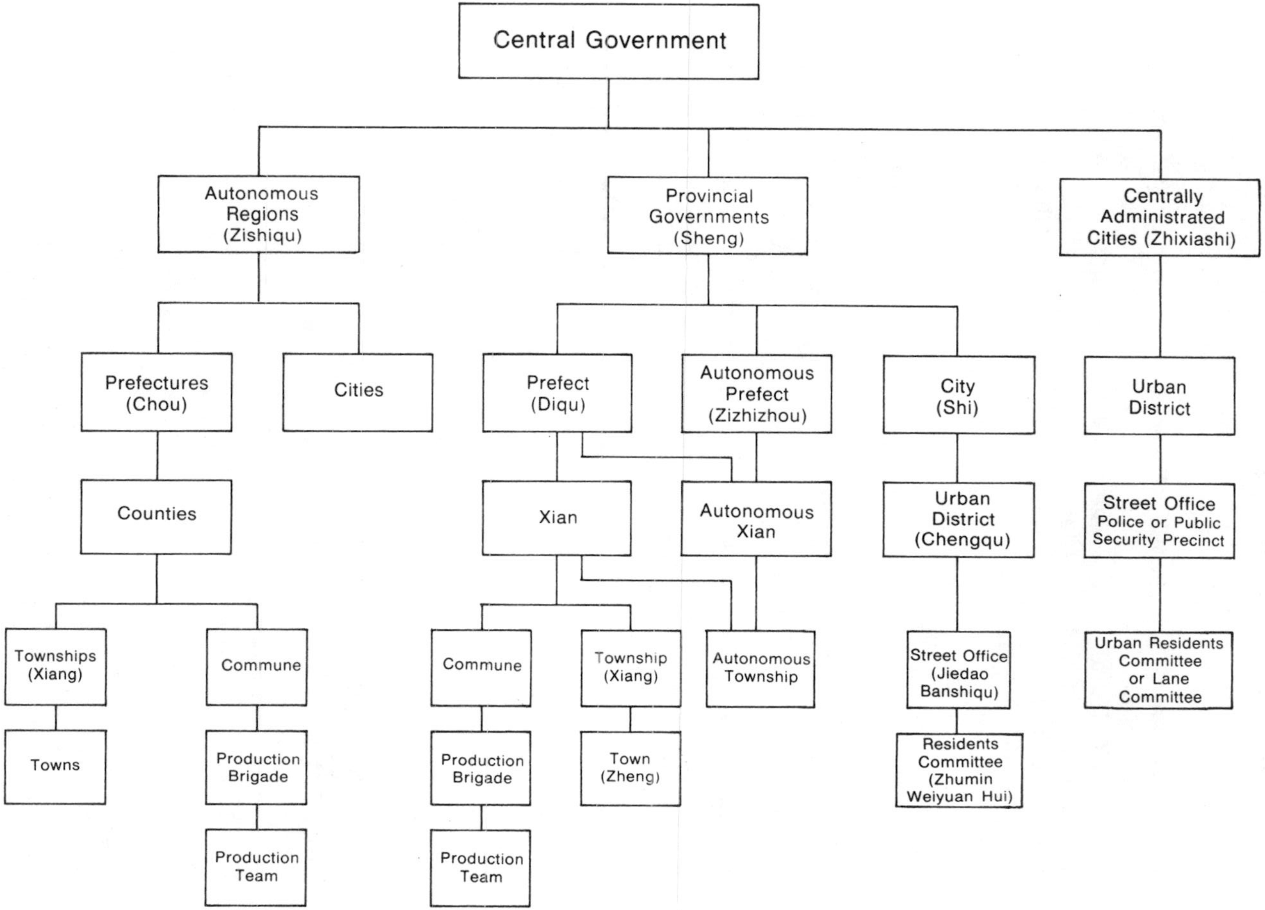

TABLE 2.1.
Major Planning Agencies of the PRC, 1980

Commissions	Banks	Ministries
State Planning Commission	People's Bank of China	Foreign Affairs
State Agricultural Commission	Bank of China	National Defense
State Economic Commission		Foreign Trade
State Capital Construction Commission		Economic Relations with Foreign Countries
State Energy Commission		Agriculture
State Scientific and Technological Commission		State Farms
Foreign Investment Control Commission		Forestry
State Import and Export Administrative Commission		Water Conservancy
		Metallurgical Industries
		Machine Building 1-5
		Agricultural Machinery
		Education
		Coal Industry
		Petroleum
		Chemical
		Electric Power
		Building Material
		Textile Industry
		Light Industry
		Finance
		Food
		Commerce

Source: 1981/82 China Official Annual Report (Hong Kong: Kingsway International, 1981).

It should be noted that, in addition to this bureaucratic model, there also exists a parallel structure set in place by the Chinese Communist Party (CCP). (See Figure 2.2 for a typical linkage pattern between the central political-economic authorities and a major city, Shanghai.) The CCP communicates fundamental political and ideological guidelines and the bureaucratic structure engages in the actual implementation of the various components of the plans. Plans are formulated for long, medium, and short-term periods. Although long-term and medium-term plans are important for forecasting and projecting purposes, for practical purposes it is the annual plan that is most important. Plans include both command

Figure 2.2   Central - Local Linkages: Shanghai

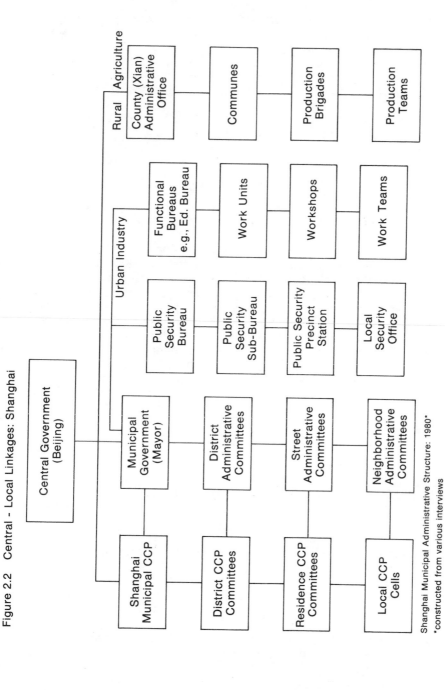

Shanghai Municipal Administrative Structure: 1980*
*constructed from various interviews

Source: Constructed from various interviews.

25

requirements (things that must be done) and expectation requirements (things that central and local officials expect to accomplish during the period of planning under consideration). Depending upon the scale of the project to be undertaken, ascending levels of authority are required for design and development (e.g., a national curriculum plan would require Ministry of Education initiation and completion, whereas elementary and secondary school construction could involve provincial and subprovincial authorities to bypass the ministry level). When determining the command and expectation requirements for the educational component of an annual plan, discussions are held between the various ministries concerned (the Ministry of Education, of course, and other concerned ministries, such as Culture, Machine Building, Transport, and so on), fiscal organizations such as the Bank of China, and provincial Education Bureau representatives as well as representatives from major cities such as Shanghai, Beijing, and Tianjin.

Plans are transmitted by a variety of mechanisms, ranging from the formal directives from the central level to local officials, to informal meetings, telephone calls, mass organization meetings, and so on. The Ministry of Education is currently attempting to bring more order to this process and it is likely that a more systematic transmission process will emerge in the near future. Once approved by the State Council (and in theory by the National People's Congress), plans are transmitted to the provinces, where they are built into the provincial plans. At the subprovincial level (municipalities, cities, and counties), relevant portions of the plans are received, adapted, and implemented. Most evident at this level is the constant tension between the forces of centralization and decentralization.

In the rural sector, the commune organization is the operational unit (renmin gongshe) that presents its own organizational and educational structure (see Figure 2.3). In brief, the commune consists of four integrated units: commune, production brigade, production team, and household. Although the total number of communes has varied, (and the entire structure is currently being questioned), in 1974 50,000 were reported. It is difficult to describe a typical commune; however, some generalizations can be made based on evidence received from a variety of communes visited by foreign scholars in the recent past.(3)

The most common observable unit in the Chinese countryside is the natural village. This unit and the property surrounding it constitute the production brigade and form the intermediate level between the production team and the commune. There may be 15 production brigades to one commune (or 15 villages) and each of these is further subdivided into smaller units of production teams (about 6 teams to one brigade, or 100 to one commune). The production team is the smallest permanent production unit.

The combination of the brigades and the teams then constitute the commune, which may have as its headquarters one of the larger brigades or villages. The commune is linked organizationally with higher levels of administration, especially the county level (xian). With respect to education, levels of authority reside at the commune level in at least six divisions: culture and education departments; library; primary schools; peasants' primary schools; part work, part study; and experimental research stations. Some larger communes also have responsibility for secondary schools and various postsecondary training institutions, but these typically reside at the county level (with the exception of agricultural and vocational middle schools).

Having provided this general model, we can now show in detail the structure of the Ministry of Education and the overall administrative pattern that is currently being utilized (see Figures 2.4 and 2.5 respectively). While details over the past 30 years have changed, these two models are representative of the evolution of China's educational bureaucracy. As can be seen from Figure 2.4, the Ministry of Education consists of two major components: departments/bureaus and enterprises/institutions.

The former constitutes the primary units of China's collegiate and precollegiate educational system. Higher education is broken down into two departments by field of study. (In the past, higher education consisted of a ministry of its own.) Appropriate departments are provided for science and technology, political theory and education, student affairs, various forms of secondary education, teacher training, general education including primary education, minorities, physical education, adult education, and planning matters (including construction, educational resources, foreign student and scholar exchange, and so on).

The second component consists of specialized enterprises and institutions relating to such areas as educational publishing, pedagogy, and educational extension (e.g., TV University). It is important to remember that many other ministries have educational responsibilities, especially with respect to worker and staff education. Various machine industry ministries operate worker schools located in factories and other large industrial enterprises. The Ministry of Railroads, for example, operates its own system of schools at the secondary and collegiate levels. This proliferation of educational systems is a topic of debate and there has been some suggestions of unifying them under the Education Ministry, at least with respect to standards and procedures.

On the other hand, others argue that spreading them out in this manner provides for more innovative approaches to curriculum and instruction and is less bureaucratic. The role played by the central government through its ministries in the field of education was one of the most hotly debated issues during the two periods of the GPCR and the Four Modernizations, as will become evident in the chapters

Figure 2.3 Commune Organization and Management: Education Functions

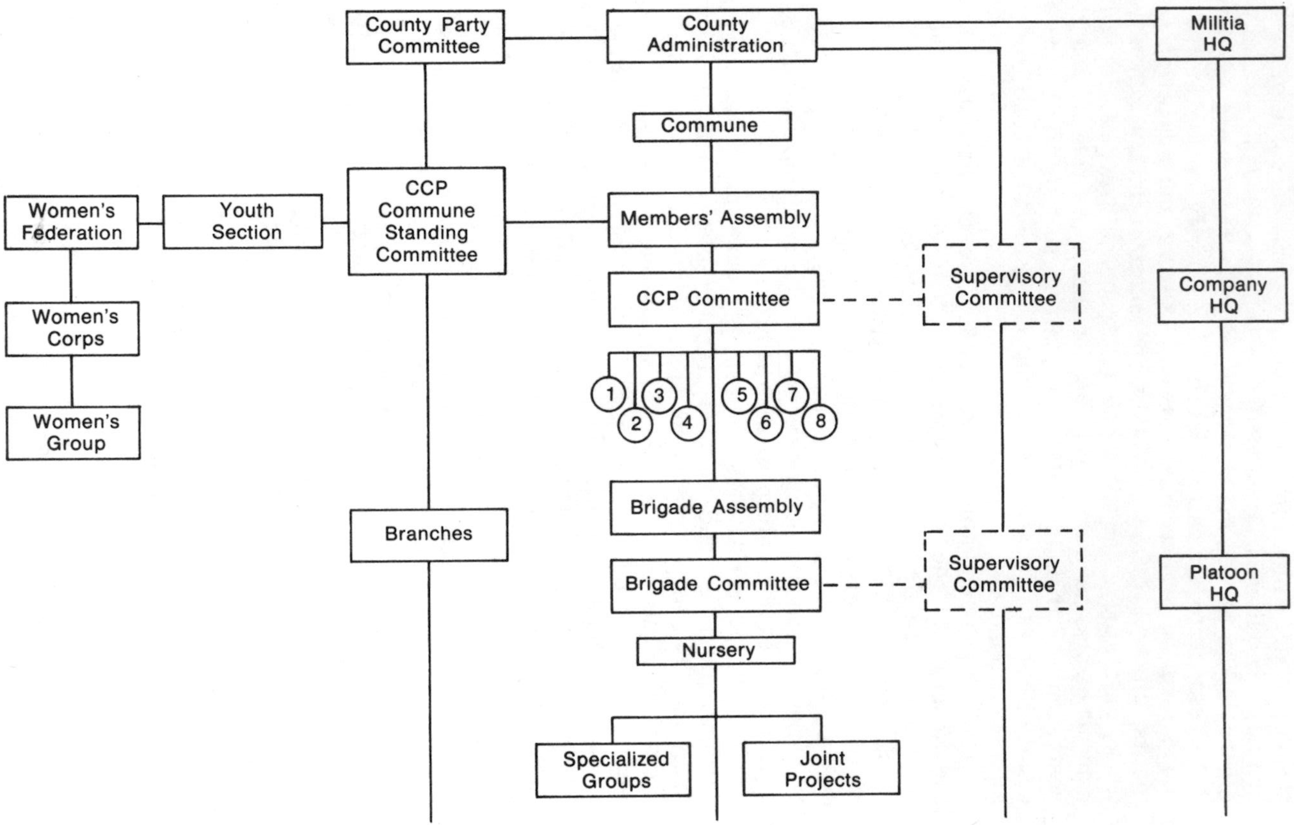

Militia HQ

Company HQ

Platoon HQ

Supervisory Committee

Supervisory Committee

County Administration

Commune

Members' Assembly

CCP Committee

1 2 3 4 5 6 7 8

Brigade Assembly

Brigade Committee

Nursery

Joint Projects

Specialized Groups

County Party Committee

CCP Commune Standing Committee

Branches

Youth Section

Women's Federation

Women's Corps

Women's Group

28

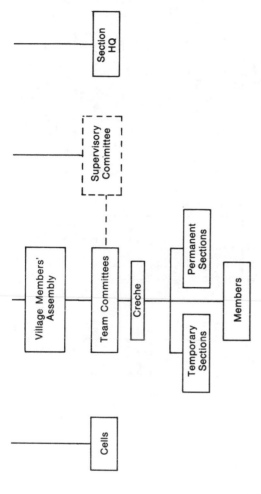

Section
HQ

Supervisory
Committee

Cells

Village Members'
Assembly

Team Committees

Creche

Permanent
Sections

Temporary
Sections

Members

1. Culture & Educational Department
2. Library
3. Primary Schools
4. Peasants' Primary Schools
5. Part-Work; Part-Study Schools
6. Experimental Research Station
7. Broadcasting Station
8. Cultural Work Group

Source: Kieran Broadbent (adapted): *A Chinese/English Dictionary of China's Rural Economy* (Farnham Royal: England; Commonwealth Agricultural Bureau, 1978). Reprinted by permission.

Figure 2.4   Organization of Ministry of Education in China

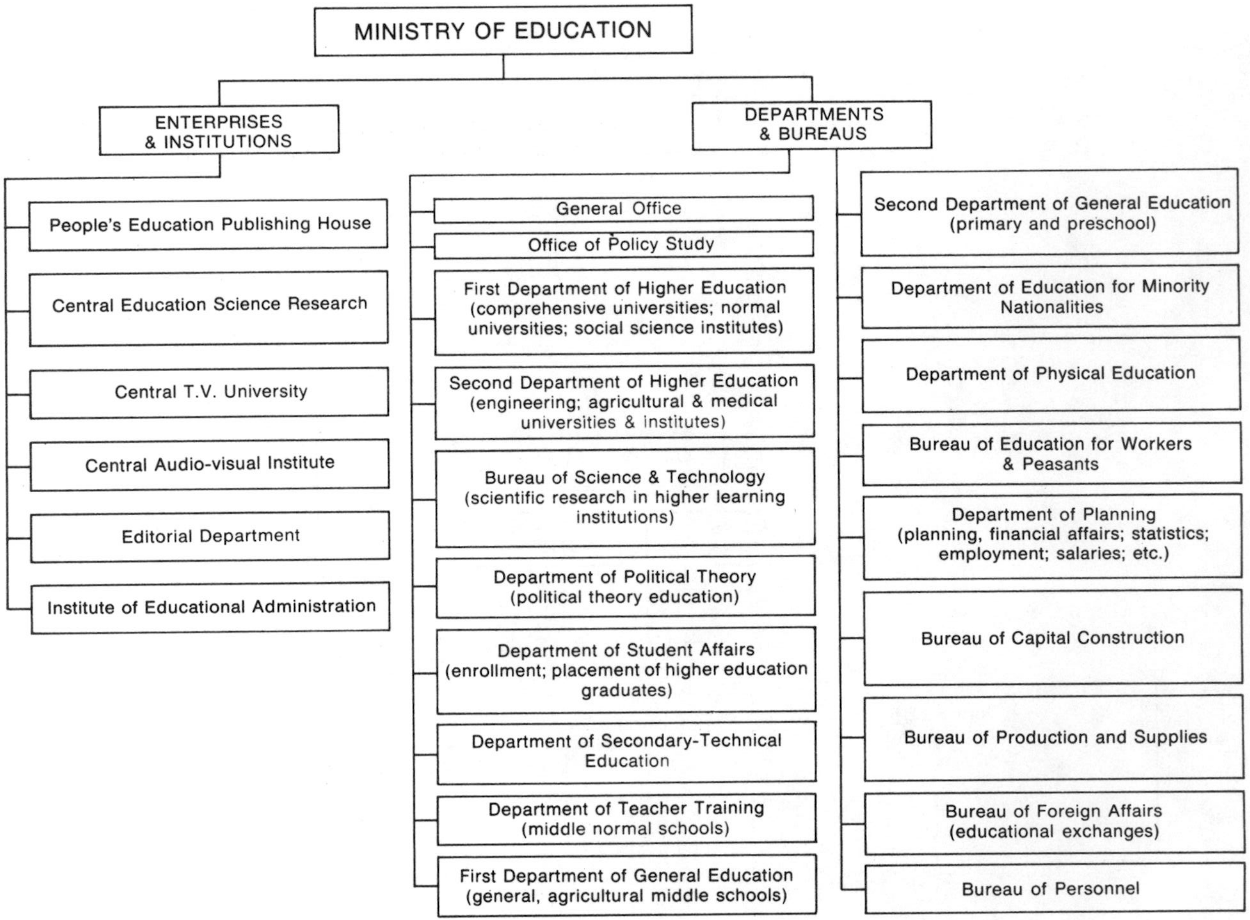

MINISTRY OF EDUCATION

ENTERPRISES & INSTITUTIONS

- People's Education Publishing House
- Central Education Science Research
- Central T.V. University
- Central Audio-visual Institute
- Editorial Department
- Institute of Educational Administration

DEPARTMENTS & BUREAUS

- General Office
- Office of Policy Study
- First Department of Higher Education (comprehensive universities; normal universities; social science institutes)
- Second Department of Higher Education (engineering; agricultural & medical universities & institutes)
- Bureau of Science & Technology (scientific research in higher learning institutions)
- Department of Political Theory (political theory education)
- Department of Student Affairs (enrollment; placement of higher education graduates)
- Department of Secondary-Technical Education
- Department of Teacher Training (middle normal schools)
- First Department of General Education (general, agricultural middle schools)
- Second Department of General Education (primary and preschool)
- Department of Education for Minority Nationalities
- Department of Physical Education
- Bureau of Education for Workers & Peasants
- Department of Planning (planning, financial affairs; statistics; employment; salaries; etc.)
- Bureau of Capital Construction
- Bureau of Production and Supplies
- Bureau of Foreign Affairs (educational exchanges)
- Bureau of Personnel

that follow. The relationship between the Ministry of Education and other educational levels of authority can be seen in Figure 2.5. Subministry levels of authority generally follow the administrative pattern discussed earlier in this chapter and displayed in Figure 2.1. Provinces, municipalities, and autonomous regions have responsibility for implementing ministry level plans in such areas as higher education, middle technical schools, key schools, and selected middle normal schools. Prefectures have educational departments as well, with primary responsibility for vocational and technical education and selected key middle and primary schools. The county level focuses on ordinary middle and primary schools and the communes and brigades have responsibility for their various levels of education. This pattern is at a high level of generalization, but serves as the basic model that has guided China's educational planners through the past three decades. The implementation of specific educational tracks has differed since the 1960s and the three most prevalent models will be briefly described below.

THREE BASIC EDUCATIONAL LADDERS

The efforts in the 1950s to expand and consolidate the existing educational system met with success and by the 1960s, impressive collegiate and precollegiate educational structures had been erected. Figure 2.6 displays a dual track system as representative of the educational system that emerged following the consolidation of the 1950s, the period of the Soviet influence and the Great Leap Forward (GLF) of 1958.

The first track consisted of regular nurseries and kindergartens, primary schools, junior middle schools, senior middle schools paralleled by vocational middle schools, technical colleges and regular universities, and research institutes. Within this track special elite schools also existed (now called key-point schools). In short, this track was a K-12, lock-step system catering to urban and more developed rural sectors.

The second track consisted of a variety of short-cycle educational programs. At the lower level a spare-time primary school system was in place both for literacy education for adults and basic primary education for urban and rural youngsters left out of the regular system. At the middle level, short-cycle programs existed for workers and peasants at both the junior and senior levels. Special political middle schools termed "red and expert" were left over from the Great Leap Forward period and were generally officially ignored.

Finally in this track, red and expert colleges, also remnants of the Great Leap Forward, were in place and offered some upward mobility for those youths unable to find places in the regular collegiate track. This dual track has been credited with raising the

Figure 2.5   Administration of Education in China

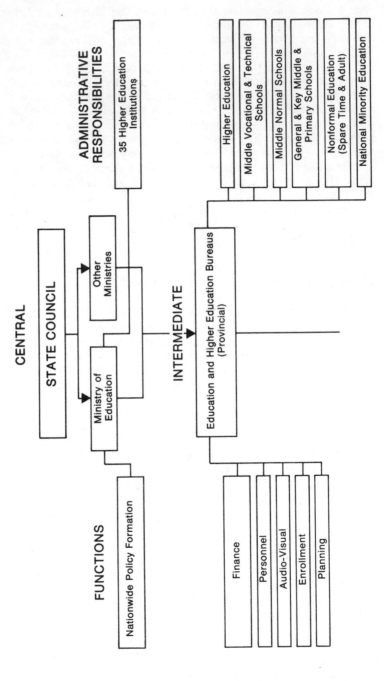

CENTRAL

ADMINISTRATIVE
RESPONSIBILITIES

STATE COUNCIL

Other Ministries

Ministry of Education

35 Higher Education Institutions

INTERMEDIATE

Education and Higher Education Bureaus (Provincial)

Higher Education

Middle Vocational & Technical Schools

Middle Normal Schools

General & Key Middle & Primary Schools

Nonformal Education (Spare Time & Adult)

National Minority Education

FUNCTIONS

Nationwide Policy Formation

Finance

Personnel

Audio-Visual

Enrollment

Planning

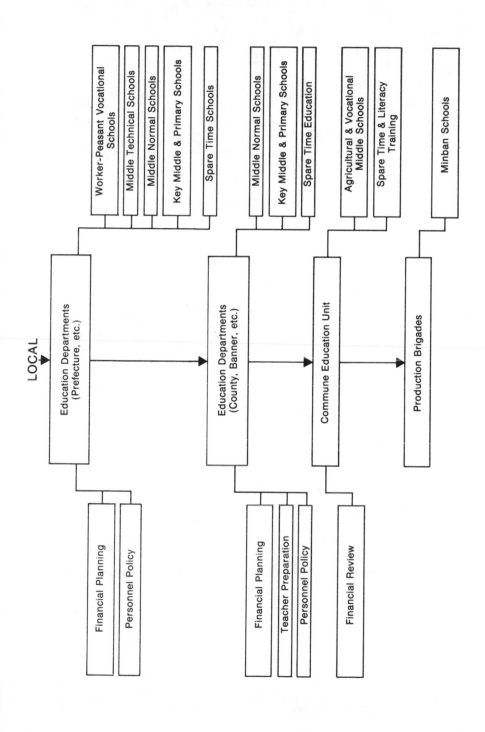

LOCAL

Education Departments (Prefecture, etc.)
- Financial Planning
- Personnel Policy
- Worker-Peasant Vocational Schools
- Middle Technical Schools
- Middle Normal Schools
- Key Middle & Primary Schools
- Spare Time Schools

Education Departments (County, Banner, etc.)
- Financial Planning
- Teacher Preparation
- Personnel Policy
- Middle Normal Schools
- Key Middle & Primary Schools
- Spare Time Education

Commune Education Unit
- Financial Review
- Agricultural & Vocational Middle Schools
- Spare Time & Literacy Training

Production Brigades
- Minban Schools

Figure 2.6   Education in China: Dual System of the Sixties

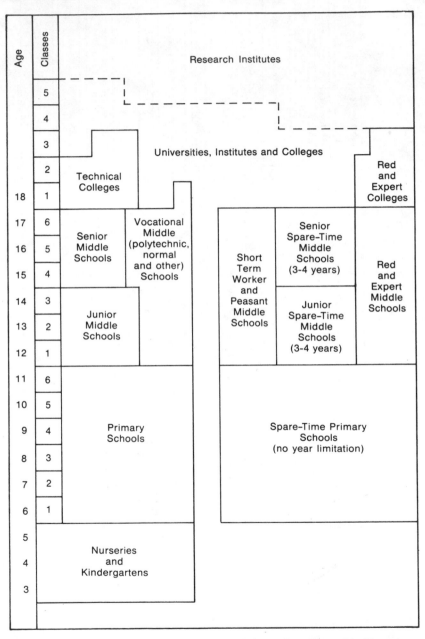

Reprinted with permission of Stewart E. Fraser: Originally appeared in Stewart E. Fraser and John N. Hawkins, "Chinese Education: Revolution and Development," *PDK*, April 1972.

academic quality of those students in the regular track, while assuring some form of education and training for those left out of the system.(4)

Dissatisfaction with this track, along with a complex array of political problems, brought about a revision in form and content as part of the GPCR (shown in Figure 2.7). This model emerged in the late 1960s and prevailed to 1976. Several features of the previous model were revised substantially but the primary change consisted of the merging of the two track system into one basic format for both collegiate and precollegiate levels. At the precollegiate level, elite schools were eliminated and the spare-time track was merged with the regular schools. In most places the K-12 elementary and secondary cycles were trimmed to K-9. A spare-time program continued to operate in industry and agricultural areas but was primarily for adults. The major division in this system was between rural and urban schools, where differentiation in quality between these two sectors continued to exist.

A second major change in this model was the breaking up of the lock-step mechanism whereby it was theoretically possible for a student to continue through the system without break to the completion of higher education. Under this model all students were required to have a break in education following the completion of the senior middle school and to engage in some form of work moratorium. Following at least three years of service to the nation, it was then possible to apply to one of the various postsecondary institutions. The curriculum was also shortened to accommodate the reduced number of years in the system.

In general, the entire educational structure was to become a mixture of formal and nonformal pedagogical formats. The stated educational goal of this system was to equalize educational oppor-tunity, to focus on mass education, and to blur the distinction between school and society. In theory, there were to be no key schools or special programs; rural and urban educational gaps were to be reduced or eliminated; and the precollegiate level was given priority over the collegiate.(5)

The launching of the Four Modernizations Movement and the inauguration of a new political administration in Beijing in 1976 brought about the third model of China's educational system (as seen in Figure 2.8). Several features of the first model have reemerged, although in an adapted format. In contrast to the dual track of the 1960s, and the single mass track of the GPCR period, an articulated three-track system is now being consolidated and put in place. As seen in Figure 2.8, key institutions have been reintroduced and are at the top of the educational ladder.

The key institutions receive more funding, better facilities, and more highly trained instructors than the regular schools. This elitist concept is justified in terms of the need to identify and train China's most talented youth in order to speed the process of modernization,

Figure 2.7 Education in China: Development for the Seventies

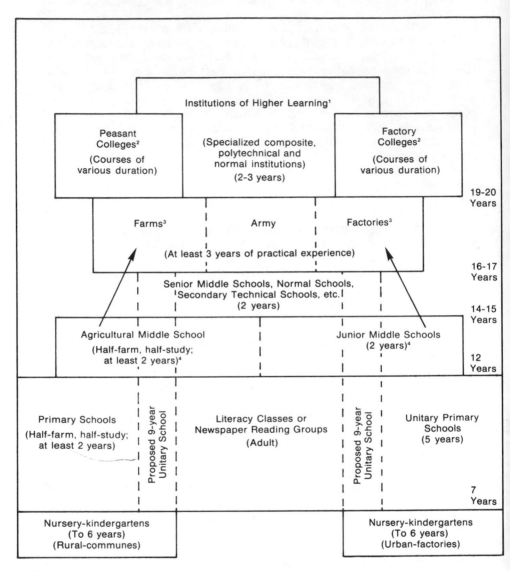

1. Supported and administered by the state.
2. Supported and administered by communes or factories.
3. Schools run by factories, farms and military or political organs (cadre schools for 1, 2 or 3 years) are not represented.
4. Short-term schools and specialized short courses are not represented.

Reprinted with permission of Stewart E. Fraser; originally appeared in Stewart E. Fraser and John N. Hawkins. "Chinese Education: Revolution and Development," *PDK* (April 1972).

Research and Development; Graduate Studies

Key Universities

Standard Universities

Key Secondary Level

Standard Secondary Level

Urban Secondary Technical School Program

Rural Secondary Level Program

Commune & Factory Post Sec. Programs

Key Primary Schools

Standard Primary Schools

Kindergarten

Kindergartens and Nurseries

Rural and Urban Literacy Programs (No Year Limitation)

Key Institutions

Standard (regular) Institutions

Nonformal, Alternative Institutions

Classes	1	2	3	4	5	6	1	2	3	4	5	6	1	2	3	4	5
Age	3	4	5	6	7	8	9	10	11	12	13	14	15	16	17	18	

Source: Constructed by author.

37

thus eventually benefiting the entire society. Rigorous examinations are held at all levels to screen youngsters attempting to enter key schools. Mass education is conducted through the regular pre-collegiate and collegiate system, which is directed toward a more rigorous preparation of students, greater discipline in academic matters, and the ultimate selection of the most promising students for higher forms of education. The number of years required to complete the precollegiate level has been increased to 12 and the curriculum has been expanded as well.

The lock-step system is back in place and those students able to complete all 12 years and pass the entrance examinations with high marks can now go straight through to some form of higher education. The total number able to do so, however, is extremely small (about 4 percent), thus in practice assuring a work moratorium of indeterminant length for the masses of China's youth.

The attempted blurring of the distinction between formal and nonformal education has also been revised and a more institutional and more bureaucratic approach to monitoring and controlling the nonformal sector has been initiated. The nonformal level is now geared primarily for the adult population (see Chapters 6 and 7), and a ministry-level body has been established for planning purposes.

In sum, this third model is perceived by China's current leaders to be more efficient, organized, and able to meet the needs of the Four Modernizations Movement. Levels of authority are more clearly defined with a highly centralized Ministry of Education formulating plans and policy and a decentralized school-level administration given the responsibility of carrying out the plans and policies and the responsibility for success or failure of the various educational programs.(6)

The three educational ladders discussed above are symbolic of differing educational philosophies, goals, and objectives, and of differing perceptions of the mechanisms of social change. They have served as the structural skeleton for various educational programs during the past 30 years. As China's educational leaders are faced with specific pedagogical issues, they have utilized one or more of the models to attempt to resolve critical problems. As they have disagreed over policy and practice, they have revised and dramatically shifted the educational structure and all its components. It is this revision and shifting policy of specific issues that will be examined in Part II. Before turning to this discussion, however, it will be useful to sketch a statistical educational profile to provide a better frame of reference for the interpretative essays that follow.

CHINA'S EDUCATIONAL SYSTEM: THE NUMBERS

The gathering and interpretation of educational statistics in China has been always a hazardous enterprise, whether it has been attempted by the Chinese themselves or by some outside agency such as the recent World Bank Study.(7) On a macro level there is the overwhelming fact that approximately 1 billion people live in China, half of whom are under the age of 25. This presents an enormous school-age cohort. This fact alone is overwhelming without even considering the extensive adult education needs of a developing country like China.

As we have seen, primary and secondary education have generally been conducted on separate levels except during the GPCR, when an attempt was made to merge the two into a unified nine-year cycle. It is estimated that 90 percent of those eligible to attend primary and secondary schools are enrolled, although there is considerable wastage.(8) Yet primary schooling is generally available and secondary education enrolls approximately 50 percent of the school-age cohort.

The fundamental fact facing secondary school graduates, however, is that only 4 percent can locate openings in regular colleges and universities. The solution to this dilemma is found in the current effort to expand and reform the quality of secondary technical schools.(9) The progress achieved in each of these levels since 1949 can be seen graphically below.

In Table 2.2 and Figure 2.9, the 30-year development of higher education is shown. The fluctuation in numbers of institutions is a reflection of political and economic movements, such as the Great Leap Forward in 1958 and the GPCR in 1966-67. In both cases there was a net reduction in the numbers of institutions and students in higher education. Despite these statistical aberrations, the growth of higher education in China has not been declining spectacularly, either in students or in institutions, even prior to the GPCR. However, the commitment to higher education has not been made clear until recent times (or possibly during the 1950s, the period of Soviet influence) and current projections are to increase the number of students at the higher education level by 300,000 annually for the next decade.(10) In comparison with other developing nations, China's enrollment ratios are considerably lower with respect to higher education (about 4.1 percent for 92 selected developing nations, while China enrolled 1.2 percent).(11)

The development of regular secondary schools since 1946 (and more particularly since 1965) has been spectacular (see Table 2.3 and Figure 2.10). There has been a steady increase over the past three decades in the numbers of students and institutions, with a slight decrease in the 1960s and a dramatic increase during the GPCR. A slight reduction followed until 1982. When the student and institutional figures declined (post-Great Leap Forward and post-GPCR), the explanation was that quality had been sacrificed for quantity, expertise for equalitarianism. Yet the fact remains that, during these periods of rapid political change (GLF and GPCR), China greatly expanded its secondary educational school oppor-

Figure 2.9   Development of Higher Education in PRC: 1947-1980

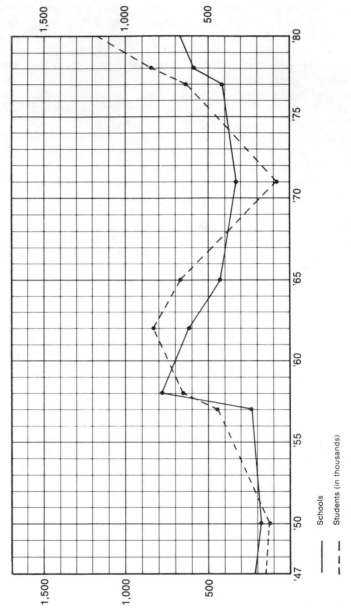

Schools
Students (in thousands)

Source: Interview with Beijing Normal University professors and Ministry of Education officials, 1982.

Figure 2.10   Development of Secondary Education in PRC: 1946-1980

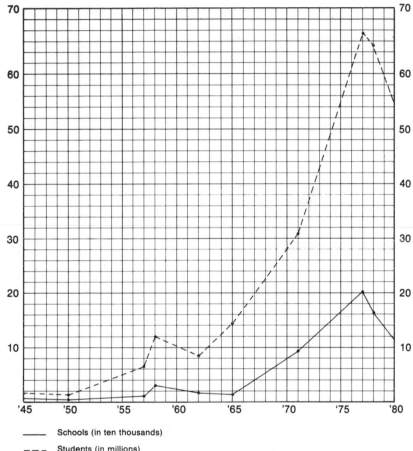

——— Schools (in ten thousands)

– – – Students (in millions)

Source: Interview with Beijing Normal University professors and Ministry of Education officials, 1982.

TABLE 2.2
Development of Higher Education in the PRC, 1947-80

	1947*	1950	1957	1958	1962
Schools	207	193	229	791	610
Students (in thousandths)	155	137	441	660	830

	1965	1971	1977	1978	1980
Schools	434	328	404	598	675
Students (in thousandths)	674	83	625	856	1.161

*Highest before 1949.
Source: Interview with Beijing Normal University professors, 1982, and Ministry of Education officials.

TABLE 2.3
Development of Secondary Education in the PRC, 1946-80

	1946*	1950	1957	1958	1962
Schools	4,266	4,013	11,096	28,931	19,521
Students (in thousandths)	1.496	1.305	6.281	8.520	7.528

	1965	1971	1977	1978	1980
Schools	18,102	94,765	201,268	162,345	118,400
Students (in thousandths)	9.338	31.276	67.799	65.483	55.081

*Highest before 1949.
Source: Interview with Beijing Normal University professors and Ministry of Education officials, 1982.

tunities for its massive precollegiate cohort. In comparison with other developing countries, China clearly leads its enrollment ratio (20.6 percent and 50 percent respectively).(12) This steady increase in both student enrollments and facilities has been an important factor in China's economic and political development since 1950, which provided a cadre of skilled human resources and politically conscious youth. Efforts are currently being directed toward the raising of quality of secondary school graduates to prepare them for the work place and a small elite group for higher education.

An increasingly important educational level is composed of secondary technical schools. The position of these schools in China's educational hierarchy has varied widely since 1949. The extreme fluctuations in both numbers of students and institutions can be seen in Table 2.4 and Figure 2.11. The rise and fall of this level over the past three decades can be attributed to the ideological uncertainty in the CCP regarding the place of vocational-technical education in a socialist country. Viewed as a separate stream, secondary technical schools have been criticized as substandard for China's working class and designed to screen into the work place the majority of worker and peasant children, while the more fortunate move on to white-collar and bureaucratic employment or higher education.

TABLE 2.4
Development of Secondary Technical Schools
in the PRC, 1946-80

	1946*	1950	1957	1958	1962
Schools	724	500	728	2,085	956
Students (in thousandths)	137	98	482	1,084	353

	1965	1971	1977	1978	1980
Schools	871	455	1,457	1,714	2,052
Students (in thousandths)	392	98	391	529	761

*Highest before 1949.
Source: Interview with Beijing Normal University professors and Ministry of Education officials, 1982.

Figure 2.11 Development of Secondary Technical Schools: 1946-1980

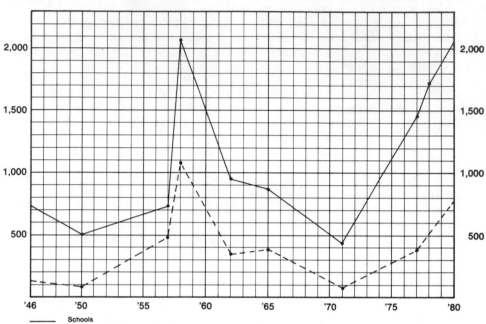

Source: Interview with Beijing Normal University professors and Ministry of Education officials, 1982.

During the GLF and GPCR periods, we can see a sharp decline in these types of schools as vocational and technical education was integrated into the regular secondary school curriculum; consequently, many of the schools were closed. During these periods, the argument was that all students should acquire some secondary technical skills as well as more general academic skills. This reform partially accounted for the rapid increase of regular secondary schools and their number of pupils.

The current Four Modernizations Movement presents another critique of this mainstreaming approach; the gradual elimination of secondary technical schools during the GPCR was roundly criticized. The secondary technical school program today is designed to attend to the many problems associated with the proposed expansion of the economy and of the modernization program, such as the lack of space for students at the collegiate level, the shortage of skilled middle-level technicians, and the fit between the regular secondary school curriculum and the entry-level requirement for China's rural and urban industries. The ratio between the regular schools and the secondary-technical schools is at this time, however, lopsided with about 55 million students enrolled in regular schools and only about 880,000 in secondary technical schools.(13)

The role of the secondary technical schools is likely to increase in importance during the next few years. Many are in the process of being upgraded into a type of community college, the numbers of students and institutions are expanding rapidly, and they are being viewed as a major solution to many of China's education and development-problems, especially for the large urban areas. As an example, in Shanghai, the city leading the nation in innovative approaches to secondary technical education, the Shanghai Educational Bureau coordinated 74 such schools. Thirty-seven of them are related directly to Shanghai's food and agricultural needs.

Although the Educational Bureau coordinates the curriculum, teaching, and other matters relating to the day-to-day operation of the schools, each school has its own administrative authority reporting directly to the appropriate municipal office. This pattern is followed as well in other major cities. The curriculum is being expanded, the course of study in some cases raised from two to four years, and emergency research programs initiated on an "as needed" basis (e.g., in Shanghai during 1980 a bacterial infection adversely affected the rice production in the Songjiang district, and appropriate secondary technical students and faculty assisted in the combat of the problem).(14)

Finally, with respect to primary education, there has been since 1946 a steady growth of student enrollments and, with the exception of a peak in 1962-65, a moderate growth of primary schools (see Table 2.5 and Figure 2.12). China ranks very well with other developing nations and its enrollment ratios approach those of most industrialized nations (about 92 percent).(15) Thus education at the primary level is almost universal. The main debate is over the role

Figure 2.12   Development of Primary Education in PRC: 1946-1980

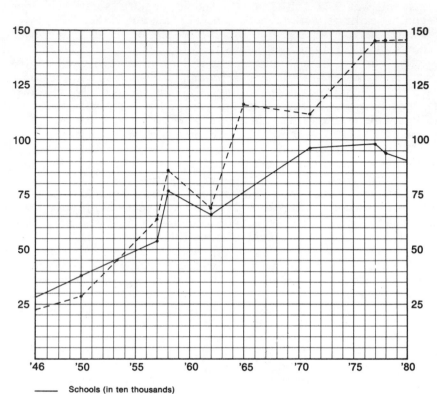

——— Schools (in ten thousands)

– – – Students (in millions)

Source: Interview with Beijing Normal University professors and Ministry of Education officials, 1982.

key primary schools will play, what should be the quality of teacher education required for this level, and the curriculum development reform efforts currently under way.

TABLE 2.5
Development of Primary Schools in the PRC, 1946-80
(in ten thousandths)

	1946*	1950	1957	1958	1962
Schools	28.93	38.36	54.73	77.68	66.83
Students	2368.3	2892.4	6428.3	8640.3	6923.9

	1965	1971	1977	1978	1980
Schools	168.19	96.85	98.23	94.93	91.73
Students	11620.9	11211.2	14617.6	14624.0	14626.96

*Highest before 1949.
Source: Interview with Beijing Normal University professors and Ministry of Education officials, 1982.

CONCLUSION

In summary, the Chinese have experimented with varieties of structural mechanisms to provide precollegiate and collegiate education of both formal and nonformal types. There has been a great deal of quantitative success in solving immense educational problems. Yet there has also been a great deal of dispute over the quality of these efforts as political interests have sought on numerous occasions to revise and reform the system.

The discussion above serves as baseline data for the issue-oriented chapters in Part II. The rather mechanical aspects of China's educational structure are merely the framework for significant and intensive policy and practice disputes that have raged since 1949.

NOTES

(1) Those ministries and committees related to education prior to the GPCR are discussed in Tsang Chiu-sam, Society, Schools and Progress in China (Oxford: Pergamon Press, 1968), p. 80.

(2)   Several useful studies are available analyzing and describing China's political-economic system as it has evolved since 1949. The distillation of these discussions and the outline contained in this chapter draw from the following sources and the author's own interviews with planning authorities in China: Alexander Eckstein, China's Economic Revolution (Cambridge: Cambridge University Press, 1977); Harry Harding, Organizing China: The Problem of Bureaucracy, 1949-1976 (Stanford, Calif.: Stanford University Press, 1981); Ramon H. Myers, The Chinese Economy: Past and Present (Belmont, Calif.: Wadsworth, 1980); Gilbert Rozman, ed., The Modernization of China (Riverside, N.J.: The Free Press, 1981).

(3)   This summary of the structure of the commune is based on the author's own observations and those of others, e.g. Jan S. Prybla, The Chinese Economy: Problems and Policies (Columbia, S.C.: The University of South Carolina Press, 1978).

(4)   Hard data for this period are unreliable; for a general discussion, however, see: Julia Kwong, Chinese Education in Transition: Prelude to the Cultural Revolution (Montreal: McGill-Queens University Press, 1979); and Stewart E. Fraser, Chinese Communist Education: Records of the First Decade (New York: Wiley, 1963).

(5)   This system is briefly discussed in Stewart E. Fraser and John N. Hawkins, "Chinese Education: Revolution and Development," Phi Delta Kappan (April 1972): 487-500.

(6)   The three educational ladders are discussed in more detail in John N. Hawkins, "Educational Reform and Development in the People's Republic of China," in Comparative Education, ed. Robert Arnove and Gail Kelly (New York: Macmillan, 1982), pp. 411-32.

(7)   The educational statistics in this section are an approximation based on three primary sources: first, official Chinese announcements in the media and from the State Statistical Bureau; second, the recent World Bank study; third, the author's interviews with officials from the Ministry of Education, 1981-82. The World Bank statistics are the most complete single source for the education sector, but are not entirely consistent with other reliable sources. The variations, however, are slight and it is not likely that completely reliable statistics will become available for several years, especially in light of the three-year period projected for China's current major census effort.

(8)   Of the 90 percent of school-age children enrolled, only 30 percent graduate. There are currently an estimated 140 million illiterates in China; FBIS, April 21, 1980.

(9)   Author's interview with the Minister of Education, Jiang Nanxiang, June 16, 1980.

(10)   BJRB, April 4, 1980.

(11)   World Bank estimates, 1982.

(12)   Ibid.

(13)   "Stress on Secondary Technical Education," Beijing Review 37 (September 14, 1979).

(14)   John N. Hawkins, Shanghai: An Exploratory Report on Human Resource Development and Food for the City (Honolulu: East-West Center, 1982).

(15)   World Bank estimates, 1982.

PART II
EDUCATION AND SOCIAL CHANGE— CRITICAL ISSUES

3

EDUCATIONAL MANAGEMENT AND ADMINISTRATION: COMPETING STRATEGIES

J.N. Hawkins

Since the formation of the Chinese Communist Party in 1921, China's leaders have experienced and agonized over a variety of administrative styles. They sought to manage Chinese society through an organizational structure, allowing them simultaneous multiple goals. Not surprisingly, this resulted in division among the ruling elite and among middle and local-level interest groups. By necessity their approach to management and organizational change, especially in the early years, was very flexible due to the humble origins of the CCP and, following the destruction of the Party apparatus in 1927, the difficult road of reconstruction that lay ahead. It is a truism that as the organization of which it was a part grew, management and administration grew more difficult. The problems of the Jiangxi Soviet period (1927-34) were most certainly a different order than were those problems of the Yan'an period (1935-49); yet neither period could in anyway compare with that following the establishment in 1949 of the People's Republic of China. Since then several very powerful forces formed as China's leaders charted roads toward both a revolutionary and a modern society. Among these were the centripetal forces of centralization and the centrifugal forces of decentralization. These contradictory paths that frame much of China's developmental experience since 1949 will be discussed. Traveling both roads – growth aided by centralization and equity promoted by decentralization – produced differing approaches to change as well as conflict within the leadership.

Nowhere was this more evident than in the field of education and nowhere more apparent than in the contrasting styles of management and organization of the GPCR and the current Four Modernization's Movement. Additional recent studies are available that provide more detail than what was reviewed in Chapters 1 and 2.(1) We will now review general principles of management found in studies of several developing societies as they evolved and will provide an overview of educational management in China during the past two periods under discussion. This section will be followed by discussion of two cases of educational management and organization, one from the GPCR period and one from the Four Modernizations period. Highlighted will be the contrasting organizational and management styles of these two periods. Both are micro studies of technical-training educational programs, one rural and one urban.

These cases have been chosen because they encapsulate details of the conflict in the administrative procedures that characterized both political periods and prove more insightful than would general discussions of the educational system per se.(2) Case studies of educational projects in China are in short supply and, while it is risky to generalize on the basis of specific cases, they do offer benchmark data for future case-study comparisons.

EDUCATIONAL MANAGEMENT AND ADMINISTRATION: SOME GENERAL PRINCIPLES

Voluminous literature exists on the management and administration of enterprises such as education but not all is relevant to the developing nations and even less to those with socialist political economies. Despite these shortcomings in the literature, a great deal of progress has been made in defining some fundamental principles of enterprise management. Taken selectively much of this material is useful in analyzing the Chinese case.

Most sources agree that in its most basic sense, management means "the achievement of objectives by identifying and utilizing material and human resources."(3) Five basic components can be identified. Those particularly relevant to the educational management and organization involving China's leaders for three decades are: planning, organization, staffing, direction, and control. These five functions link central and local administrative levels through information, communication, and authority channels (Figure 3.1).

In terms of the process followed in the PRC, the first function — planning — has already been discussed. Here, it is referred to as a function of preparing for the commitment of resources in the most economical fashion, and by preparing, of allowing this commitment to be made less disruptively.(4)

In most nations well-established enterprises such as education have already demonstrated their legitimacy, and planning as it now exists in the Four Modernizations Movement is thus more often planning for improvement. However, during periods of radical social

Figure 3.1   Basic Elements of Management

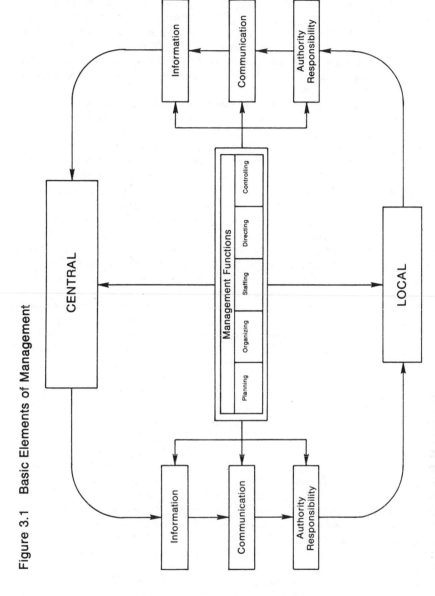

Source: Constructed by author.

change, when the legitimacy of the enterprise is being questioned as it was during the GPRC, planning is from the ground up. Planning from the ground up is more closely associated with project planning, a point discussed later. Planning, then is not a static function but relates directly to the prevailing political-economic climate. Planning for improvement and planning from the ground up are both related to conflicting forces of centralization and decentralization of educational management.

A second major management function is organization, defined for our purposes as "the procurement of human and non-human factors, the grouping and alignment of personnel and physical resources, the delegation of authority and responsibility within the organizational structure."(5) This somewhat neutral definition must be viewed in context of the degrees of social change political and educational officials seek to follow. If the overall goal is to be the maintenance and refinement of an existing educational policy, then the most appropriate organizational style may be functional, where standard operating procedures with minor refinements prevail. If the goal is to be massive reorganization and radical institutional change, then the most appropriate organizational mechanism may be the task force, a highly decentralized organizational change structure designed to focus on specific problems and the redesign of institutions responsible for resolving problems. Each approach contains implications for forces of centralization and decentralization. The former concentrates authority and responsibility in hierarchical bureaucratic institutions and the latter disperses political and economic power to the local project levels.

Staffing the educational enterprise refers to how human resources are utilized, organized, controlled, and monitored, with implications for awards and sanctions. Effective staffing must involve at least four major considerations: first, technical expertise combined with career goals, practical training, and experience in at least one senior study area; second, a broad-based working knowledge of several fields of study sufficiently different from the manager's own technical expertise (including cognizance of the overall political picture); third, a broad understanding of problems of general management involving personnel, or stated otherwise as having a commendable work style; and fourth, an active interest in the upgrading of skills and of being a teacher-trainer for subordinates.(6) Successful staffing also suggests that managers be selected at the planning stage from among those involved, ideally those recruited from below and then promoted. In short, early involvement in planning with an anticipated move into management should be the objective.

In light of the distinction raised between function and task, it is clear that a manager associated with function does not necessarily perform well in the task mode. Ideally a one-man management approach works well within functional systems where refining and fine-tuning are the primary responsibilities. However, if the approach is task or project oriented and requires rapid and dramatic change, the more viable staffing approach is a management team (e.g., the three-in-one committees utilized during the GPCR).(7)

Directing educational management refers to the day-to-day process of coordinating available resources, of attending to personnel matters, and of working closely together at the implementation level. One major study demonstrated that this function of management is one of the most conflict ridden in these seven primary respects: first, scheduling of work assignments; second, technical quality control; third, human resource development; fourth, establishment of priorities; fifth, personnel interaction; sixth, fiscal and cost constraints; and seventh, the establishment of standard operating procedures.(8) The degree of success in resolving these conflicts is related directly to the overall management and organizational style of the enterprise being studied, particularly as related to centralization and decentralization.

Finally, all managers must develop skills for effective control of enterprises and projects, ". . . that is, coordinating the action of all parts of the organization according to the plan established for attaining the objective."(9)

Confusion often surrounds the term "control," attributing to it a negative connotation. In a strict management sense, the meaning is more closely associated with monitoring to assure a smooth operation. However, in command economies such as China's, it appears there is a tendency to exert a more control-function than a monitoring-function system. Thus, depending on one's outlook, a manager could be guilty of either "commandism," or on the other hand be rewarded for running a tight ship. The controversy over what constitutes correct project control is one that during both movements of the GPCR and the Four Modernizations was divergent.

Referring again to Figure 3.1, we see that the glue binding the management functions to the different policymaking levels consists of three interrelated systems. The information system is essential at all function levels, but especially at the direction and control levels, where it must provide the proper amount of information at reasonably frequent and accurate intervals. This information that chain links top to bottom and bottom to top in two-way feedback loops is crucial to management of educational enterprises, particularly in planned economies such as China's. Substandard reporting or inadequate information causes gross errors among planners and implementors, as during the Great Leap Forward when, in 1958, a lack of clear direction for managers and administrators at the local level was present. On the other hand, an over reliance on the dazzling array of sophisticated data gathering and dissemination techniques and the newer equipment replacing manually obtained data resulted in larger volumes of computer printouts. Receivers were overloaded with useless information, (occurrences reported in the current Four Modernizations Movement).(10)

Related to the necessity of an appropriate information system are the various communication channels currently being utilized. Communication travels along several paths: upward from middle-level managers and administrators to superiors, sideways to colleagues, and downward from superiors to subordinates. Each requires clarity with lack of distortion as well as the utilization of multiple communication forms such as memos, meeting minutes, directives, use of technology, and so on.

Successful project managers agree that, "emphasis should be on helping to overcome problems and not on allocating blame."(11) One common liability facing managers and administrators is that they are charged with varying degrees of responsibility yet lack the authority to carry out these responsibilities. In a strict sense, authority and responsibility form the legal framework of management. Authority is defined as "the right derived from some legitimate source to direct the efforts of others. It is the power to act."(12) Responsibility and authority functions are found in varying degrees at all five management-function levels. The effective discharge of responsibility and authority depends on the level of formal authority that has been granted: the ability to award recompense to employees for correct behavior, the power to sanction subordinates for mistakes, the respect one can engender because of perceived expertise in political as well as managerial matters, and the ability to induce subordinates to properly identify with the manager and the project. Responsibility also involves reporting, either by one's self or collectively, to superiors possessing the same attributes of responsibility.

These three systems interact dynamically with all management functions in a complex societal framework that imposes many political-economic and sociocultural administrative constraints. These general considerations are relevant to China's experience but have been adapted and improved upon as needed. Contained in these functions and systems are contrasting management and administrative styles that, when applied to education, present models potentially divergent. China's experience with educational administration provides evidence of experimentation with different management approaches. It is against this background that the two cases will be discussed.

EDUCATIONAL ADMINISTRATION AND MANAGEMENT IN CHINA: AN EVOLVING STRATEGY

Through trial and error China's leaders developed an administrative strategy within the ideological context of Marxism-Leninism as practiced by the Chinese Communist Party. Although the CCP had several years of organizational and administrative experience prior to the Jiangxi Soviet period, it was during this period that Mao Zedong and leaders in the CCP had the opportunity to administer a government, formulate public policy, and make decisions affecting a sizable proportion of people. At this time an administrative structure evolved that included a central authority for development of an educational system.(13) Much of the organizational impetus was informal and was criticized at a later time for having no governmental or CCP control.(14)

Gradually, a balance between central and local administration evolved. Youth and student groups (provided they were already attending one of the "people's schools" and were literate) were encouraged to participate actively in the management of the schools.(15) The school principals were to be chosen from the local regions and were not required to be literate, the primary requirement being that they possess "enthusiastic leadership ability," have compatibility with people, and have the ability to manage what administrative details might arise. The principals, too, (if they had not yet been through the primary school cycle) were required to attend classes.(16) As a result of these rulings, the administration and management of schools resembled a human relations approach, with much more in the way of horizontal relations than line and staff, and being much more task oriented than function oriented.(17) The net result was a system composed of a vertically organized CCP, a governmental structure that provided loose leadership over educational policy, and a locally controlled school system in a more horizontal and informal fashion.

As the Jiangxi Soviet came under military attack in 1934, the CCP was forced to tighten up its organizational structure, which affected the administration of education. CCP leaders criticized the lack of direction and control over education. They suggested a special branch of education be established with placement of more constraints over local educational units.(18) This was clearly a period of experimentation from which China's leaders deduced that a delicate balance existed between decentralized, task-oriented administration and control and centralized, functional educational planning and practice.

The next major formative period in the evolution of China's educational administrative strategy was the Yan'an period (1936-48), when a more complex system developed composed of many horizontal staff and line relationships. The administration of the border regions resembled as a whole an interlocking system that included the CCP organization, the People's Liberation Army (PLA), the formal government, and a variety of mass organizations. Extensive information and communication channels were developed that linked all levels. The CCP rose to the top as the most responsible and authoritative body in the system.

Responsibility for the administration of education fell within the government's domain. At the regional level one of the eight departments was the Department of Education. Assigned to the Department of Education, as well as to the mass organizations involved in educational affairs such as youth groups, student and youth groups, teachers' unions, and so on was one or more cadres of the CCP. While the CCP provided central leadership, by 1944 a viable system that linked the village to higher administrative levels had been established and local participation and decision making was balanced with centralized planning.(19) At this time, school credos of self-sufficiency, self-reliance, and popular management (minban) evolved, as did the concept of basic school administrative units of leading groups (lingdao gugan).(20) Educational administration and management was therefore to be spread widely, and responsibility and authority for the five management functions discussed above were to be lodged between central and local "leading groups." Central authorities in both the CCP and formal government were not to interfere in local management. Their role was focused on overall planning and problem resolution.(21) This concept of the mass line in educational management remained a central theme in the evolution of China's administrative and management style.(22)

The contrasting outlook toward centralization and decentralization which was present during the Jiangxi and Yan'an periods intensified tenfold following the establishment of the People's Republic in 1949. It has been suggested that if one had to choose one primary difference between political interest groups in China, it would be their view regarding the relative roles of central and local responsibility and authority.(23) Should schools be controlled by provincial and ministry-level experts and bureaucrats or should there be a transfer of control to local leading groups and/or CCP cadre? During the political campaigns that waged from 1949 to the period of the Four Modernizations, this was the central question.

These two competing tendencies were referred to respectively as the branch dictates (tiaotiao zhuanzheng) and the area dictates (kuaikuai zhuanzheng). The former pertained to a central, ministry, top-down administrative style and the latter to a local, CCP (or other committee) administrative and management system.(24) The line of direction ran toward the central (the branch dictates) from between 1950-58 and in the early 1960s, and was reintroduced in 1980. During these periods, one-man management was dominant, with school principals, university administrators, and ministry heads granted authority in preference to local CCP committees and leading groups.(25) Emphasis was on the utilization of experts and professionals for educational management, with consequent implications for each of the five management functions and for such components as curriculum (with stress on academics), student selection and advancement (emphasizing hierarchical and meritorious criteria), and the role of the teachers in school and student government relationships (teacher-centered, focus on discipline).

Decentralization (the area dictates) tendencies were most visible during the Great Leap Forward and the GPCR. Local units such as the communes, the CCP committees, and factories and their three in one committees were urged to establish and maintain their own schools according to their particular needs, except that the school cycles were to be trimmed from 12 to 8 or 9 years.(26)

In the administrative structure of the schools themselves, CCP committees and mass organizations were to play a cooperative, if not a dominant, role in the administrative process.(27) The GPCR was the most dramatic exponent of the credo that "red" replace "expert" as a management style, that "politics" rather than "rules and regulations" take command, and that schools and other institutions merge rather than separate. In school management wide levels of participation were encouraged among students, teachers, the People's Liberation Army (PLA), and the restructured CCP. The envisioned model was to comprise a working-class group leadership decentralized to the level of the schools themselves. The three in one committees that evolved included personnel from the PLA who were gradually replaced by the CCP committees, teachers and students, activists from among local industrial workers, or peasants from rural schools.(28)

But when branches replaced areas, expert replaced red, line and staff replaced committees, and the total educational structure was brought under central ministry and provincial control, an abrupt end came to this model of decentralization. The advent of the Four Modernizations Movement had arrived.

With the changing of China's administrative and management experience, no single model initiated by the various political interest groups since 1949 has prevailed. At different times highly centralized and decentralized approaches have been emphasized. Western observers as well as China's leaders have disagreed over the relative merits of each approach. The stability provided by a more centralized bureaucratic management process is, of course, favored by those whose ideology supports a linear, hierarchical development strategy. The use of mass campaigns and of conflict as a development strategy is preferred by those whose ideology supports a mass-participation approach.

With respect to the developmental advances that China has achieved in the past 30 years, there is evidence to support both points of view.(29) Neither approach has been monolithically entrenched for any length of time. In each major campaign, elements of centralization and decentralization have been present that present us with a picture of a broadly based management and organizational structure with contradictory approaches.(30) One way to focus on these two management and administrative styles is through micro-case studies. The next two cases and the concluding discussion will illustrate the relative aspects of both approaches.

EDUCATIONAL MANAGEMENT AND THE GPCR:
TECHNICAL TRAINING FOR RURAL DEVELOPMENT

For the past 30 years, a priority of the Chinese government has been the effort to transform rural China into a more productive, modern, and integrated economy.(31) Despite the many factional disputes involving leadership, this still remains the case. Whichever administration holds sway in Beijing, broad econmic policy guidelines reinforced the promotion of rural development through a policy of "walking on two legs," or giving equal attention to the transformation of indigenous small-scale technology and techniques to more modern methods. In reality, however, the different administrations emphasized one "leg" over the other. This often has been the case with technical training programs, one of the more critical educational efforts of China's rural development schema.(32)

The technical training program discussed here was associated with a small-scale hydroelectric project known as Yaocun Project. The project was in an area located in North China near the county seat of Linxian, Henan province, and consisted of an extensive canal system known as the Hongqi Canal (Red Flag Canal). Construction of the massive canal began in 1957 and was completed in 1969. Over several years following its completion, numerous other small-scale projects associated with the canal were also built. For example, over 70 small factories and 80 small hydroelectric stations were erected along the canal route.

For the period of 1970-75, all of these projects conformed to the development plan specified by Linxian county, and coincided with the GPCR. Therefore, there were some common characteristics in each: they were rural based, utilized indigenous technologies, supported the development of agriculture, were low in cost, were labor absorbing, and were locally financed, managed, and controlled. In addition, all trained personnel were derived from and trained in the area. These characteristics were consistent with the national policies to be self-reliant, combine theory with practice, combine mental and manual labor, and merge school with society.

Planning for the Yaocun Project was set at the county seat or below, with equal decision-making power emanating from the three production brigades involved. To choose the site, feasibility studies were conducted and designs for the project drawn. The project required about four years to complete and was put into operation in 1974. During the construction phase, the project was organized in a paramilitary fashion. The project manager was in "command" of the headquarters (si ling bu), which consisted of committee members from the county and production brigade. The production brigade consisted of highly experienced personnel who required little, nor asked for little, direction from county officials.

During the initial stage of the project, the major concern had been the selection for future management and technical positions of adequately trained men from among the 220 workers on the site. To absolve this difficulty, a technical training program was initiated whereby master craftsmen assigned to small groups of young laborers taught stone masonry and other construction crafts. Another method was to assign older skilled workers to monitor the work of younger unskilled workers to correct their shortcomings. The skilled trainers and the unskilled laborers met daily to discuss the overall progress of the trainees and to identify the more promising from among the force. At least 30 such bright people were needed for recruitment into a more sophisticated electrical-technical training program. These programs were to be conducted on-site during the installation of the electrical components.

But before the second stage of the training program could be implemented, several political events occurred that had a decided impact on the Yaocun Project. By 1974 the national economy had continued to erode. Widespread factional disputes involving several industrial cities were reported and were particularly critical in the steel and transport industries. Conditions deteriorated so drastically that in mid-1976 the military was called to settle the discord in the railroad industry. Zhengzhou, the capital of Henan province weathered such disruptions to its industries.

At the central level of government, the so-called moderates and pragmatists (Deng Xiaoping and Zhou Enlai) demanded that professional managers and technicians centralize their operations and tighten up management. More radical factions associated with the GPCR claimed that experts contributed little or nothing to the development of small-scale industrial and educational projects and that the mass movement model should be the guideline in all project activities.(33)

The Yaocun Project was nearing completion at this time of conflict and the second stage of technical-educational training was being initiated. This second stage was a more formal process and involved middle-level training programs for management, electrical engineers, and maintenance personnel. The identification and selection of superior workers had begun and appointments were finalized for those who would be trained for positions in the completed plants.

Such training had begun during the construction of the project, and had culminated during this period. The workers had been given on-the-job training and short-term classes at the Yaocun brigade area. This particular form of training program became known as the Yaocun May 7 Peasant College (since renamed the Yaocun Secondary Agricultural Technical College) and was similar to many in the GPCR. These peasant colleges of 1973-77 were locally managed and stressed practical studies.

Enrollment at the Yaocun College ranged from 100 to 200 students at any given period and their training was in some area of agro-technical science. The course of study ranged from a few months to three years, few reaching the maximum. The program was intense and specialized. A short two to three month course might focus on the skill of becoming a tractor driver, an electrician or a paramedical person. A five to seven month course would train in the areas of basic veterinary science, machinery repair, and water conservation and power. The longer periods of study, one to two years, provided training in more technical matters such as plant protection, insect control, microbiology, animal husbandry, teacher education, and project management.

Responsibility for management of the college rested with the county CCP committee, in cooperation with the revolutionary commune and brigade committees, and linked horizontally the county and provincial agricultural departments (Figure 3.2). Students were enrolled without age or educational restrictions, although a middle-school education of six to nine years was preferred. Once admitted, the student was required to finish the curriculum, but could leave when sponsors felt the material had been mastered and he could return when refresher courses were needed or when advanced technical problems arose. While a student, he would continue to be paid in work points from his production brigade and his course of study was so arranged that he could continue to work at the project during the daylight hours.

After daily on-the-job training stints, the Yaocun trainees were released early to attend classes at the May 7th College. As advanced students, their course of study focused on electrical engineering, water conservation, power, and project management. These trainees soon became known as the backbone of the construction crew. The plants were eventually handed over to them for control once the project was completed. Once on their new duties, they were relieved from their work in agriculture and retained their regular work-point payment rate plus receiving an additional subsidy paid for by the county government.

County officials and the project manager at Yaocun felt this method of technical education to be time consuming and inefficient. Yet, given the small pool of technically trained personnel in rural China, they felt it an educationally well-suited strategy to further China's developmental needs and, because of the nature of local controls, a strategy that created high levels of motivation for both students and teachers.

The third and last stage of this technical training program was the dissemination and diffusion process occurring after the plants were completed and the "backbone" students trained. The basic goal was to demonstrate to the production brigade and the farmers innovative technology such as that of the small-scale hydroelectric plants. The mechanism for transmitting this knowledge was a technical exchange station. The station served as a demonstration and a consulting agency giving short introductory classes directed to leaders from other brigades that were also developing similar plants. Field trips were organized to bring these personnel to the project

Figure 3.2   Urban Secondary-Technical Training Structure and Linkages

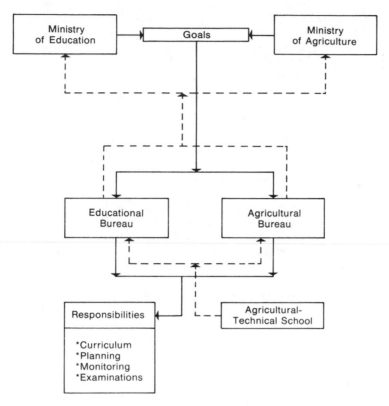

Source: Constructed by the author.

site to demonstrate to them benefits of the small-scale hydro-electric plants. To further educate, the station produced easy-to-read publications discussing the project, the technical skills required, and a how-to-do-it guide for other brigades and communes.

The final activity of the technical exchange station was its sponsorship of forums and seminars for purposes of exchange of information across the brigade/commune lines. Such approaches continued until the target population had been reached. With the establishment of the technical exchange station, the project was fully staffed and completed. The brigade technical school continued to provide short-term training for the new project management and technical team which, in turn, became the new instructors on an as-needed basis.

This corporate training program illustrates features that are associated particularly with educational policy and planning during the GPCR. In terms of the five functions discussed, this educational project was indeed planned from the ground up; the officials from the county and production brigade cooperated in an atmosphere of equality to set in place the elements of both the project and the educational training program. Organizationally the program was task oriented, designed to solve specific problems, and to prepare personnel for specific tasks. Instructors and students associated with the educational component were selected based on their proximity to the hydroelectric plant, were recruited from the ranks, and had been involved in the initial and final phases of construction.

Given the nature of the project, the management team was committee-based rather than dependent on a one-man management approach. Complex unity existed between the county-level hydro-electric authorities, commune and production brigade committees, and various agricultural departments, and this unity was given the direction and control of the technical training program. Confusion sometimes arose over which of the responsibilities a group would be in control of, but pertinent individuals indicated this approach to be preferable to a centrally planned, strict and hierarchical educational chain of command. (Figure 3.3)(34) In short, the Yaocun Project is representative of decentralized, task-oriented educational programs that proliferated during the GPCR.

EDUCATIONAL MANAGEMENT AND THE FOUR
MODERNIZATIONS MOVEMENT: TECHNICAL TRAINING
FOR URBAN DEVELOPMENT

Of China's 1 billion people, roughly 20 percent live in urban areas (dushiqu). Cities are categorized according to four administrative levels: first, special municipalities (zhixiashi) governed by the central government and harboring large surrounding rural popula-tions (e.g., Shanghai, with its 5.52 million city inhabitants and 5.29

million in ten surrounding counties); second, 78 regional centers, as of 1979, made up of capitals of provincial and autonomous regions and prefectural-level cities; third, medium-sized cities; and fourth, small cities.

Cities have been the focus of major modernization efforts and have led the rest of China in putting together the most innovative educational practices. Cities such as Shanghai are centrally administered municipalities and are thus representative of the more centralized planning bodies in China. Since the inauguration of the Four Modernizations movement, Shanghai has been at the forefront of adherence to central guidelines, improvement of management and administration, and bringing order to such areas as secondary technical education, an area in which it leads the nation.

The focus of this case study is the role played by secondary technical education in relation to Shanghai's food production.(35) Because of the enormous food requirements of Shanghai, food production is a critical ingredient and the city must of necessity manage and administer well its complex linkages between agriculture, industry, and education. Debates rage over the policies of centralized and decentralized planning, and any existing problems with reference to secondary and technical education are attributed to the GPCR period. Emphasis then has been put on the reorganization of planning, management has tightened, and the quality of curriculum and instruction has been raised.

A feature of Shanghai's current educational strategy worth study is the emphasis placed on the coordination of human resources and the research done in modern agricultural methods to benefit the surrounding industries and areas. Since the 1950s it is the agro-technical education and research and training that have been given priority: however, it is since the Four Modernizations movement that high level officials in Shanghai have equated these priorities with investment in material resources.(36) A recent report from the Research Institute of the Ministry of Finance in Beijing suggests that agro-technical training be formalized and placed to the fore-front in priority, while local officials should no longer concentrate agro-technical training primarily on local agricultural and industrial production, as was done with the hydroelectric training program.(37) Again, the GPCR period was blamed for problems occurring at all levels, including those in research and development, agro-technical colleges, secondary technical schools, and various on-the-job training programs.

Although agricultural research received much attention and progressed at a remarkable rate, city officials remained critical of what they considered the poor quality achieved during the past ten years. As a consequence, agricultural science (nongye kexue) was identified as the solution to China's productivity. Through the establishment of key institutes for agricultural research and the establishment of links with other national agricultural research institutions, the municipality of Shanghai followed this theory and is in the process of reorganizing the administration and management of this educational sector. The Shanghai Educational Bureau and the Ministry of Education in Beijing hold joint responsibilities for government of this procedure.

The next two educational levels under the research institutes are related more to Shanghai's immediate developmental needs. They comprise the secondary technical colleges and the nonformal training programs associated with industry. The Shanghai Educational Bureau maintains greater authority over these levels and coordinates the program content of the 70-plus secondary technical schools.(38) Each school in turn has its own administrative staff linked directly to an appropriate municipal office. For example, an agricultural-technical school would report to both the Shanghai Agricultural Bureau and the Educational Bureau. They in turn would report jointly to the Ministries of Agriculture and Education in Beijing. At this ministry level, goals regarding teaching policies, terms of instruction, curricular plans, and the balance of specializations are established and communicated to the municipal bureaus. Returning again to the Shanghai Agricultural Bureau and the Educational Bureau, they have responsibility for implementing these goals in such areas as enrollment, examination, ideological studies such as political education, in-service education, and municipal planning (see Figure 3.4). The organizational model presented reflects the more centralized policies of the Four Modernizations movement and expresses the desire by educational officials to bring order to bear, first on education in general and second on technical education.

A profile can be drawn from some selected examples of Shanghai's secondary schools and nonformal programs.(39) Of the former is the Songjiang Agricultural College at which, since 1956, middle-level agricultural technical training has been taught to solve food needs of the Shanghai municipality and environs. Since its inception, the school has graduated about 4,000 students and is subsequently increasing its enrollment and administering stricter entrance requirements. The term of study has been increased from three to four years, reversing the trend set by the GPCR in 1972 of decreasing the number of years required. A curriculum has been organized with five discrete specializations: cultivation, plant protection, agricultural meteorology, agricultural mechanization, and veterinary science. Forty percent of the curriculum is devoted to six basic studies: Chinese, English, politics, mathematics, physics, and physical training. The remaining 60 percent is devoted to advanced courses in one of the five specializations.

The previous practice of recruiting teaching staff from among brighter graduates has given way to a centralized staffing plan developed by the Shanghai Educational Bureau. The college is also in the process of separation from its companion factory, with which it was associated during the GPCR years, and is in the midst of a battle over management of land claimed mutually by both. This is indicative of the current conception of separation of jointly managed schools and factories to be replaced by discrete administrative structures. Also, the process of committee management of secondary technical school administration has also been replaced by a one-man management by principals (xiao zhang).

Various rural and urban nonformal educational programs are also in practice throughout the Shanghai area. Rural programs are conducted at local secondary-schools that focus their attention on production brigade cadres and agricultural technicians. Work points are offered as an incentive to those individuals who take specialized, short-term courses in plant protection, fertilizer production, agricultural machinery repair, and truck driving. Specialized courses are offered also for cadres in charge of agricultural management. Over the past six years, Shanghai's educational officers found that management cadres attached to communes were greatly deficient in number and that those who were available lacked the technical knowledge to meet China's new mechanization and modernization drive. Consequently, a new policy stipulates that managers of rural units must be examined annually to determine the extent of their ideological level, performance, and technical and general skill. If their abilities are judged inadequate, the examinee must resume study and be reexamined at a later date. A continuing study program has been suggested for agricultural managers as well so they can be kept abreast of new developments.

Nonformal classes are also being maintained for peoples involved in urban industry. Factories are encouraged to offer spare-time classes to raise employee skill levels and to keep in step with the modernization effort. According to the director of the Shanghai Educational Bureau, roughly 25 percent of the industrial workers take advantage of this opportunity, however the performance level remains disappointing.

Workers receive pay for time spent in day classes or ·study in night classes for one or two years depending on the subject matter. Standards have been raised to overcome the former lack of quality charged to have prevailed during the GPCR. Rigorous examinations are given, yet achievement levels remain low; in 1981, only 6 percent passed the course examinations. Educational officials have been astounded by both the inferior quality of instruction and the poor motivation of the workers. Efforts are underway to improve instruction, and the new policy stipulates that without progress in their course of study, those who fail will be denied bonuses and promotions.

It is not sure how successful this new hard line will prove to be, but a commitment has been made to improve the skills of rural and urban workers. Moreover, the involved officials are stressing the importance of the development of human resources for the modernization program, while clearly viewing education and training as functional; the focus is on serving the interests of industry and agriculture while at the same time having the ability to shift quickly enough to new developmental priorities. The answer, it seems, is to strengthen centralized planning, administration, and management, while reducing the flexibility of program content characteristic of the GPCR period.

To raise instructional quality and to reward or punish workers attached to the program, standard operating procedures are being initiated. Strict line and staff relations are being implemented, and strong links forged with other educational institutions. It has been suggested that educational planning be left to the planners and not be delegated downward to include groups associated with the educational program in question (e.g., brigade members, students, factory workers, and so on).

The model followed in Shanghai has been that of planning for improvement, in contrast to the GPCR practice of planning from the ground up. Control and monitoring responsibilities have been strictly adhered to by experts in the Shanghai Educational Bureau. Efforts to clarify authority and responsibility have been introduced to dispell confusion as to who is in charge and who gets the blame when things go wrong. In short, educational programs have been viewed as only one important ingredient among the many in China's modernization and production drive and as such must be integrated into the mechanism of national central planning and implementation.

CONCLUSION

The cases discussed reflect two very different administrative and management styles. With respect to the five management functions, the GPCR period can be characterized as representative of a massive effort at decentralization of responsibility and authority. Planning was a combination of local, intermediate, and central inputs with emphasis placed on local communes, factories, individual schools, and so on. The organizational style was task-oriented and the personnel recruited for advancement was contingent upon a variety of criteria. The direction and control functions were accountable to committees and coalitions, rather than to central planning bodies. This remained true for all rural and urban schools as well as for the secondary technical programs.(40)

By contrast, the current Four Modernizations movement has reintroduced the hierarchical, centralized planning and administration pattern of previous years; albeit, with some new innovations. The first major effort to bring the educational structure under control was the introduction of a report by the CCP Central

Committee at its Fifth Plenary Session in 1980 that stressed strengthening control over all levels of education.(41)

At the same time, a new program was inaugurated to recruit and train educational personnel in a formal, pedagogical manner, rather than from within the organization and from the bottom up as described in the Yaocun Project.(42) For example, a special School Administrator's College has been set up in Beijing for the training of principals in special subjects and in such subjects as pedagogy, psychology, and philosophy. This program has been introduced at precisely the time when the United States and other industrialized countries question such an approach.

Each of the five functions noted are assigned to specific bodies for implementation and control. Whereas educational officials of the GPCR stressed management and administration according to local conditions, present-day officials state that educational administration should emphasize optimization of manpower and material resources, acting according to objective rules.(43) To be operational on a massive scale, a centralized educational planning system has been proposed. This would include recruitment of students, selection of locale and model of the physical plant's companion buildings (school, libraries and ancillary structures), assignment of personnel, and so on. Computers could be used to execute this centralization process more efficiently. It has been suggested that China avoid imitating the West, and instead use foreign things to serve China (yang wei zhong yong). There is considerable fascination with Western principles of management but without the understanding of the political-economic process involved.(44)

Among supporters of the GPCR movement, it was widely believed that with politics in command everything else would follow rationally. The current group has preferred to shift their emphasis to one with science in command. GPCR educators considered educational administration impractical as a science and inappropriate for a field of study. As a guide it would prove useful, but nothing more. Far more useful would be experienced personnel with good work style recruited from within an organization, rather than those with formal training.

This GPCR belief continues to plague China's new leadership. This leadership now suggests that a complex network be established of educational administrative branches linked to the Educational Academic Society. This network would establish also educational administrative research bodies, textbooks would become required reading for school administrators, administrative control central to all educational levels would be tightened, and, as mentioned, foreign administrative practices would be studied.

The argument can be made that China's educational officials have learned that operating through a centralization process involves many limitations and consequently are beginning to decentralize key functions. Thus far, however, the decentralization has been limited to relieving the financial burden placed on central bodies, such as municipalities, provinces, and the Ministry of Education in Beijing.

Two administrative and management styles have been presented in the form of discrete cases. Obviously, the national picture is quite complex.(45) Nevertheless, it is clear that there has been a tendency in Chinese educational policy to swing dramatically centrifugally (as in the Great Leap Forward and GPCR) or centripetally (as in the current Four Modernizations Movement) with respect to management and administration. Some educational officials feel that the former model is more suited to rural development where rapidity of response to change and the resulting innovations required are the key, while the latter model is more attuned to change and development of urban large-scale, capital-intensive projects.(46)

In other words, a strategy must be developed to utilize both the positive aspects of centralized and decentralized administration and management but the strategy should not reflect a domination by either the forces of centralization or decentralization. Chinese educational officials are sometimes hampered by the political need to attribute to the GPCR period all their educational problems. This dynastic history approach of inappropriately analyzing the past, if not soon abandoned, may evolve into the use of blinders similar to those worn during earlier Chinese regimes that contributed to their downfall. With centuries of societal management and administrative experience to draw from, and in light of the many innovative approaches used in problem solving, China's educational leaders are now in a position not only to produce theoretical and practical breakthroughs in educational administration but to serve as a stimulating example for others.

NOTES

(1)   Ramon H. Myers, The Chinese Economy: Past and Present (Belmont, Calif.: Wadsworth, 1980); James R. Townsend, Politics in China, 2d ed. (Boston: Little, Brown, 1980); James C.F. Wang, Contemporary Chinese Politics: An Introduction (Englewood Cliffs, N.J.: Prentice-Hall, 1980); Gilbert Rozman, ed., The Modernization of China (Riverside, N.J.: The Free Press, 1981); Harry Harding, Organizing China: The Problem of Bureaucracy, 1949-1976 (Stanford, Calif.: Stanford University Press, 1981).

(2)   Many fine studies of this sort are available, see for example: Jonathen Unger, Education Under Mao: Class and Competition in Canton Schools (New York: Columbia University Press, 1982); Susan L. Shirk, Competitive Comrades: Career Incentives and Student Strategies in China (Berkeley: University of California Press, 1982); Ronald F. Price, Education in Communist China (London: Routledge & Kegan Paul, 1979).

(3)   The terms "management" and "administration" are used in close proximity in this chapter; management refers to overall process and administration to specific educational units. This section draws heavily from a study by the author and an international team of scholars and practitioners from Asia, the Pacific, and the United States, the results of which are contained in Louis J. Goodman and Ralph N. Love, eds., Project Planning and Management: An Integrated Approach (New York: Pergamon Press, 1980); Clark Bloom, "Project Identification and Formulation," in Goodman and Love, Project Planning and Management, p. 22; John N. Hawkins, "Refinement of Policy and Planning," in Goodman and Love, Project Planning and Management, pp. 233-44.

(4)   E. Kirby Warren, Long Range Planning: The Executive Viewpoint (Englewood Cliffs, N.J.: Prentice-Hall, 1966), p. 21.

(5)   David I. Cleland and William R. King, Systems Analysis and Project Management (New York: McGraw Hill, 1968), p. 5.

(6)   These recommendations are based on several recent studies and coincide with traditional staffing strategies; See Goodman and Love, Project Planning and Management; Paul Gaddis, "The Project Manager," Harvard Business Review (May/June 1959): 93.

(7)   See Hawkins, "Refinement of Policy and Planning" for current theory attempts to predict the abilities of managers to adapt to one or the other approach; and Douglas Bray, The Assessment Center Method (Pittsburgh: Development Dimen, 1979).

(8)   Hans L. Thambain and David L. Wilemon, "Conflict Management in the Project Life Cycle," Sloan Management Review (Spring 1975): 38.

(9)   Cleland and King, Systems Analysis and Project Management, p. 6.

(10)   Hawkins, "Refinement of Policy and Planning," pp. 238-39.

(11)   W.F. Taylor, and T.F. Watling, Practical Project Management (New York: Halsted Press, 1973), p. 106.

(12)   Cleland and King, Systems Analysis and Project Management, p. 7.

(13)   Mao Zedong, "Shixing guangfan shenru de chatian yundong," in Mao Tse-tung chiv, 4 vols. ed. Takeuchi Minoru (Tokyo: Hokubosha Press, 1970), III: 224.

(14)   This criticism came from chief of the general staff of the PLA Lo Ruijing in 1957. Mao and Lo clashed over administrative control of the PLA in 1959 and Lo was later purged. See Franz Schurmann, Ideology and Organization in Communist China (Berkeley: University of California Press, 1966), p. 193.

(15)   Mao Zedong, "Xingguo diaocha," in Mao Tse-tung chi, II: 249-50.

(16)   Mao Zedong, "Changgang xiang diaocha," in Mao Tse-tung chi, IV: 158.

(17)   The human relations approach to management is outlined in Jacob W. Getzels, James M. Lipham, and Ronald F. Campbell, eds., Educational Administration as a Social Process (New York: Harper and Row, 1968), pp. 30-39.

(18)   Mao Zedong, "Zhonghua suweiai gongheguo zhongyang," in Mao Tse-tung chi, IV: 262-63.

(19)   Administrative practices during the Yan'an period are discussed in Schurmann, Ideology and Organization in Communist China, and especially in Mark Selden, The Yenan Way in Revolutionary China (Cambridge: Harvard University Press, 1971), pp. 144-60, 274.

(20)   Mao Zedong, "Some Questions Concerning Methods of Leadership," in Selected Works of Mao Tse-tung (Peking: Foreign Languages Publishing House, 1965), III: 118-19.

(21)   This policy is suggested in a document published by the Shenganning Border Region Government and contained in a collection of Chinese documents published in Japan: "Hanrei kenkyu no teisho oyobi mintei shogaku shiko ni kansuru no tegami," in Mo Taku-to kyoiku ron, ed. and trans. Saito Akio and Niijima Atsuyoshi (Tokyo: Aoki Shoten, 1957), p. 260.

(22)   The mass-line concept is discussed in John Wilson Lewis, Leadership in Communist China (Ithaca: Cornell University Press, 1963), pp. 70-100.

(23)   Unger, Education Under Mao, p. 143.

(24)   Ibid.

(25)   Ibid., p. 124.

(26)   Mao Tse-tung, "Summary of Talk to Heads of Education Departments and Bureaus of Seven Provinces and Municipalities," in Current Background, no. 888, August 2, 1969, p. 7.

(27)   Mao Tse-tung, "Instruction Given on an Inspection Tour of Tientsin University" (excerpts) in Current Background, no. 891, October 8, 1969, p. 30.

(28)   Mao Tse-tung, "Educational Revolution" in Mao Papers: An Anthology With Bibliography, ed. Jerome Ch'en (New York: Oxford University Press, 1970), p. 155. Even such conservative leaders as the former President Liu Shaoqi, posthumously rehabilitated, agreed with many aspects of the GPCR critique of current conditions in the mid-1960s; see Lowell Dittmer, "Death and Transfiguration: Liu Shaoqi's Rehabilitation and Contemporary Chinese Politics," Journal of Asian Studies 40, no. 3 (May 1981): 427.

(29)   An insightful comparative, qualitative, and quantitative analysis of the effectiveness of the mass-campaign approach to social change is presented in Charles P. Cell, Revolution at Work: Mobilization Campaigns in China (New York: Academic Press, 1977), p. 173.

(30)   The struggle between forces for decentralization and those for centralization leading up the GPCR is discussed in depth in

Parris H. Chang, Power and Policy in China (London: Pennsylvania State University Press, 1975), pp. 176-90.

(31)   This section is a condensed case study of a rural development project in north-central China. This study is based on data gathered during the summer of 1979 by the author and during a two month research site visit to the PRC and appears in full in John N. Hawkins, "The People's Republic of China: Energy for Rural Development," in Small Hydroelectric Projects for Rural Development, ed. Louis J. Goodman, John N. Hawkins, and Ralph N. Love (New York: Pergamon Press, 1981), pp. 21-60.

(32)   For a more complete discussion of the transfer-transformation dilemma, see John N. Hawkins, "Technique Transformation and Rural Education in the People's Republic of China," Technology Forecasting and Social Change (April 1978).

(33)   Hongqi, no. 6 (1973).

(34)   The leader of the project management team was more explicit: "we prefer not to have Beijing (central government) or Zhengzhou (provincial government) interfering and telling us what to do and how to train personnel."

(35)   Based on a study conducted by the author in Shanghai during the period March 4-31, 1981. See John N. Hawkins, Shanghai: An Exploratory Report on Human Resource Development and Food for the City (Honolulu: East-West Center Press, 1982).

(36)   Foreign Broadcast Information Service (FBIS), February 22, 1980.

(37)   FBIS, April 21, 1980.

(38)   This level of education was referred to both as "schools" (xueyuan) and "colleges" (daxue), and appeared in a state of transition from middle level to higher level education.

(39)   Eight such institutions were part of the broader study; the programs presented are representative of those researched in the complete study.

(40)   This process is described at the national level in: Suzanne Pepper, "Education and Revolution: The 'Chinese Model' Revisited," Asian Survey 18, no. 9 (September 1978): 847-90. It can be contrasted with the previous period in: Susan Shirk, "The 1963 Temporary Work Regulations for Full Time Middle and Primary Schools, Commentary and Translation," China Quarterly, no. 55, 1973.

(41)   FBIS, March 17, 1980.

(42)   FBIS, March 11, 1980.

(43)   Lou Huguan, "Yao janjiu jiaoyu guanlixue," Renmin Jiaoyu, January 1981, pp. 31-32.

(44)   FBIS, January 15, 1980. See also Qian Jiaju, "Increasing Educational Funds as an Important Strategy for the Realization of the Four Modernizations," Jiaoyu Yanjiu, no. 21, 1980, pp. 5-15.

(45)   On recent research visits (1979, 1980, 1981), the author found many GPCR management patterns still being followed,

particularly in the rural sector. In private conversations some educators voiced reservations about the current modernization policy.

(46)   This dichotomy is similar to one presented in John Friedman, Retracking America: A Theory of Transactional Planning (New York: Anchor Press, 1973), pp. 49-85.

4

THE POLITICS OF
CURRICULAR CHANGE IN THE
PEOPLE'S REPUBLIC OF CHINA

Irving Epstein

During the past 15 years, curricular change within the People's Republic of China's educational structures has been premeditated, swift, and substantial. The degree to which such change has occurred within the world's largest educational system attests to the importance policymakers have placed upon the school as a potential transmission agent for identifiable political, social, and cultural values. Indeed, it would be difficult to find a clearer example whereby specific curricular forms have been endowed with such a wide-ranging degree of cultural capital. This process has occurred within the domains of both the concrete and the hidden curricula; it has held true for the actual as well as symbolic forms of curricular content. At the same time, it should be remembered that the scope and quality of curricular change within the People's Republic of China has been very much influenced by different attempts at institutional reorganization, and in most instances, supplementation of those policy reforms.

As in the case with most educational systems, Chinese institutions repeatedly have been assigned roles that complement and are interrelated with each other. This is certainly not surprising in a state dedicated to central planning, and with a strong historical tradition that encouraged at least some measure of centralized educational control through the operation of the Confucian examination system. Nevertheless, it must be reiterated that to speak of specific institutions, such as primary, middle level, or university structures, as possessing autonomous institutional roles is misleading. Each of these institutions has derived its role in relation to its counterparts with curricular issues directly affected during various historical periods. In this chapter, some attention will be given to the two periods of the Great Proletarian Cultural Revolution (GPCR) and the reforms inacted since 1976, many of which have replaced dramatically the curricular pattern set ten years earlier. Questions will be raised concerning the costs and benefits of each curricular model, models which have been inextricably intertwined with the political fabric of Chinese life. Many must remain unanswered.

EVOLUTION OF A CURRICULAR PATTERN

During the years prior to the advent of the Cultural Revolution, the Chinese educational system experienced rapid expansion until the primary school enrollment was nearly universalized. Such expansion occurred within a framework closely modeled after the Soviet educational system, with its emphasis upon structural hierarchy, early streaming into vocational and academic tracks, teaching technically oriented subject matter, and the separation at the highest levels of the educational system of scholarly research from instruction. In particular, in the 1950s at the secondary level a heavy curriculum was established that included 30 class periods or more of 50 minutes each per week including plane, solid, and analytical geometry; trigonometry; geography; and foreign languages. The curriculum was dominated by examinations and the result was a dual-track system whereby only the academic elite were permitted a secondary school education. The nonelite eligible to enter school were forced to seek postprimary training in one of the numerous vocational-technical schools. This was a sharp departure from the universal, polytechnical dimension of education as discussed by both Karl Marx and Mao Zedong. The exact content and nature of the curriculum, especially at the secondary level, was determined by the Ministry of Education in Beijing and was communicated to the provincial and county educational authorities. Thus, decision making with regard to curricular development was highly centralized, with strong controls exerted upon it by the professional pedagogues and administrators.(1)

The expansion of educational opportunities gradually exascerbated the problem of access into the country's higher educational institutions. While it appears to be obvious that the country's universities would have obtained an increased sense of social importance during early 1969, increased access pressures also enhanced the status of the senior-level middle school, with its largely college preparatory curriculum. And, while specific admissions policies rejected the political influence of local elites, favoring at specific times either the children of intellectuals or party cadres, upward access channels for the majority of students were never significantly widened. The exception was access to nonformal institutions such as <u>minban</u> half-work, half-study schools whose social status was consistently lower than that of their formal counterparts.(2) Efforts to expand opportunity at the lowest rungs of the educational ladder, while maintaining traditional limits upon widescale advancement onto the higher rungs of the ladder, have certainly existed outside of the Chinese case. This tendency has been especially true of Western European educational systems during the late nineteenth and early twentieth centuries.(3) But it was perhaps Mao's own charismatic genius that allowed him to successfully portray a personal intraparty leadership struggle as a mass-line struggle against the perceived abuse of privilege and the existence of social inequality, much of which was rife within the educational system. This struggle, of course, culminated in the Cultural Revolution.(4)

REVOLUTIONARY CURRICULUM REFORM:
PROBLEMS OF IMPLEMENTATION

Those institutional changes initially adapted in hopes of redressing outstanding structural inequalities within the educational system were largely negative in tone. Some universities were shut down for up to four or five years. The distinction between senior and lower level middle schooling was, in some cases, also abolished. And treasure pagoda or elitist middle schools, which often served as feeder schools for the country's leading universities, were similarly dismantled, at least in name if not in actual fact.

However, the consequences of such policies were not entirely negative. Middle school expansion increased dramatically in the countryside, and nonformal educational programs also multiplied. The attempt was, in short, one of cutting off the top of the educational pyramid while expanding the base.(5) Curricular reform played its own role in facilitating the process.

Primary education has historically been assigned the dual tasks of socializing a nation's youth by articulating those political and social norms deemed important enough to be internalized if the country's children are to exhibit desirable behavior, while also teaching functional literacy and numeracy skills. In China, the pattern was followed stringently during the 1950s and 1960s.

Charles P. Ridley, Paul H.B. Godwin, and Dennis Doolin, in their analysis of primary school readers (1964 editions), categorized the contents of these texts in terms of informational, political, and behavioral domains. From a purely informational perspective, the agrarian nature of the country, its traditional cultural forms, along with Communist institutions and personalities, were most often stressed. Political themes contrasted the evils of the preliberation period with the progress of the postliberation era, while also emphasizing Mao's personal leadership role and the necessity of remaining vigilant against external threats. Behavioral themes included the necessity of maintaining altruism and personal and social responsibility, and transforming allegiances from the traditional family unit to that of the political entity of the state. The exercise of human will, with the aim of conquering environmental circumstances, was an additional theme prevalent in some of the readers.(6)

While it is certainly arguable as to the degree to which the values expressed within these texts represented a sharp break with traditional Confucian norms, they clearly symbolized governmental attempts to overtly politically socialize the nation's youth through the use of the mechanism of the school.(7) Government-sponsored language reforms, including the use of the hanyu pinyin romanization and the simplification of Chinese characters, also figured prominently within the primary-level texts, further reflecting a commitment to the teaching of basic skills.(8) As students progressed to the higher levels of upper primary and lower middle school, the teaching of specific subject matter in the sciences and humanities was increasingly emphasized.

Reform efforts during the GPCR made some attempts at purifying in ideological terms the educational curricula purging the schools of at least some of the Soviet influence of emphasis upon technical (as opposed to general) subject matter mastery. The importance of students' experiencing practical investigations rather than memorizing theoretical knowledge was, at least overtly, encouraged. Student work experiences in school shops and laboratories and on local agricultural plots increased. Political sloganeering coupled with the ritual of group self-criticism were popularized. Teachers were asked to instruct in an interdisciplinary, open-door manner, as centralized textbooks were abandoned and authoritarian teaching practices were criticized. Year-end compulsory testing as a prerequisite for promotion to the next grade ended; peer tutoring was encouraged.(9)

In Basil Bernstein's terms, the instrumental nature of classroom rituals was at least theoretically replaced by a series of alternatives that were inherently expressive in tone, including a loosening of strict curricular framing and a delineation of the overt authoritarianism within the teacher/student relationship.(10) This change was encouraged by changes in institutional policy and structure, some of which have been mentioned previously. The xiaxiang campaigns, which required middle-school graduates to work in the countryside for a minimum of two years but usually longer, coupled with the restructuring of university curriculum into a generalist, often interdisciplinary format, served, once those institutions were reopened, to loosen the influence the university had on the traditional, college preparatory curricula of the latter years of middle-school instruction. Indeed, in many cases, the abolition of the junior level-senior level dichotomy further served to lessen the necessity of teaching at all levels of instruction specific subject matter with identifiable contours and boundaries.

There was no inherent reason why the teacher, now responsible for communicating information in an interdisciplinary manner, would lose authority within the classroom. However, the Maoist stress upon inductive, practical, investigation, along with a commitment to combining specific disciplines into a general, interdisciplinary curriculum, did attack the principle that one's teaching status was commensurate with an acquired expertise in a particular discipline. It can also be argued that Maoist ideological loyalties renounced not only the distance between theoretical and applied learning, but confronted the very raison d'etre for academic specialization of task.(11)

Despite pronouncement to the contrary, it is not surprising that in the area of teaching method few innovative techniques were clearly enacted. A traditional tolerance for a student-teacher relationship articulating dominant-submissive roles was not easily overcome. Formerly, the predominant view of the teacher-student relationship held that,

> a student must respect his teacher and learn from him all the useful knowledge (he can) with a most serious and conscientious effort. As for the fact that some students eventually surpass their teachers, this can only happen when the students have first learned from their teachers and then surpassed them on that basis. The old saying expresses it well, "Ice grows out of water but is colder than water; indigo is extracted from the indigo plant, but is bluer than the plant it comes from": this is exactly the same argument. There is no such thing as a pupil surpassing his teacher without first learning from him.(12)

While there were, indeed, concerted attacks upon teacher roles during the Great Proletarian Cultural Revolution (GPCR), too often the student-teacher relationship was never positively reconstructed.

> Only when the "sanctity of the teacher's right" has been thoroughly destroyed can a revolutionary and democratic relationship be re-established between the teacher and the student. This is called "no construction without destruction and no flowering without damming." It is a law of ideological struggle.(13)

Already assigned a relatively low degree of social status within the lower levels of the educational system, specific policy changes served to weaken further the role of the teacher.(14) Thus, while the expansion of middle schooling into rural areas allowed many primary-level teachers to move up to the middle-school level, many of these teachers remained unqualified for their new tasks. Primary level teaching vacancies were also filled with equally incompetent teachers.(15) In this way, the Maoist attack upon acquired expertise was implemented in a manner antithetical to the mandate for curricular reform. If it were to have been successful, teaching in an open-door fashion, encouraging practical investigation and allowing for a general environment that was both child-centered and group oriented would have required a greater degree of training on the part of teachers. As a result, while the negative aspects of reform efforts were often internalized (e.g., teachers subjecting themselves to self-criticism in front of students or lecturing solely according to the presumed acceptable political slogans of the day), the impetus for real experimentation was often lost.

Prior to the GPCR, the view of the student was colored by a general acceptance of Soviet psychological principles and, even during the mid-1960s, Chinese views were articulated in a mechanistic rather than in a dynamic fashion when concerned with the possibilities for human development. Personality characteristics were described in static, moralistic terms.(16) Students were thought of, to a certain extent, as unprocessed products subject to the conditioning in Pavlovian style, of their environmental circumstances and class background. Even during times of greater ideological stridence, such as the Great Leap Forward era, questions concerning the importance of individual motivation or independent consciousness affecting human behavior, while raised, were never fully articulated.(17) As a result, a truly interactive approach to developmental issues, which stresses the necessity of encountering varied external experiences while utilizing internal structures of rationality to interpret those experiences, principles distinctive of the Piagetian developmental approach, were never fully explored.

The use of traditional teaching techniques, of course, reiterated these assumptions. In practical terms prior to the GPCR students were held accountable for their success or failure in assimilating the required curricular material. Thus even the most basic of curricular requirements, such as the mastery of Chinese characters, inherently emphasized a traditional importance attached to memorization facility.(18) While it has been pointed out that the traditional use of the unison repetitive response to teacher-directed activities may at times facilitate greater group cohesiveness, its perpetual use may have had the additional effect of camouflaging differences of individual abilities.(19)

With the expansion of schooling in the mid-1950s, peer interactions and group loyalties, especially within urban areas, become more important and competed successfully for influence with traditional family loyalties. Within the senior-level middle school, practices that exascerbated the political importance of peer relations included the granting by teachers and administrators of a privileged status for Communist Youth League (CYL) members. This allowed them to perform quasi-administrative and teaching duties within the classroom. Often this was done to the irritation of their fellow students, whose political activism or class background was labeled less acceptable.(20)

Changing curricular priorities during the GPCR affected the quality of both teacher-student and student-student interactions. Thus, while attacks upon their authority had made teachers gun-shy and reticent in covering any curricular material that might have been construed as being anti-Maoist, similarly the authority of traditional organizational structures such as the CYL was attacked.

A politics-in-command strategy within the classroom setting was implemented through use of the small-group self-criticism session and through widespread participation in manual labor experiences and activities. Group self-criticism, whereby individuals were attacked publicly and forced to confess to their misdeeds in front of the group so their slate could then be wiped clean, was not a new phenomenon. But the degree of its use was extensive during the GPCR although its use produced limited results. Because students were understandably reticent about facing reprisals from their peers, they would offer only cursory critiques of observed mis-behavior.(21) It seems plausible to argue that the irregularity of the political dynamics of the environment probably took its toll on peer relationships. The substitution of a general camaraderie type of group interaction for the strong, particularistic friendship between two peers is a phenomenon within the People's Republic of China noted even before the advent of the GPCR.(22) One would have expected then, that with the continued use of the self-criticism session, and as students looked elsewhere for more significant peer relationships, strong loyalties between individual group members might have waned.

The importance of the work experience to the politics-in-command strategy should not be underestimated. As has been mentioned, participation in manual labor activity was intended to redress the perceived imbalances in social status afforded to manual, as opposed to mental, activity, while also redressing the distance between practical and theoretical investigation. But, while the sight of teachers engaging in mental labor with their students might have presented a clearer picture of the limited importance of their own mental labor, manual labor as a curricular experience had other functions. The activity, first of all, was of a general rather than a specific nature. It was not intended to be monotechnical or to require specialized training. In fact, part of its attractiveness was due to its symbolism. This was an egalitarian participatory activity with which everyone, regardless of intellectual acumen, was capable of indulging.(23)

Second, there were strong moral claims made for the utility of engaging in manual labor. The physical discipline it demanded, the discomfort it created, built character. While this puritanical strain is strong and unmistakable within GPCR ideological pronouncements, the urgency with which it was articulated represented a fundamental concern — the ability of the country's urban youth to appreciate the living conditions of the peasantry and the revolutionary importance of their historical role in contributing to the founding of the People's Republic. The pain of the experience symbolized the essence of revolutionary class struggle, and the activity allowed students to associate more concretely their personal experiences with the predetermined revolutionary mandate.(24)

The multiplicity of schemes, initiated in order to avoid being sent to rural areas with harsh environment, attests to the limits with which such symbolism was internalized.(25) However, it would be a mistake to contend during the GPCR that schools failed totally to implement their task of politically socializing children to the tunes of increased ideological stridence. The extraordinary ability of primary level students to memorize and perform intricate rituals, many with political connotations, their self-confidence in engaging in public performances, and their teachers' appeal to group cohesiveness and loyalty at all times, were characteristics of classroom environments which, during the early 1970s, impressed Western educators in their visits to Chinese schools.(26) In fact, the emphasis upon expressive classroom rituals as a means of implementing ideological tasks, especially at the earlier levels of schooling, compares favorably with traditional Chinese child-rearing patterns. In their initial stages, children are given excessive attention until age six or seven, at which time parenting (especially on the part of the father) becomes dramatically more authoritarian and aloof.(27) Basil Bernstein noted that in the British case, expressive classrom rituals were first popularized and accepted by elements of the middle class when both family members began working on a full-time basis, which transformed the quality of traditional parenting roles and spousal relationships.(28) Within the Chinese context, one of the effects of stringent birth-control measures was to create the phenomenon of the single child or two-children urban family with both spouses working. This situation was first pronounced during the early 1970s.(29) It is thus not unreasonable to speculate that the Maoist appeals to expressive classroom rituals, amidst the popularization of open-ended curricular framing, not only allowed for the expansion of day care and other schooling facilities, but also compared favorably with similar reform efforts within the British context.

At the more advanced levels of schooling though, there are certainly indications of rebellion and subversion of the normative claims of the ideological mandate. For many students, the social utility of their educational experience remained undefined as the ties between middle school graduation and university enrollment were cut. During this period, contemporary discipline problems within the schools are said to have originated not only because the attacks upon teacher authority were excessive, but also because students saw little extrinsic reason to vigorously pursue their studies.(30)

On the other hand, the countless stories of university-bound students sent to the countryside, but who independently continued their studies, often under adverse circumstances, belies the fact that the intrinsic worth of their education was for at least some, not lost. Indeed, the degree of alienation expressed by those members of the "lost generation" who in good faith went to the countryside sincerely believing in the validity of the ideological pronouncements of the time, only to be abandoned there, appears to be too great to deny totally the impact of their schooling in initially shaping their political opinions and beliefs.(31)

What one can conclude is that, at best, curricular reform efforts having been unevenly implemented in the first place, had mixed results. In noting the Maoist attacks upon both regular CCP elements and professionals with intellectual class loyalties, the degree of unevenness of implementation does not strike the observer as being surprising. In fact, even the initial aims of curricular reform were themselves often mixed and seldom clearly defined.(32) The revolutionary mandate for substantive change encouraged and tolerated wide-ranging experimentation in all educational sectors. On the other hand, curricular reform during the latter stages of the GPCR came to represent a conservative attempt to preserve the activist spirit of the initial years of the GPCR and, as such, was subject to and influenced by those elites who sought to manipulate policy changes for their own ends.

CURRICULUM REDEFINED:
QUALITY, STABILITY, SCREENING

Attempts during the post-GPCR to turn back the clock on educational reform have been clearly articulated. The reestablishment of a nationwide university examination system in 1977, fully centralized in 1978, signified a concerted effort to regulate limited access channels into the country's higher educational institutions. Aspiring university students are now tested in both core (Chinese language, mathematics, and politics) and in elective subject areas (foreign language, chemistry, physics, biology, geography, history, and literature). The testing process has served to redefine and reassert the importance of rigidly framing the various curricular disciplines.

At the primary level, in addition to the traditional course work in areas such as Chinese language and mathematics, a greater stress is being put upon the teaching of foreign languages, natural science, music, and the fine arts. Even first-grade students are being asked to attend 36 class periods a week, six days a week of instruction. Some are asked to stay even longer for extra instruction and for intensive study. Within the language component of the primary curriculum alone, students are expected to read and write, often in both full and simplified forms, about 2,500 Chinese characters by the time they complete the first grade.(33)

An analysis of the National Examination syllabuses gives an indication as to the nature of the specific subject requirements for senior middle-school students wishing advancement into the university. According to the 1978 examination syllabus, students are expected to be familiar with ancient Chinese, modern Chinese, and world history, if they decide to sit for the history exam. Climatology, topography, and cultural geography are topics that are included within the general fields of Chinese and world geography, while chemistry students are expected to be specifically proficient in organic chemistry. The physics exam stresses both applied and theoretical concepts, while the mathematics exam requires a knowledge of algebra, plane and solid geometry, exponential calculation, and trigonometric functions. The English foreign language examination concentrates heavily upon correct usage and knowledge of grammatical structure.(34)

While these subject areas are most heavily stressed during the senior-level middle-school experience, their influence upon lower level schooling is still substantial. Thus, according to one report, even sophisticated mathematical concepts such as set theory and the calculus functions of maxima and minima will be introduced into the junior middle-level curriculum.(35)

It is said that new textbooks will include additional topics in traditional subject areas, such as introductions to probability theory and statistics (mathematics); satellite, laser, and semiconductor technological advances, atomic theory, mass-energy relations and wave particle duality, and so on (physics); and microscopic qualitative determinations, nitrogen fixation experiments, environmental protection, and molecular biology (chemistry). Foreign language textbooks will emphasize to a greater degree reading proficiency in scientific and technical material.(36)

It is not surprising that the push for mastery of specific subject content has carried calls for increasing the length of schooling, the use of centralized, hierarchically structured textbooks at all levels of instruction, the reimposition of compulsory testing as a prerequisite for promotion from one grade to the next, along with the ability grouping and tracking of students at even the primary levels.(37)

In a policy change reminiscent of the elitism of the 1950s and early 1960s, universities, middle schools, and some primary schools have been designated into key school and nonkey school categories. While the criteria for obtaining such status varies, government-designated key schools receive a larger share of funding than their counterparts and are often able to draw a more select group of students. While the official pronouncements claim that the experiments and innovations practiced within key schools will be transferred to nonkey institutions, the mechanisms for such transference and institutional modeling are never clearly spelled out. Indeed, for the agricultural middle school, its traditional half-work half-study curriculum is receiving an even greater technical and vocational orientation, reinforcing its second-class status when compared to that of the urban secondary schools.(38)

Within these schools, teachers are being asked to teach the content of designated textbooks, while the urban senior-level middle-school teachers are required to teach the content of the national examination syllabus. As was the case prior to the GPCR, examination results are often published in the local press, with middle schools informally ranked prestigiously according to the number of their graduates who successfully enter the university.(39)

The teaching of politics within the school setting has been significantly revised. The previous emphasis on the group as the primary unit of a socialist society has been replaced by a focus on the individual (Self-Cultivation of Youngsters — <u>Ching shao nian xiuyang</u>). As can be seen in Table 4.1, the course on scientific socialism has been altogether eliminated. Middle-school graduates are no longer forced to the countryside to participate in manual labor. The amount of manual labor activity required of middle-school students during the school year is minimal if enforced at all, but the self-criticism sessions have not been abandoned. To some extent, there is a reluctance to totally repudiate the symbolism of previous ideological rituals. Calls for improved moral education within the schools are common, but they are voiced within a general context that rewards studiousness at the expense of political activism.(40) Communist Youth League members, in particular, have been indirectly criticized for their reluctance to perform officially recognized obligations, concentrating instead upon their own academic studies.(41) Indeed, it appears that university students prefer to enroll in mathematics and science courses, in part because their content is less political than that of their liberal arts counterparts and, therefore, appears to be more internally consistent and less subject to the external influences of overt political manipulations.(42)

The renewed sense of instrumentality attached to the values placed upon one's education is unmistakable. In a society where the typical urban middle-school graduate waits for up to two years before obtaining employment, the university graduate is, at the very least, guaranteed a job. The universities and research institutes are now beginning to award advanced degrees (B.A.'s, M.A.'s and Ph.D's) to graduate students.(43) A few universities have experimented with credit systems, granting course credit to students for the completion of required work. Of course the symbolic association that

TABLE 4.1.
Comparative Politics Curriculum

Pre-1980	Course
Junior middle school	
first grade	General History of Societal Development
second grade	General Knowledge of Scientific Socialism
third grade	General Knowledge of Scientific Socialism
Senior middle school	
first grade	General Knowledge of Political Economics
second grade	General Knowledge of Dialectical Materialism

1980-Present	Course
Junior middle school	
first grade	Self-Cultivation of Youngsters
second grade	General Knowledge of Laws
third grade	General History of Societal Development
Senior middle school	
first grade	General Knowledge of Political Economies
second grade	General Knowledge of Dialectical Materialism

Source: Guangming Ribao, April 27, 1981.

equates the value of the educational experience with that cultural capital, which is both acquirable and consumable, is a phenomenon common to the U.S. educational experience. As Pierre Bourdieu points out, the usefulness of a credit system lies in the flexibility of its utility, for its use encourages a perpetual competitiveness on the part of those elites vying for increased authority, as their own cultural dominance is never completely assured.(44) Within China though, such a policy must contend with a strong historical tradition about which, it is continually argued, the authority of its Mandarin practitioners remains unchallenged. Given the contemporary tendencies that are promoting increased curricular centralization, in addition to this historical legacy, it remains unclear as to whether or not a credit system on a large scale will ever be successfully employed.(45)

Nonetheless, two of the more prominent expectations underlying the post-GPCR curricular changes assume that students learn more in a competitive atmosphere, and that the importance in their mastering a uniformed, predetermined curriculum (at least on the primary and middle school levels) is beyond dispute. It is therefore not surprising that pre-GPCR attitudes that concern learning theory and human development issues resonate in the post-GPCR era. Piaget's works are now known and have received scholarly attention. Yet Piagetian theory is often discussed in a curious manner whereby preoccupation centers around the speed and rate of development rather than on the analysis of those learning differences that allow generalizable concepts to be independently mastered. The necessity of teaching more, faster, is an underlying assumption in at least one significant development study,(46) while a popular weekly column in Guangming Ribao published tips to parents, intent on improving their children's academic performance at even the earliest of ages.(47)

It is not the case that post-GPCR policy changes have met with universal acceptance. For primary and secondary-level students, the work load is heavy and the pressures to succeed are immense. Primary level students are often expected to complete a minimum of at least one to two hours of homework a night, and some teachers are again being accused of jeopardizing student health by piling on the work.(48) The reintroduction of a student code of behavior has been similarly accompanied by complaints concerning teacher abuse of student rights,(49) while teachers have been criticized additionally for teaching to the better students only and not giving slow learners enough attention.(50) In response to the complaints, calls have been issued to extend schooling even further so that sufficient attention can be paid to the required subject matter, and to abolish ability grouping.(51) Of course, the mere extension of years of schooling in and of itself can perpetuate dropout tendencies, especially in a system designated to encourage a sense of internalized failure on the part of individual students. It is thus not surprising to read reports of school vandalism and violence and to note in some instances, the existence during classroom hours of public security forces on school premises.(52)

The pressures for success are at their most extreme during the final two years of upper primary and senior-middle school, when decisions are made as to who will continue on to higher quality schooling. While at both levels, the final year of schooling is largely a review of previous work and preparation of students for further examinations, since only 4 percent of China's middle school graduates can continue onto some form of higher education, the failure rate on the National Examination is heavy. The social stigma attached to failure is not insignificant. During the first few years in which the examination was held, there were reports of suicide threats and suicides.(53) But as the difficulties in passing the examinations and in entering the universities have been more clearly articulated, the number of students actually sitting for the exams has further served the message that only an elect few will be deserving of higher education on a formal basis.(54)

There are, of course, schemes underway to expand access opportunities to higher educational levels. The curricula in some senior middle schools is being changed so that more vocationally oriented training will be offered to replace the university preparatory courses that have for a large majority of middleschool students become irrelevant.(55) This policy presumes that at the junior middle-school level, where an even greater degree of pressure will be placed upon students to succeed, the decision to stream students into academic or vocational tracks can be effectively pursued.

Nonformal alternatives to the formal system of higher education are similarly being encouraged (see Chapters 6 and 7). The television university is one such mechanism. In this instance it has proven difficult to get employers to allow student-workers time off to watch the televised programs or for completion of their related studies.(56) Without attending a formal institution, one is to receive the official equivalent of a university degree by passing an examination, but the value of such certification will probably be limited. It is the university graduate who will receive first priority in job placement.(57)

For those senior middle-school graduates failing their examinations and who remained unemployed, there are buxiban schools or study centers where they can receive assistance in preparation for retaking the national examinations.(58) It is interesting to note that arguments in favor of school expansion speak not only of the necessity of training competent workers able to contribute significantly to the country's long-range modernization efforts, but also to the extension and expansion of schooling as a practical alternative to current as well as long-term employment issues.(59) A recognition as to possible tension between the acquired custodial function, as opposed to purely educational purposes of these institutions, does not appear to be forthcoming, although it should be recognized that credential inflation and institutional expansion are, for the most part, occurring within the nonformal sector of the educational system. The status and the authority of the nation's higher educational institutions, for example, remain intact as the access channels to established institutions continue to be narrowly defined.

CONCLUSION

Aside from the institutional and structural influences upon curricular formation, a fundamental question concerns the perceived role of curricular content in promoting the country's modernization drive. It has been previously mentioned that the renewed emphasis upon scientific and technological investigation is due in part to the perception of science as being politically value free and neutral as well as logically ordered. It is important to recall that much of the current educational leadership gained not only initial prominence during the 1950s, but were intellectually influenced by the May Fourth Movement. China's original impetus to quickly modernize arose from an acute sense of crisis experienced by the country's intellectual community concerned with the continued viability of the Confucian tradition, in the face of perceived institutional, political, and cultural collapse. It has been pointed out that to the thinkers of this era, scientific method represented order and structure, rather than the innovative experimentation American progressives thought would solve Western social problems.(60) Within the contemporary context, one notes that the skepticism with which the West has come to view technological development, in terms of recognizing its very real limits as well as possibilities, is not present in China today. Technology is spoken of as an inherently productive force while at the same time emanating from the country's socioeconomic superstructure. The drive to modernization has assumed for itself an ideological importance counterbalancing much of the Maoist rhetoric of the last 30 years.(61)

To a certain degree, the educational mood of the post-GPCR era is reminiscent of the American educational community's response during the Sputnik era to Soviet technological advances. Both movements capitalized upon external threats to perceived internal weaknesses in rationalizing a greater degree of elitist educational practice as well as increased centralization of educational authority. In both instances, concerted efforts were made to increase cultural contacts and foreign language training.

However, in the Chinese case, the commitment to cultural borrowing remains curious, for policymakers earnestly maintain that such an enterprise can be implemented successfully on a selective basis. China, it is assumed, can learn from the West without repeating Western mistakes or imitating Western weaknesses.(62) The inherent difficulty with such an assumption is that it necessarily postulates an a priori ability on the part of the Chinese authorities to know ahead of time, in fixed fashion, their own curricular needs and priorities. The danger is that the entire process of cultural exchange can degenerate into self-fulfilling prophecy. It is thus, perhaps, too simplistic to view recent policy changes as comprising little more than a Chinese style back-to-basics movement. To some extent, the possibility must be recognized that Chinese officials are neither blindly following conservative Western educational trends nor in recent years are they totally unaware of the voluminous criticism and debate many of their espoused policies have raised. Their intentions must be seen within the context of an elite that was initially traumatized by the loss of its political power and has only recently regained its preeminence. Thus, the need to symbolically legitimize their return to power in curricular terms is quite apparent.

A campaign that associates modernization with the preservation of order, rather than the encouragement of independent initiative glorifying individual competition within strictly defined social hierarchies, and that essentially sees the learning process as occupying within the context of extrinsic rather than intrinsic reward systems, many of which are negative in tone and impact, is a strange creature indeed. It is clearly in sharp contrast with the GPCR emphasis on self-reliance, local control, and development of curriculum, all within the context of class conflict. Because its potential for continued success remains unknown, interested observers will have to stay tuned for further details as the Chinese educational scenario continues to unfold.

NOTES

(1) Jan-Ingar Lofstedt, Chinese Educational Policy (Atlantic Highlands, N.J.: Humanities Press, 1980), pp. 60-64. Tsang Chiu-sam, Society and School Progress in China (New York: Pergamon Press, 1968), p. 183; Ronald F. Price, Education in Communist China (London: Routledge & Kegan Paul, 1979), p. 115.

(2) Jonathan Unger, "The Chinese Controversy Over Higher Education," Pacific Affairs 53, no. 1 (Spring 1980): 29-31; "Bending the School Ladder: The Failure of Chinese Educational Reform in the 1960s," Comparative Education Review 24, no. 2, pt. 1 (June 1980): 221-37.

(3) Fritz K. Ringer, Education and Society in Modern Europe (Bloomington: Indiana University Press, 1979), pp. 84-85.

(4) Lowell Dittmer, "Thought Reform and the Cultural Revolution: An Analysis of the Symbolism of Chinese Politics," American Political Science Review 61, no. 1 (March 1977): 84-85.

(5) See Suzanne Pepper, "Education and Revolution: The 'Chinese Model' Revisited," Asian Survey 18, no. 9 (September 1978): 547-90.

(6) Charles P. Ridley, Paul H.B. Godwin, and Dennis Doolin, The Making of a Model Citizen in Communist China (Stanford, Calif.: Hoover Institution Press, 1971), pp. 87-183.

(7) For both sides of the debate see Roberta Martin, "The Socialization of Children in China and Taiwan: An Analysis of the Elementary School Textbooks," China Quarterly 62 (June 1975); and R.F. Price, "Chinese Textbooks, Fourteen Years On," China Quarterly 83 (September 1980): 550.

(8) See Peter J. Seybolt and Gregory Kuei-ke Chiang, eds. Language Reform in China (White Plains, N.Y.: M.E. Sharp, 1979), pp. 2-7.

(9)   Mao Tse Tung, "Talk at the Spring Festival Forum," February 13, 1964, "Letter to Lin Piao," May 7, 1966, in "Chairman Mao on Revolution in Education," Current Background (Hong Kong: American Consulate General, no. 888, August 22, 1969), pp. 11-12, 17; "Establish a New Proletarian System of Examination and Assessment," Renmin Ribao (Peking), August 31, 1969, and "Draft Program for Primary and Middle-Schools in Countryside," New China News Agency, May 13, 1969, in Toward a New World Outlook, ed. Shi Ming Hu and Eli Seifman (New York: AMS Press, 1976), pp. 230-36, 239-40; See also Sylvia Chan, "Revolution in Higher Education," in China: The Impact of the Cultural Revolution, ed. Bill Brugger (New York: Harper and Row, 1978), pp. 95-125; and John Gardner and Wilt Idema, "China's Educational Revolution," in Authority, Participation and Cultural Change in China, ed. Stuart R. Schram (Cambridge: Cambridge University Press, 1978), pp. 257-89.

(10)   Basil Bernstein, Class Codes and Control, vol. 3, Towards a Theory of Educational Transmissions (London: Routledge and Kegan Paul, 1975), pp. 54-150.

(11)   Rensselear W. Lee III, "The Politics of Technology in Communist China," in Ideology and Politics in Contemporary China, ed. Chalmers Johnson (Seattle: University of Washington Press, 1973), pp. 314-15.

(12)   Yang Yi, "Equality and Respect," China Youth News (Beijing), July 20, 1961, translated in Chinese Education 12, no. 4 (Winter 1979-80): 96.

(13)   Sheng De, "On Drawing a Dividing Line," Wenhuibao (Shanghai), April 30, 1966, translated in Chinese Education 12, no. 4 (Winter 1979-80): 96.

(14)   See Joel Glassman, "The Political Experience of the Primary School Teachers in the People's Republic of China," Comparative Education 45, no. 2 (June 1979): 159-74.

(15)   Suzanne Pepper, "Chinese Education After Mao: Two Steps Forward Two Steps Backward, and Begin Again," China Quarterly 81 (March 1980): 11-12; Joint Publications Research Service (JPRS), no. 74165, September 12, 1979, pp. 79-80.

(16)   Robert and Ali S. Chin, Psychological Research in Communist China: 1949-1966, (Cambridge, Mass.: M.I.T. Press, 1969), pp. 161-62.

(17)   Robert and Ali S. Chin, ibid., p. 207.

(18)   Richard Solomon, Mao's Revolution and the Chinese Political Culture, (Berkeley: University of California Press, 1971), p. 111.

(19)   Lilian Weber, "Early Childhood Education," in China's Schools in Flux, ed. Ronald Montaperto and Jay Henderson (White Plains, N.Y.: M.E. Sharpe, 1979), pp. 127-28.

(20)   Susan Shirk, "The Middle School" (Ph.D. diss., Cambridge, Mass.: M.I.T. Press, 1973).

(21)   Martin King Whyte, Small Groups and Political Rituals in China (Berkeley: University of California Press, 1974), pp. 111-13.

(22)   Ezra Vogel, "From Friendship to Comradeship: The Change in Personal Relations in Communist China," China Quarterly 21 (January-March 1965): 46-60; "A Preliminary View of Family and Mental Health in Urban Communist China," in Mental Health Research in Asia and the Pacific, ed. William Caudill and Tsung Yi Lin (Honolulu: East-West Center Press, 1969), pp. 393-404.

(23)   See Donald J. Munro, "Egalitarian Ideal and Educational Fact In Communist China," in China: Management of a Revolutionary Society, ed. John Lindbeck (Seattle: University of Washington Press, 1971), pp. 290-301.

(24)   Solomon, Mao's Revolution and the Chinese Political Culture, p. 525.

(25)   Thomas Bernstein, Up to the Mountains and Down to the Villages (New Haven: Yale University Press, 1977), pp. 103-20.

(26)   William Kessen, ed., Childhood in China (New Haven: Yale University Press, 1975).

(27)   Margery Wolff, "Child Training and the Chinese Family," in Studies in Chinese Society, ed. Arthur P. Wolff (Stanford, Calif.: Stanford University Press, 1978), pp. 223-25.

(28)   Bernstein, Up to the Mountains and Down to the Villages, pp. 157-73.

(29)   Hou Wenruo, "Population Policy," in China's Population: Problems and Prospects, ed. Liu Zheng, Song Jian et al. (Beijing: New World, 1981), pp. 69-72.

(30)   Foreign Broadcast Information Service (FBIS), September 15, 1978, E4; JPRS, no. 76971, no. 146, December 10, 1980, pp. 76-82; FBIS, October 16, 1981, K1.

(31)   See Gordon A. Bennett and Ronald Montaperto, Red Guard (London: George Allen and Unwin, 1971).

(32)   R.F. Price, "Education – Why a Reversal?" in China Since the Gang of Four, ed. Bill Brugger (London: Croom Helm, 1980), pp. 202-30.

(33)   Wang Hsueh-wen, "Elementary Education Reform on the Chinese Mainland," Issues and Studies (April 1981): 42-44.

(34)   See Robert D. Barendsen, ed., The 1978 National College Entrance Examination in the People's Republic of China (Washington, D.C.: Government Printing Office, 1979).

(35)   Jerry Becker, "Mathematics Education," in Chinese Education, 13 (Spring-Summer 1980): 119.

(36)   FBIS, September 14, 1978, E22.

(37)   See Susan Shirk, "Educational Reform and Political Backlash: Recent Changes in Chinese Educational Policy," Comparative Education Review 23, no. 2 (June 1979): 183-217.

(38)   Hubert O. Brown, "Recent Policy Toward Rural Education in the People's Republic of China," Journal of Public Administration (Hong Kong) 3, no. 2 (December 1981): 168-88.

(39)   Summary of World Broadcasts (SWB), December 1, 1981, FE/6894/BII/12-14; FBIS, August 7, 1980, L8.

(40)   SWB, November 9, 1981; FE/6875/BII/4, November 10, 1981; FE/6876/BII/4, and FBIS, February 5, 1979, E 10-11. The comparative curriculum chart is from "Gaijin (zhongxue) kejin qiushi yongxin jiaocai," Guangming Ribao, April 27, 1981.

(41)   Xinhua News Agency, no. 121837, December 19, 1980, pp. 25-26; JPRS no. 74165, September 12, 1979, p. 65.

(42)   Suzanne Pepper, "Western Influences on Chinese Universities," Asian Wall Street Journal, September 9, 1981; FBIS, February 25, 1980; Beijing Review, no. 30, July 28, 1980, pp. 22-24.

(43)   Xinhua News Agency, no. 12829, December 19, 1980; no. 092114, September 22, 1981; no. 010412, January 25, 1982; SWB, December 1, 1981; FE/6894/BII/15.

(44)   Pierre Bourdieu and Jean-Claude Passeron, The Inheritors (Chicago: University of Chicago Press, 1979), pp. 95-97.

(45)   Pepper, "Western Influences."

(46)   Zhang Muyan and Wang Jizhen, "Research into the Developmental Potential of Children in Thinking First Graders in their First Semester of Study How to Read and Write 8 Digit Numbers," translated in Chinese Sociology and Anthropology 13, no. 2 (Winter 1980/81): 32-53.

(47)   Guangming Ribao, March 13, 1982, p. 2 is especially representative.

(48)   Hugh Thomas, ed., Comrade Editor: Letters to the People's Daily (Hong Kong: Joint Publications, 1980), pp. 90-91; FBIS, August 7, 1980, L8-9.

(49)   JPRS, no. 74595, November 19, 1979, p. 83.

(50)   FBIS, August 7, 1980.

(51)   SWB, December 5, 1981, FE/6898/BII/10.

(52)   SWB, October 10, 1981, FE/6850/BII/9, p. 13; SWB, December 30, 1981, FE/6915/BII/4-5; JPRS, no. 79808, January 6, 1982, p. 51.

(53)   JPRS, no. 74165, September 12, 1979, pp. 83-84.

(54)   FBIS, July 7, 1980, p. L16.

(55)   FBIS, August 7, 1980, pp. L8-9; JPRS, no. 78792, August 20, 1981, p. 59; SWB, December 5, 1981, FE/6898/BII/10; SWB, December 31, 1981, FE/69161/BII/13; Xinhua News Agency, no. 010511, January 6, 1982, p. 7; Beijing Review, no. 46, November 17, 1980, pp. 7-8.

(56)   "Changing Faces of China's TV," The Asian Messenger 5, nos. 1 and 2 (Winter 1980/Spring 1981): 35-36.

(57)   Xinhua News Agency, no. 1211718, December 18, 1981, pp. 11-12.

(58)   Xinhua News Agency, no. 113005, December 1, 1980, p. 42; FBIS, December 3, 1980, pp. 5-6.

(59)   Li Yining, "The Role of Education in Economic Growth," Social Sciences in China, no. 2 (June 1981), pp. 66-84; FBIS, September 13, 1978, E29-30; JPRS no. 78678, August 5, 1981, p. 49.

(60)   Peter Buck, American Science and Modern China 1876-1936 (Cambridge: Cambridge University Press, 1980), p. 206.

(61)   Li Kejing, "Is Education a Superstructure or a Productive Force," Social Sciences in China 1, no. 3 (September 1980): 17-18.

(62)   FBIS, November 13, 1979, pp. L14-L16.

5

EDUCATION AND THE POLITICAL SOCIALIZATION OF CHINESE YOUTHS

Stanley Rosen

To Western observers who have followed events in China over the last 20 years, some of the recent reports that have appeared in China's newspapers and magazines must have been simultaneously shocking and enlightening. Advanced or progressive individuals "who study, work hard and make outstanding achievements in production and other work or who are commended by Party organizations for their achievements . . . are subjected to freezing irony and burning satire, are deliberately harassed or are beaten up."(1) There is a widespread feeling among youths that an impassable gap exists between the older and younger generation and that this gap cannot be eliminated.(2) Many youths have lost their faith in Marxism(3) and believe that the present leadership in China has degenerated into a new class of bureaucrats.(4) Opinion polls have revealed an overt skepticism regarding China's ambitious modernization program and state-defined goals. National and local magazines and newspapers intended for students at various levels of schooling, from primary school on up, frequently contain letters reflecting the confusion among youths over issues that in the past had been much less controversial. Thus, one sees letters inquiring about the criteria for membership in the Communist Youth League (CYL) under today's new economic conditions,(5) complaining about the isolation felt by progressive CYL members and class cadres,(6) groping about for the meaning of life,(7) and so on. All this is a far cry from the familiar Maoist dictum of "serve the people" that reportedly has been instilled in Chinese youths from their earliest days in school. Something appears amiss in China's socialization process.

How are we to account for these developments, for this crisis of faith among Chinese youths? This chapter argues that the roots of the present demoralization and even cynicism of youths can be found in part in the contradictions inherent in the educational system and student relationships characteristic of socialist societies stressing economic development; that these contradictions had already appeared by the 1960s, before the Great Proletarian Cultural Revolution (GPCR); that the contradictions were greatly exacerbated during the GPCR years (1966-76); and that the attempt to reverse the now-discredited policies of the GPCR in education and other areas and return to earlier policies has created serious ambiguities in the minds of youths as to what constitutes proper behavior and has left many of China's youths with few remaining ideals.

POLITICAL SOCIALIZATION

Political socialization – a term that was virtually unheard of as recently as the late 1950s – has become an integral part of the study of political science with an ever-burgeoning literature.(8) The term can be narrowly conceived as "the deliberate inculcation of political information, values, and practices by instructional agents who have been formally charged with this responsibility," or interpreted more broadly to encompass all political learning, including nonpolitical learning that affects political behavior, for example, the learning of social attitudes and the acquisition of personality characteristics that are politically relevant.(9) Our interpretation will be still broader, and will focus on student attitudes and relationships, contrasting the model of a good citizen fostered by the state to the actual values and behavior of Chinese students.

Since Chinese textbooks, even in the sciences, frequently have contained a strong measure of political content, an analysis of the specific, formal political messages being imparted to students is important. However, of even more relevance for political socialization are the lessons to be learned outside one's textbooks. Most significantly, the emphasis on the value of education in a collective environment, with its stress on cooperation, small group criticism and self-criticism, and so forth, was imparted to the students through less formal mechanisms. In fact, we will show that the formal and informal processes of political learning were sometimes in contradiction. One of our basic arguments will be that the political and behavioral lessons rendered in Chinese textbooks to train citizens of a socialist society were often incompatible with an educational system that stressed contest mobility. As the basic themes in citizenship training have been fully developed by the time one graduates primary school, while contest mobility normally begins in earnest only in secondary school, we will examine the political-behavioral themes emphasized in primary school readers and then look at actual student behavior in secondary schools.

EDUCATION AND POLITICAL SOCIALIZATION UNDER MAO: THE MODEL CHILD-CITIZEN

In a sense, of course, Mao Zedong's prescriptions for education and political socialization have never fully been put into practice in post-1949 China.(10) For one thing, given his distrust of the intellectuals, who as teachers were responsible for the transmission of political values, and the institutional isolation of schools from the society at large, Mao favored a much less institutionalized school system.(11) He advocated a more open school system in which members of society at large — such as workers and peasants — would play an important role. In turn, society itself should become a school, with education provided through institutions ranging from the neighborhood and the work place, to the mass movement.(12) The educational reforms introduced during the GPCR decade, while coming closest to meeting Mao's prescriptions, nevertheless fell far short.

But, even Mao conceded that schools were still necessary. The school system and the process of education could be used to transform traditional values and instill a successor generation with values deemed appropriate for a revolutionary society. Thus, for example, courses on politics were a part of the regular curriculum. But, as noted, political learning was not limited to those courses specifically devoted to the subject. Political and moral themes permeated storybooks for Chinese children.(13) Primary school readers published at various times have been scrutinized by a number of scholars and found to be greatly consistent in content. Many of the same stories and lessons, practically word for word, that were used before the GPCR continued to be used during the GPCR years, and even down to the present.(14) A number of themes, both political and behavioral, were emphasized most forcefully. The stories in the readers were designed to produce a "model citizen," to make clear the differences between proper and improper behavior, between what to love and what to hate.

The political theme most stressed was patriotism, with students taught to treasure the sacred symbols of nationhood associated with the Chinese Communist Party and socialism, for example, the red flag, Tiananmen Square in Beijing, and Mao himself. Support for communism was inspired by the stress on past and present struggles against the Chinese Nationalists, the Japanese and American imperialists and, by the 1960s, the Soviet revisionists.(15) The most important of the behavioral themes were: first, social and personal responsibility, including such subthemes as devotion to duty, the performance of social obligations, protection of public property, and so forth; second, achievement for the good of society; third, altruism, including heroic self-sacrifice and service to others; and fourth, collective endeavor, accomplishing tasks through cooperation rather than through individual activity.(16) The child was also taught, through the stories in these readers, to accept his role in society. The most predominant of the roles differentiated were those of worker, peasant, and soldier. Most especially, even in readers used in large cities like Beijing and Shanghai, there was a heavy emphasis on rural, not urban life. The countryside was shown to be exciting, satisfying, and not at all forbidding. The role of the peasant was portrayed not just as the most common, but also the most desirable, in Chinese society.(17)

The political and behavioral themes were clearly united in the lessons the child received regarding "class education." Particularly after 1962, when Mao sought to revitalize a society he felt was drifting away from revolutionary values, the dictum "never forget class struggle" permeated all learning. Altruism, for example, was to be selective. The exploiting classes (most often depicted as landlords and capitalists) had opposed the revolution before 1949 and had remained unreconciled to the new society. One must therefore draw a clear line between these "enemies" to be isolated and the "people," who should be served wholeheartedly.

Ideally, the model child was to be oriented toward "new" China, aware of the evils of "old" China, and prepared to defend the new society against all enemies at home and abroad. The child would be able to envision his own role within the new society as a part of a larger whole. Personal individual ambitions were to be subordinated to group interests. Thus, while the child was expected to study diligently, any success achieved would be attributed to the opportunities created by the new society and would be shared with others for the benefit of the nation. An individual concerned only with developing personal competence through study (Expertise), but not with communist ideology or with political education (Red), has been improperly socialized. The ideal citizen was one who could combine both Redness and Expertise.(18) Models worthy of emulation were introduced, and most represented ordinary people.(19) By demonstrating that those performing the most common social roles were capable of exhibiting the most cherished values of the new society — such as service to society, sacrifice of personal ambitions, and achievement through hard work — the authorities sought to instill the belief that "all work is for the revolution." Some model personages, for example, were praised for giving up the opportunity of a university education in favor of a life in the countryside.(20) Model children with whom the students could identify were frequently presented as members of an officially sanctioned organization, the Young Pioneers, to which all children aged 7 to 14 were expected to belong. These basic values imparted in primary school were continued in more sophisticated form at the junior and senior high levels.

EDUCATION AND POLITICAL SOCIALIZATION UNDER MAO: STUDENT INTERACTION AND CLASSROOM BEHAVIOR

While formal political study was required in Chinese schools, it would be a mistake to assume that the most important political and moral lessons were to be found in books or course work. Even at the secondary level, politics courses generally emphasized current events, the Party line, official interpretation of past events, and simple explanations of basic concepts of Marxism-Leninism. These courses were not considered demanding nor even crucial by the students and teachers. Much more important to the authorities – and to the students as well – were the informal moral and political lessons to be learned in school. As several recent studies have pointed out, the Chinese approach to political socialization was to penetrate and control this informal side of schooling.(21) A student's political manifestation (zhengzhi biaoxian) could best be gauged not by scores on politics tests, but by participation in collective school activities. This was, in fact, part of a more general emphasis in China on "collective education," which had been modeled on Soviet educational experience.(22) The key to political socialization by means of the collective was to deemphasize the role of the teacher as a socializing agent and to rely more heavily on student leaders and peer groups as primary agents of political socialization. Student leaders were recruited into officially sanctioned youth organizations and were delegated significant powers over their peers. Although almost all students between the ages 7 and 14 were expected to become members of the Young Pioneers, already in primary school classrooms students were actively recruited by their teachers to serve as class cadres or Young Pioneer officers, to act in effect as intermediaries between the teacher and the rest of the class. In the last year of junior high, when a student reached the age of 15, he was eligible to apply for membership in the more elite organization of the CYL.(23) Only the most advanced were to be recruited into the CYL, with the number of members rarely exceeding half the class. The CYL was an organization separate from the class as a whole, holding its meetings privately; simultaneously, however, the organization was expected to maintain strong roots in the class. League members were required to monitor the political behavior of the ordinary members of the class and to raise the level of activist involvement of nonleague members by engaging the latter in heart-to-heart talks, small group discussion, and criticism sessions, and by their own personal examples of activist behavior. League members actively sought to "develop" (fazhan) new league members from among their classmates as the latter met the qualifications for membership.(24) Opportunities to demonstrate one's activism and qualification for league membership most frequently were provided by collective endeavors. For example, enthusiastic participation in manual labor, which before the GPCR engaged the students approximately one month each year, provided aspirant activists with such an opportunity. Small group discussion and criticism meetings likewise accorded the students an arena in which to show their mettle.

In short, ideally there was a congruence between themes depicted in primary school readers and the organization and operation of a well-functioning secondary school classroom. Activities were to be engaged in collectively; more advanced students (league members) were to be concerned about raising the political level of backward students; and all were to strive for excellence in their own work.

THE REALITY OF POLITICAL SOCIALIZATION IN CHINESE SCHOOLS: CONTRADICTIONS BEFORE THE CULTURAL REVOLUTION

While an argument can certainly be made that the GPCR was bad for China, it was ironically a boon to those engaged in research on various aspects of Chinese politics and society. The revelations concerning Chinese political and social processes — most frequently obtained from interviews with former residents who left China beginning around 1967, and in material published in the Red Guard press — greatly expanded our knowledge of how the Chinese system works. Far from presenting the image of a smoothly functioning collective unit, with selfless activists serving as models for aspirant activists among their classmates, the picture of Chinese classrooms before the GPCR that has begun to emerge in the most recent scholarly literature stresses rather the serious tensions and contradictions among students.(25)

As we shall see below, the primary source of tension in secondary schools stemmed from two competing, seemingly irreconcilable, goals of the state. The educational system had the task of training people to be both Red and Expert, to serve joyfully in whatever capacity the state deemed necessary, and to be fired by a strong sense of shared interests and unity rather than of competition and individual benefit. With these goals in mind, many students' activities such as labor cooperation, mutual help, small group meetings, and so forth were fostered. At the same time, however, it was at the secondary school level that a student's future occupation was decided. With opportunities to continue on to a university (and even senior high) narrowingly sharply by the mid-1960s, the secondary schools often became competitive arenas in which successful students would be rewarded by promotion to the next level of schooling, while the less successful might be allocated urban jobs and, as the Cultural Revolution drew near, the least successful would be asked to depart for the countryside to serve the nation on the agricultural front.(26)

To a certain extent, this dual mission was reflected in the primary school readers we have referred to earlier. Analysts of these readers have uncovered conflicting values in the stories children read. For example, one major conflict pits themes emphasizing achievement and self-reliance against themes of self-sacrifice for the benefit of others, acceptance of limited occupational roles as workers or peasants, and collective behavior.(27) A related set of conflicting values appears in the contrast between stories that stress the importance of ingenuity in solving problems and stories that accentuate the necessity for obedience to rules and deference to authority.(28) Although primary school students may have been unaware of these internal contradictions in their readers, students in secondary school classrooms were fully conscious of the contradictions dividing them, and this awareness was reflected in their behavior. Before examining this behavior, let us turn to a brief account of the educational structure in the 1960s.

As was mentioned above, the schools were charged with providing students with proper moral-political training while also determining which students would advance up the educational ladder. The most desirable fate was to enter a university. In fact, the aspirations of students to enter a university were reinforced by secondary school officials who, in their own interests, sought a high promotion rate to university for their students. In turn, official policy, as transmitted through the media, consistently urged all eligible students to sit for the university entrance examinations, arguing that China's future required large numbers of qualified intellectuals.

Until 1960, this congruence of interests was not a problem, and most senior high graduates were able to go on to a university. By the early 1960s, however, university entrance became more difficult, as did entrance to a good senior high school. State expenditures began to be diverted to an expansion of the less costly primary and junior high education, along with technical and vocational training. Graduates of primary schools and junior highs became more and more reluctant to seek to climb the increasingly steep educational ladder. By 1965, a year before the start of the GPCR, China's educational pyramid had been filled out by many different kinds of schools. Although only a small number could gain university entrance, there were numerous options at the secondary school level.

Those not dissuaded from making the climb toward university found it necessary to step up their competitive efforts to succeed. Moreover, industrial stagnation and a neglect of urban services in most cities raised the stakes for these competitors. By refusing to opt for the technical or vocational training that would lead to a secure job, a student unable to gain university entrance might well find himself mobilized to settle in the countryside.(29)

Under these conditions, the criteria the state adopted for entrance to university and the best senior high schools were a source of continuing concern for the students. Generally, three criteria were to be taken into account: academic achievement, class origin, and political manifestation. Since the priorities of the state varied from year to year, the weight given to each of these criteria likewise varied. When economic development and the training of experts was stressed, as in 1962, academic achievement was given pride of place. When the state was most concerned with redistributing opportunities in favor of formerly deprived classes, class origin rivaled academic achievement as a criterion. Since the state had as a permanently stated goal the cultivation of intellectuals who would be both Red and Expert, a person's political manifestation was also considered, no matter which of the other two criteria were being stressed.

The process of political socialization and the moral transformation at the secondary school level was, ideally, to be a uniform one, with little variation from school to school or student to student. The values that were espoused in primary readers were to be internalized by all students. In reality, however, as a student made his way up the educational ladder opting for a particular form of secondary schooling, he developed perspectives in accordance with his place in the educational structure. A student who had aspirations to attend a university and had gained entrance to a regular senior high school had the most difficult road still ahead of him, while a student who had gained admittance to a specialist school was assured of a secure and prestigious job upon graduation. Those in technical schools also had been assured a job, if perhaps for somewhat less prestigious occupations, while students in the urban vocational schools established in 1963-65 were often there only because they had been unable to gain admittance to any other form of school. They had enrolled in the vocational schools to avoid an even worse fate: the strong possibility that they would have to migrate to the rural areas.

Generalizing broadly, three patterns of classroom relationships in China's secondary schools on the eve of the GPCR can be distinguished. The classrooms that came closest to the desired model tended to be in specialist and technical schools. Since many of the specialist schools were prestigious in their own right, students attending these schools felt privileged to be there.(30) Having their futures more or less assured, there was a certain esprit among classmates, with most students eager to be CYL members and activists. Cooperation among students was common, and competition was not likely to interfere with the future prospects of the students.

On the other hand, students at many of the vocational schools, which tended to half-work and half-study, were a much more disspirited group. In the same manner that desirable job prospects contributed to activist behavior by those in specialist schools, the certainty of less than satisfactory employment upon graduation discouraged activism.(31) Variations on this second pattern of class-room relationships were exhibited by students in neighborhood junior high schools and urban minban (privately run) high schools. Many of the neighborhood schools were of recent establishment — built during the Great Leap Forward or slightly afterward — and of poor quality. They lacked senior high sections and only a minority of their graduates went on to senior highs in other schools. As many students in these neighborhood schools were from working class homes, and were expecting to move on to factory jobs upon graduation, it was difficult for school authorities to stimulate the creation of "model" classrooms in which desire for CYL membership was high and political activism was a source of status within the peer group.(32)

Likewise at the schools that prepared students for university, classroom relationships seldom resembled the models students had read and been taught about since primary school. As previously mentioned, three basic criteria were considered for university entrance, and the relative weight of these criteria differed from year to year. The ideal student would be one with high academic achievement, impeccable class origin (the best class origins were revolutionary cadre, revolutionary military, revolutionary martyr, worker, and poor and lower-middle peasant), and excellent political manifestation. In practice, few students were able to measure up in all three areas. What developed was the attempt by each student to maximize his chances by emphasizing one or another of these three criteria.(33) Thus, children from intellectual homes, realizing that class origin was ascriptive and beyond their control, felt their best chance for university entrance lay through scholastic achievement. Children of good class origin — particularly those from cadre or military families — tended to take advantage of the prevalent assumption of school authorities that, emulating their parents, they would be "naturally Red" and enthusiastically became activists. The third criterion — political manifestation — was often interpreted in terms of the other two criteria. When academic achievement was stressed by state policy, political manifestation could best be demonstrated by studying hard and making good grades. When the state gave greater preference to those of good class origin in distributing opportunities for educational advancement, there almost seemed to be a deterministic relationship between class origin and political manifestation in the eyes of the authorities.

The changing criteria for membership in the CYL reflected this interpretation of political manifestation. Such membership was the most obvious indicator that activism had been rewarded. In the early 1960s, it was reportedly difficult for students whose grades were mediocre to gain entrance to the league, no matter what their class origin or political activism. By 1964 league policy had altered; the previous reliance on grades was considered a deviation. The league was now enjoined to concentrate on recruiting as many students of good class origin as possible.

The league, generally, even more than the classroom, became subject to division into cliques. In schools with substantial numbers of children of party and military officials, such students often formed a separate group within the league. Decisions on the recruitment of new league members became caught up in the academic achievement/class origin imbroglio. As a vanguard organization intended to be the training groups for future party members, the league's lack of unity was of serious concern to the authorities.

Aware of divisions within the classroom and the league, responsible authorities introduced various campaigns designed to bring the students closer together. These campaigns seem not to have been overly successful, however. For example, the Red Pairs campaign, in which an activist was paired with a nonactivist in an attempt to produce a pair of activists, foundered because activists were primarily concerned with distinguishing themselves from their fellow classmates and the more backward members of the pairs in turn resented the patronizing airs of their tutors.

Campaigns in which model youths were to be emulated originally were intended to set an ideal that all youths, regardless of their particular attributes, could strive to emulate. The organizers of the campaigns quickly discovered, however, that one model was unlikely to appeal to all youths, and that differences – particularly in class origin – would have to be acknowledged. The most prominent campaign of this type – the Learn from Lei Feng Campaign that began in 1963 – appealed most readily to youths of good class origin. Since Lei Feng's deep class consciousness and his ordinary but great communist spirit were inseparable from the fact that he came from a family of hired peasants and had suffered great hardships at the hands of the landlord class, and from the exploitation and oppression by the ruling class in the old society, many youths who had not been so deprived in the past found it difficult to match Lei Feng's communist spirit. Another hero, from a middle peasant family, who had also expressed doubts about his ability to live up to Lei Feng's example, was provided as a model in November 1965. Thus began the Emulate Wang Jie Campaign. There was even a model for those from landlord background. Named Tan Jianhua, his successful moral transformation was studied primarily by those who had already become CYL members.

Ultimately, cooperation among students in China's regular high schools tended to prevail most often when the cost of helping others was low, i.e., when such cooperation was not likely to damage one's own chances for success. Thus, cooperation was most likely in such group activities as performance of manual labor, athletic contests, and cultural events. On the other hand, activities in which students were being measured as individuals directly against their class-mates, with the reward for success being higher education, offered little incentive to students to cooperate. Both academics and politics were therefore among the most competitive activities in which students engaged.(34)

THE CULTURAL REVOLUTION REFORMS

In June 1966, most of China's schools closed to enable the students to take part in the GPCR. Although there were many targets that came under fire during the acute phase from 1966-68, perhaps the most prominent of the targets was the revisionist system of education. Indeed, when the smoke had cleared and the schools were reopened, the structural changes introduced were substantial. The crucial contradiction that had led to competition rather than cooperation among students — the schools as both inculcators of the moral-political ideology and arenas for educa-tional contest mobility — had been excised from the new structure.

Most fundamentally, the new educational structure sought to eliminate the inequalities of the old.(35) Distinctions between schools and between students were to be eradicated. The entrance examinations for junior high, senior high, and university were all abolished. Urban students were expected to progress all the way through senior high. After graduation from senior high, all students were required to spend at least two years performing manual labor before becoming eligible for university education. To guarantee equality between students and between schools, many junior high schools and technical, vocational, and work-study schools, were transformed into regular middle schools with junior and senior high sections.(36) Distinctions among the regular middle schools — the best ones had been called "key points" before the GPCR because they were allocated the best teachers, had the highest university promotion rate, received the most funding, and so forth — were also erased. Students were not to be held back, to skip grades, or be divided by ability within grades.

One clear result of these changes, as might be expected, was an expansion of secondary school education. Enrollment in regular high schools went from below 10 million in 1965 to over 58 million in 1976, even though the length of such schooling had been reduced from six years to five.

But with pre-GPCR education the lack of educational equality was considered to be only part of the problem. The social and political content of education and the separation of the schools from society were considered equally serious defects. To remedy these problems, political study, manual labor, and practical training all were to receive increased emphasis within the shortened curriculum. Of the time spent in class, 60 to 70 percent was to be devoted to general knowledge and productive labor courses, and 30 to 40 percent to politics.(37)

The GPCR reforms in education were designed in part to foster the ideal model-citizens that had been depicted in the primary school readers. As has been pointed out, aside from further emphasis on the importance of manual labor and a somewhat greater attention to politics, the readers prepared during the GPCR were remarkably similar to previous readers. By introducing structural changes negating advantages for high academic achievers, and by a renewed stress on manual labor, which had always elicited cooperative behavior in the past, it was anticipated that student relationships would alter accordingly. Even the renewed stress on politics, a source of keen competition previously, was not expected to drive a wedge between the students. Under the new system, students were headed for rather similar stints of manual labor before decisions on their uiltimate futures would be made. The sequence of the 1960s, in which a student's decision to become an activist was frequently tied to his hope that such activism would be recognized by admission into the CYL, which in turn would aid in university entrance, had been short-circuited. Activism in GPCR schools could not be so rewarded. In fact, the CYL had to be completely rebuilt, a process that was not complete until 1975.(38)

In a sense, the GPCR reforms were too successful. In removing student experience in primary and secondary school from future educational or occupational prospects, a certain equality was in fact achieved. The differences in behavior between students in the former key-point schools and students in less prestigious neighborhood schools were markedly reduced. But it came at a price. In removing the competitive atmosphere, in equalizing schools, in detaching secondary education from higher education, the power of the schools as socializing agents was fatally weakened. The schools had few incentives and disincentives with which to influence student behavior. One potential lever for controlling behavior was the determination of which high school graduates would be sent to the countryside and which would be allocated urban jobs. But, although the criteria varied from year to year, the decision normally was based on one's family situation, i.e., whether or not one was an only child, how many siblings were already in the countryside, and so forth. Significantly, even in this decision, the role of the school was minimal.

With the schools considered by many students as merely an interlude in their lives, some sought to spend as little time there as possible. An odd phenomenon developed. The marked competition to advance to senior high in the 1960s was now replaced by a desire on the part of a fair number of students to forego such schooling entirely. With larger cities enthusiastically striving for a system of

universalized senior high education to demonstrate their commitment to the new egalitarianism, students who sought to avoid senior
high had to submit a petition indicating special family difficulties.
The large number who remained in school were reportedly guilty of
chronic absenteeism and antisocial behavior.(39) But the teachers
had little control over the situation. One of the indictments against
the "revisionist" educational system of the 1950s and 1960s was that
it maintained the teacher-student relationship typical of traditional
China. The GPCR offered a vivid lesson that the total authority of
the teacher in the classroom and the submission of youths to their
elders were no longer acceptable. To drive the point home, a
primary school student named Huang Shuai, who had used her diary
to criticize her teacher for acting in an authoritarian manner, and in
turn had been publicly upbraided by the teacher, was praised in the
national press as a model of "going against the tide." This incident
led to the publication of letters and big character posters by other
youths complaining about their teachers. The latter quickly absorbed
the lesson.(40)

The weakened authority of teachers and schools as important
socializing agents gave the peer group greater independence from
authority. As described above, pre-GPCR schools had relied heavily
on student leaders and peer groups as primary agents of political
socialization. The system had worked relatively well in classrooms
and schools in which activism and CYL membership were valued by
peer groups. Thus, students in quality senior high schools, anxious to
continue on to a university, were much more interested in league
membership than those in junior highs who had little aspiration to
continue their academic careers.(41) In this sense, the GPCR schools
— both junior and senior high — were more similar to the dead-end
junior high schools of the 1960s.

Recognizing this problem, the schools tried several mechanisms
to encourage appropriate behavior. For example, they enhanced the
role played by small classroom groups in criticizing deviant
behavior. Moreover, appraisals of student behavior by the small
group for the first time became part of a student's report card sent
to his parents, and were placed in his permanent dossier to follow
him to his work unit.(42) There were also attempts to increase the
appeal of political education by linking it with spare-time classes in
technical education and with cultural and recreational activities for
youths still in school as well as those who had graduated. With the
regular school curriculum unappealing to many students, classes in
such subjects as machine maintenance and repair, basic industrial
design, and so forth, which were organized by the CYL, found a
ready audience. Youths were told that the acquisition of these skills
would better enable them to serve the revolution and, in fact,
admittance to such programs depended on one's political manifestation.(43)

But the reforms of the GPCR proved transitory. Given the scale of the changes envisioned, and the entrenched interests to be overcome, the new educational model required a much longer period in which its costs and benefits could be assessed. Seeking a thorough transformation of the 1960s structure, some of whose advocates were still influential, the radicals were repeatedly faced with challenges to their innovations. In the final analysis, many of their policies seemed designed as much to fight off these challenges and to repudiate the earlier system as to develop fully their own model.(44)

CHINA AFTER MAO: RETURN TO THE 1960s?

The death of Mao Zedong in September 1976 and the political demise a month later of the GPCR faction, known popularly as the Gang of Four, once again led to a striking modification of the educational structure. Just as the pre-GPCR educational system had been uniformly condemned as a dictatorship of bourgeois intellectuals who had blocked the implementation of Mao's educational line, the new assessment averred that, on the contrary, there had been great strides made in education from 1949-66, only to be negated by the ten years of catastrophe that followed.(45)

The major thrust of the post-Mao educational system has been the concentration on restoring educational quality in the schools. Such one-sidedness was acceptable, even essential, to the leadership in spite of anguished cries from some quarters.(46) After ten years in which the prevailing attitude among both students and teachers had been that studying was useless, by its initial policies the new government made it clear that everything except studying was useless. Displacing the more egalitarian structure the radicals had painstakingly attempted to erect was a structure more hierarchical than that of the 1960s. The key-point school system was reintroduced. The catch phrase became "cultivate talent early" (zaochu rencai). Arguing that the original rankings of schools had been invalidated by GPCR adjustments, schools and students were encouraged openly to compete academically. Students in the same year were divided into fast and slow classes, with the very best students forming a separate classroom (key-point classroom). The university entrance examinations restored in December 1977 became virtually the sole basis on which university entrance was decided. The successful schools, with success, as always, measured by promotion rate to a university, would be given key-point status; the successful students would be chosen for a university.(47) From 1977 to 1980, China's leaders made the adjustments considered necessary for a return to the "golden years" of Chinese education, as the 1961-65 period was called.(48) Just as the egalitarian ideals of the GPCR had led to the attempt to universalize senior high schools in Chinese cities, the commitment to academic quality dictated the retransformation of these schools into technical, vocational, or junior high schools, with the weakest academically (read low promotion rate) to be so transformed. To avoid such a fate, most of the urban high schools stepped up their competitive efforts. By autumn 1980, school rankings had become clearer. In each province and municipality, pecking orders were established, with scarce resources allocated according to a school's status. In Tianjin, for example, of the 66 key-point secondary schools, 27 were to be given priority, with the others aided as conditions permitted. Five of the 27 were given the right to recruit throughout the city; the rest could only recruit within their districts.(49) Moreover, throughout China, the better schools were lengthening senior high schooling from two years to three. In Liaoning province, the best schools were to introduce the three-year program in autumn 1980, with the rest of the key-point schools to follow within two years, and ordinary schools to join in only in 1985.(50)

Correlative with the renewed stress on academics came a diminution of the GPCR's stress on politics and morality. Whereas before the GPCR the expressed aim had been the development of students who were good intellectually, morally, and physically, the GPCR indictment objected to a de facto stress only on intellectual education. Accordingly, the balance was shifted mightily toward moral education. With the denunciation of the GPCR reforms came a new set of articles in the Chinese press protesting the overemphasis on morality and politics in the schools at the expense of academics.(51) Adding substance to this argument, the most well-known model units and individuals, having won praise as embodiments of the new activist morality, now either acknowledged they had been hoodwinked by the Gang of Four or were condemned outright as Gang of Four elements.(52)

STUDENT REACTION TO THE POSTCULTURAL REVOLUTION CHANGES

Had it been feasible to move rapidly from the GPCR educational system to the desired new model, perhaps student reactions would have been different. It was not possible, however, to implement concurrently all the measures required for the new system. Priorities were set. Most important was the restoration of academic quality and the identification and training of China's most talented students and scholars. In part, this meant the dispatch abroad of thousands of scholars in the sciences to study the advanced methods of the West. At home it meant that secondary schools – and, to some extent, even primary schools – were concerned almost exclusively with those students who showed academic promise. Students in provincial key points were considered more promising than those in municipal key points, who in turn were considered better than those in district key points. Within ordinary schools, only the key-point classrooms received attention. Students in schools targeted for transformation into technical, vocational, or junior highs received little attention. Those in junior high school were also frequently ignored. Because the transformation of the educational structure has been a relatively slow process, China has in recent years bemoaned the large number of students still attending regular senior and junior high schools and being turned out much faster than they can be absorbed in the job market. With few opportunities available for tertiary or secondary technical education at present, many students see junior or senior high school as similar dead ends. For example, in 1980, four years after the fall of the Gang, there were 6,160,000 senior high graduates. In 1976, there had been just 5,172,000.(53)

What has developed is something of a two-tiered system, with a distinctly competitive atmosphere among students in key-point schools and in key-point classrooms at the senior high level. Unlike the 1960s, however, when students were examined on the basis of class origin, academic achievement, and political manifestation, by 1979 and 1980 only academic achievement carried much weight. Students became reluctant to engage in any activities unrelated to university entrance examination preparation. But because the educational structure is still in transition from the GPCR years, only a small number of senior high graduates (around 4 to 5 percent) can actually enter a university. The remainder must seek employment. Although the situation has improved recently, it is still common for high school graduates to remain unemployed for a year or more before finding work.

If students with superior academic ability see the present system as a great advance over the GPCR model, the large majority of students are in many ways faced with a situation bearing no small resemblance to that earlier model. Most strikingly, for many students there once again seems little relationship between their schooling and their future. Although the prospect of a lifetime in the countryside no longer threatens, students who have no hope of postsecondary education have shown little motivation for studying. The renewed emphasis on academic quality has not trickled down to the ordinary junior high schools. Startling numbers of junior high students come out uneducated.(54) As in the GPCR years, many students see little point in attending senior high. A surprising number drop out early because it may enable them to find jobs more quickly.(55) The schools themselves foster these negative attitudes among the students. Students who reach the ninth grade (the last year of junior high) and show little promise are considered "senior middle-school rejects." Some schools have abandoned the teaching and supervision of ninth grade students, holding classes only half a day, allocating few teachers to this work, and even urging students to drop out of school and seek work.(56)

Published surveys reveal that the return to diversity in education has once again produced a diversity in student attitudes, based on the type of school attended. For example, partial results (from Beijing) of a ten-province survey of ideals, motivations, and interests of secondary school students revealed that more key-point school students are motivated to serve the state and work for the Four Modernizations than are those in ordinary schools (64.5 percent for key points, 48 percent for rural schools, 36.4 percent for general-urban). Far fewer key-point school students have "unclear motivation" (7.8 percent compared to 15 percent for general-urban, 13 percent for rural, and greater than 50 percent for work-study students).(57)

Perhaps even more ominous is a November 1979 study of the aspirations and learning interests of primary school students from grades 3, 4, and 5 of six primary schools in the city of Wuxi. In all, over 800 students were surveyed. It was discovered that a sizable proportion of the students did not want to continue to study, but wanted early employment, to replace parents as workers; the higher the grade, the greater the number of such pupils. When asked their favorite subject in school, only 0.84 percent chose politics, which was the least favored subject.(58)

Most damaging from the government's point of view is the cynicism openly displayed by today's students. Nor is the cynicism limited to those still in school. The three most recent generations of high school students — the pre-GPCR group of the 1960s, the GPCR generation of the 1970s, and the current crop — have each, for different reasons, developed an overt skepticism toward the political system and its leaders as well as toward their own future prospects. The former Red Guards had been products of the educational system of the 1960s when idealism and political activism were still prevalent. Many had fully expected to go to a university. Having experienced the twists and turns of the GPCR as members of one or another faction claiming allegiance to Chairman Mao, the majority of these idealistic youths were sent to the countryside as the movement wound down in 1968. The privations of the countryside, along with the progressive dismantling of the GPCR reforms (including their own recall to the cities after the youth to the countryside program was acknowledged as unsuccessful) gave many the feeling that their youth had been wasted and their educational opportunities denied.

Those who went to high school during the GPCR years of the 1970s generally had not harbored such ambitions for university entrance, nor were they much concerned with academic achievement, but at least some of the GPCR ideals still held some attraction for a fair number of these students.(59) Current denunciations of the "ten wasted years" have likewise caused many of these youths to feel, as one recent newspaper report put it, that they "were born at the wrong time." Now that the large majority of youths educated in the 1960s and 1970s have been allocated urban jobs, they have carried their frustrations and cynicism with them.(60)

In dismissing the GPCR uniformly, in disparaging the achievements of the most well-known model units and individuals as in one way or another "phony" or fabricated, China's leaders have created an atmosphere in which any current model put forward will likewise be viewed skeptically. In fact, at present anyone who is an activist is suspected of possessing ulterior motives. Yet the continued success of the party depends precisely on producing an uninterrupted procession of activists. Richard Solomon argued persuasively over a decade ago that the critical measure in evaluating the strength of the party's links to society, and its ability to operate successfully, is not really the ratio of party to population. Rather it is the number of nonparty people willing to compete for party membership, willing to carry out the daily tasks of policy implementation in hopes of eventually being chosen for party membership. If the party attracts five competitors for each new member chosen, its effective operational cadre has increased fivefold and has gained control of the motive power that derives from ambitious people anxiously competing for elite status.(61)

In this light, the present plight of those willing to be activists is a major cause for concern. One recent letter to a local youth magazine described the activist's dilemma well:

My good friend Little Chen was always positive and serious about her work, willing to undertake hard work and accept criticism. The masses praised her highly and the leadership had a good impression of her. She has been chosen many times as an advanced producer in the factory. But after she became well-known, there was much criticism of her. Some people said that she only wanted to ingratiate herself with the leadership and gather all the glory herself. Others felt that having to work with her was distressing, bad luck, or constituted a loss of freedom. Still others considered that her striving to be advanced was for the purpose of becoming an "official." Actually, Little Chen has no intention of being an "official." The leadership had decided to promote her to a leadership post, but she considered herself unqualified and did not want to stir up trouble, so she sincerely declined. Still, others criticized her more, and the leadership constantly pressured her, so that she was in total agony, and often her cares and concerns were piled one on top of another. Unfortunately, she recently made a mistake in her work so that the leadership told her to guard against arrogance, and some people slandered her even more. I sympathize with

Little Chen. Seeing her treatment after becoming an advanced element really makes me tremble with fear.(62)

Having witnessed the political dislocations of the past 20 years, many youths have adopted a wait-and-see attitude with regard to China's long-term prospects. Recent surveys conducted in China reveal a seemingly unprecedented lack of confidence. For example, a poll conducted at Shanghai's Fudan University in September 1980 revealed that 78 percent of those polled had doubts about the success of China's Four Modernizations. When asked about the possibility of Gang of Four type people regaining control over the government within the next ten years, 39 percent replied that it was inevitable. Fifty-five percent felt that the greatest social problem in China today was cadre privileges. When asked to state their faith or belief, 33 percent listed communist, 25 percent mentioned fate, 25 percent said nothing, with a small number listing capitalism.(63)

More limited surveys — conducted by foreigners — have turned up equally distressing figures. Kyodo news agency surveyed 28 sophomores majoring in Japanese at Sichuan University. When asked whom they now admire, not one student brought forth a name. Of six juniors asked the same question, one replied Zhou Enlai and five had no reply.(64) When students in a college class in Chongqing were asked on a CYL questionnaire whether they believed in socialism, capitalism, religion, atheism, or fatalism, 85 percent chose fatalism, none chose socialism.(65)

Although some officially published surveys have revealed rather less negative student responses, there have been many articles in the press acknowledging that the government is aware of widespread rejection by youths of the official ideology.(66) Reports in People's Daily and Guangming Daily lament the indifference, even hostility, shown by university students toward Marxism-Leninism. With their heavy work load, many students do not attend politics classes, since they are considered of little relevance to present society and the Four Modernizations.(67) Following official criticisms of the emphasis on combining education with productive labor charac- teristic of the GPCR years, students virtually stopped participating in labor.(68) The CYL has recruited large numbers of students who are indifferent to the organization's ideology and do not participate in its activities. Many joined because their school simply recruited all students considered to have a chance to pass the university examinations.

RECENT DEVELOPMENTS: SOLUTIONS OFFERED

Alarmed by the decline in socialist morality, the government has begun to move rapidly to win back the confidence of Chinese youths. Blaming much of the current dissatisfaction with the party and

Marxist-Leninist ideology on the "pseudo-Marxism" practiced by the Gang of Four, the present emphasis has been less on theory and more on practice. The current "crisis of faith" is said to stem from a contradiction between theory and reality. Those aspects of Marxism that are incompatible with the current needs of society are to be jettisoned, as Marxism continues to develop. Making a virtue out of necessity, the crisis of faith has, perhaps euphemistically, been termed a "great thought-emancipation movement."(69)

In terms of specific policies, there has been a return to political, moral, and labor education in primary and secondary schools. Primary school courses in politics are gradually being turned into classes in ethics, with the stress on building a "socialist spiritual civilization" side by side with increasing wealth.(70) For example, the contents of the courses on morality introduced into Shanghai's primary schools in autumn 1981 are very similar to what had been stressed in the pre-GPCR primary readers. Rules of conduct for primary and middle school students, first designed in 1953 but neglected during the GPCR, have been reissued with appropriate revisions.(71) A central document issued in late 1980 stressed the necessity of reintroducing political lessons into the middle school curriculum.(72) Returning to fundamentals, political education is to be centered on education in the Four Basic Principles. Widely publicized after April 1979, these principles include keeping to the socialist road, upholding the dictatorship of the proletariat, party leadership, and Marxism-Leninism-Mao Zedong thought.

Moreover, history and geography courses are once again to contain a heavy dose of patriotism; dialectical materialism will be used in math, physics, and chemistry courses. Education through labor is also to be stepped up.(73) Youth magazines and newspapers have carried articles and forums on the close relationship between academics and politics.(74) In this regard, China's foremost model youth — Lei Feng — has been recycled for those who have been concerned only with study. For example, the well-known self-taught mathematician Chen Jingrun, himself a post-GPCR model, has been called a good student of Lei Feng.(75) Students are being urged to study and apply — albeit selectively — the works of Mao Zedong. Even Mao's dictum that "education must serve proletarian politics" has been reaffirmed, so long as it is not stressed too one-sidedly.(76)

Although it is obviously too early to assess the effects of the increasing emphasis on political and moral education, there are indications that success will not come easily. While the youth problem is often acknowledged, there has been a reluctance by social institutions to tackle the problem. Schools, which were stripped of much of their power to control the fate of their students during the GPCR decade, have yet to recover this power. School officials therefore argue that there is little they can do to strengthen ideological and political education; the major influence on students comes from family and society. If such influence is negative, the schools are helpless.(77) Party officials as well, witnessing the declining prestige of the CYL among youth, have been neglecting the league. At best, youth work seems to have been given low priority at the basic levels. Some argue that, "there would be no steel if we neglect industry; there would be no grain if we neglect agriculture; but children grow up all the same even though we neglect them."(78) There has also been resistance from those who argue that the active promotion of communist morality will inevitably lead, once again, to leftist mistakes and that ideological consciousness will in any event spontaneously develop in accord with the development of the productive forces and the improvement of material conditions.(79)

Perhaps the most disturbing to league cadres is the reflection within the CYL of the two-tiered competitive/noncompetitive atmosphere currently marking Chinese secondary schools. A recent investigation by the schools section of the Shanghai Municipal Youth League Committee discovered that only 12 percent of eligible (in terms of age) secondary school students in Shanghai were league members. Moreover, they were very unevenly distributed, with the large majority to be found in key-point schools, schools containing both junior and senior high sections, and the graduating classes of senior high. In nearly 50 percent of Shanghai's secondary schools, there were fewer than 30 league members per school. League committees in many junior high schools simply did not function due to small membership. The investigation found that when students reach the age of 14, after their second year of junior high school, they simply are dropping out of the Young Pioneers, and the CYL is making no attempt to recruit them.(80) At the other extreme, there have been reports of schools simply pulling every student in a classroom into the league en masse (chuang tuanyuan ban), most commonly in senior high graduating classes, in the hope that league membership will enhance a student's chances of gaining entrance to university.(81) Not surprisingly, visitors have discovered very high rates of CYL membership at key-point schools. One secondary school in Chengdu told a visitor that close to 92 percent of ·its students were league members by their last year of senior high; Nankai Middle School in Tianjin reported that 70 percent of its senior high students were league members.(82)

Lei Feng's reappearance has reportedly also been met with less than unqualified enthusiasm. Many have indifferently reacted to a model they consider outmoded, as an anachronism from the 1960s.(83) Interviewees – including some who had been CYL officers – reacted to the connection between Lei Feng and the mathematician Chen Jingrun with surprise and laughter. As one put it, "everyone knows Chen was a bookworm, interested only in studies." The following letter from a local youth magazine is typical of many other letters and newspaper reports:

Since the "Five Stresses and Four Beauties Campaign" began, we have wanted very much to learn from Lei Feng and do more good deeds. However, faced with the ridicule of some people, we find the situation unbearable. Even before you do anything, some will say your "phony activism is rather advanced." Or, they will say bitingly, "Didn't you say you wanted to do a good deed? Help me wash my socks!" Confronted by such sarcasm, we become very apprehensive. What should we do?(84)

The time-honored technique of small group criticism and self-criticism also seems to be functioning less effectively at present. Once again, the legacy of the GPCR has left its mark. In reaction to the superheated political atmosphere prevalent during the GPCR years, when praise and benefit, criticism and disfavor depended heavily on factional or personal connections, current attempts at recreating a political atmosphere within individual units have been met with suspicion. Turning the ideal model on its head, it is the objects of criticism who now receive group support and sympathy; the rancor, hostility, and isolation are reserved for their critics.(85)

Those youths eagerly responding to the new calls for public service by becoming class officers have fared little better than the Lei Feng activists. Titled "Does One Lose Out Because One Manages Affairs for the Collective?," a recent letter to a local youth magazine became that magazine's lead story:

Comrade Editor:

I am a member of the CYL and a class officer as well. After I was elected an officer, I was determined to do a good job, but got no support from my classmates. Sometimes when I allocate tasks to be done, everyone procrastinates and no one carries it out. When I ask them why, some will say: "Doing things for others of necessity takes away from your own study time. If you want to get into a university, it's your grades that will be examined. Anything that interferes with studies will cause you to lose out." When I hear this, my own enthusiasm declines. I figure that if everybody feels this way, why should I foolishly put out any effort? But as soon as this thought comes to mind, I feel it is incorrect. Still, I can't get rid of it. Can you please help me to solve this vexing problem?(86)

Although activists before the GPCR had been faced with rather similar problems, the elimination of class origin as a factor in educational mobility, the reaction against the "empty politics" of the GPCR years, and the undisguised primacy of academic achievement combine to make the current situation qualitatively different.

A forum attended by educators responsible for ideological education for youths revealed some of the obstacles to the reintroduction
of political education for students. One participant from a key-point
school told how key-point schools had not considered ideological and
political education an important task. If, under the present circumstances, we should become concerned with this question, he asked,
how should it be done? Another participant explained that it had
become common to stress ideological education for poor students,
the ones unlikely to climb the educational ladder, and intellectual
education for those of superior academic ability. A third
complained that the necessary reduction of physical labor following
the downfall of the Gang of Four had led schools virtually to
eliminate such activities completely.(87)

EDUCATION, YOUTH, AND POLITICS IN THE
CHINESE COUNTRYSIDE

A number of recent reports in education and youth magazines,
including surveys of student attitudes, have shown that the greatest
casualty of GPCR policies and their replacement by the Four
Modernizations strategy may be youth perceptions of the countryside and peasant life. Primary school readers from the late 1950s on
had sought to orient both urban and rural students toward a life in
rural China. The countryside was presented as a vast arena in which
youths armed with scientific and technical skills would cooperate in
improving life in rural China. While possessing fewer amenities than
life in the city, participation in the great adventure of rural
transformation was seen to possess its own psychic rewards.
Now that the vast majority of urban-educated youths who —
willingly or unwillingly — answered this call have been allowed to
return to the city, as China is importing advanced technology on a
large scale, and as the desire to study abroad has reached a fever
pitch among China's students and intellectuals, a life in the countryside has lost all its attraction. For example, the study of primary
school students in Wuxi cited earlier found that only 4 out of 839
(0.47 percent) answered peasant/farmer when asked "What work
would you like to do when you grow up?"(88) A survey investigating
the ideal future occupations of 1,122 youths in Liaoning province in
1980 — which included students in 3 urban and 2 rural middle schools
— found that only 2 youths (0.18 percent) listed peasant as their
choice. In 1979, the same researchers had found that only 1 youth of
the 523 surveyed listed peasant.(89) Another survey, this time
encompassing eight full-time secondary schools in one city, three
county capitals, and two communes in Guangxi province, found
peasant the least favored of eight possible future occupations listed.
Of those in junior high, 2.3 percent chose peasant; in senior high, the
corresponding figure was 3.2 percent. Even among senior high

students in commune schools, many of whose hopes to leave the countryside had presumably already been dashed, only six percent looked forward to a life as a peasant.(90) Interestingly, this same survey showed that while 94.8 percent of senior high students in the rural areas felt that the Four Modernizations would definitely be achieved, only 56.08 percent in urban schools expressed such confidence.(91)

These surveys are consistent with other reports in the Chinese press complaining that students attend secondary school in the countryside only because it gives them the opportunity to "leap over the village gate" (tiaochu nongmen).(92) This desire to escape the tedium of village life has been described by a number of scholars investigating villages in Guangdong, where escape to Hong Kong seemingly had reached epidemic proportions prior to the recent change in British policy toward illegal immigrants, but it now seems clear from the Chinese press that the phenomenon is not limited to those in the proximity of Hong Kong.(93)

School authorities are cognizant of student aspirations to use advanced education as a ticket out of the countryside. Moreover, for their own reasons, and similar to their urban counterparts, they focus almost entirely on intellectual education. In many schools there is either no one assigned to conduct ideo-political work or a feeling that, unlike other specialties requiring expertise, anyone can do such work on an ad hoc basis.(94) Thus, students in rural secondary schools tend to be divided into those with good academic achievement who study eagerly and make every effort to be noticed, and those with poor academic achievement who make use of the opportunity to fool around for two years until it is time to return to their families and take part in labor. In neither case are the students concerned with politics nor labor education.(95) In fact, the Guangxi survey of urban and rural schools cited above found that most students in junior high rated the subject of politics last (fifteenth) when asked their favorite courses, with only 0.37 percent rating it highest. Respondents in senior high were a bit more favorable, with 2.49 percent citing politics as their favorite subject. Similar results appeared when students were asked their favorite reading matter outside the class. Perhaps surprisingly, history courses and history books were equally unpopular with the students.(96)

Government authorities as well acknowledge the desire of rural youths to leave the villages, arguing that it is a consequence of the present poor and backward state of China's rural areas. The solution offered is the new production responsibility system (shengchan zerenzhi), which "grant(s) the right of self-determination for the collective economy to the localities and . . . pay(s) attention to the peasants' material interests in order to stimulate their enthusiasm for work," and is expected to make the countryside prosper.(97) Youths are urged to remain in the countryside and become wealthy. In the same way that the favored schools are the key-point schools, the favored brigades are the rich brigades. Young peasants who remain in the countryside and prosper, under the current system, are exhibiting Red behavior.

As in the cities, the current policy has led to some confusion and demoralization among those responsible for ideo-political work. For example, some CYL cadres have found it difficult to adjust to the new stress on production over politics. One writer to a national youth magazine could not puzzle it out:

> In the past, when we looked at the standard for admittance to the CYL, most important was to see whether one worked wholeheartedly for others, loved the collective, contributed one's strength for the construction of a new socialist countryside. Now, with the fixing of farm output quotas for each household, with individuals solely responsible for tasks, with youths surrounded only by their own families, increasing production only out of selfish calculation, how do we investigate whether a youth's political consciousness is high, whether he wholeheartedly embodies the collectivist ideology?(98)

The official response emphasized that the CYL's recruitment policy must reflect present party policy. Generating higher output shows a rural youth's concern for the collective and his contribution to the building of socialism.

Indeed, a survey of provincial youth magazines reveals something of a crisis in rural CYL work under the new conditions. For example, a letter from a commune league committee in Shanxi complains that no one wants to be a league cadre since they are not compensated with work points for going to league meetings.(99) In Sichuan, in a readers' forum organized by the local youth magazine, similar objections were raised.(100) From a commune in Guangdong comes a report that in 3 of the 16 league branches, not one cent in dues had been paid in the last three years. Moreover, when a brigade league committee recently organized a celebration of May 4, only 5 of the 282 league members bothered to show up.(101) In Gansu, an investigation report revealed that CYL work had stagnated in the countryside under the new economic conditions. Political discussions had no appeal. The answer, according to the report, was to make the league more relevant to the concerns of youth.(102)

CONCLUSION

The overriding and long-standing problem of political socialization in China has been the gap between the model citizen the Chinese educational system has sought to foster and the actual product of that system. Although the government readily acknowledges that serious ideological problems currently exist among many youths, the blame is placed solely on the GPCR. Deng Xiaoping, in an interview with a Yugoslav reporter, summed up the situation:

> This is the problem of an entire generation and cannot be resolved in 3 or 5 years' time. We must begin with nursery schools. Before the Cultural Revolution the moral image, habits and ideological stands of the people were good, but they were totally destroyed during the Cultural Revolution.(103)

But our examination of the attitudes and behavior of Chinese students before, during, and after the GPCR has revealed that even before the GPCR students in China's secondary schools were deviating from the prescribed behavior characteristic of model citizens. The crucial source of this deviation was the fundamental contradiction between the two functions of the school system: as transmitters of moral-political ideology and as arenas for educational contest mobility. The structural reforms introduced in the late 1960s were in part a response to these deviant tendencies but, in suppressing the schools' mobility function and overstressing the moral-political function, these reforms in turn produced other, much more serious deviations. With the political demise of the radicals, a new educational structure emerged, designed to restore as rapidly as possible the academic quality that had been sacrificed as a concomitant of the GPCR reforms. Once again, serious deviations in student attitudes and behavior followed in the wake of these structural changes.

As reactions — or, more precisely, overreactions — to previous structures perceived as seriously defective, both the GPCR model and the Four Modernizations model were transitional, not finished products. Just as the GPCR model varied from year to year in the 1970s, the current structure is being altered to cope with the serious side effects that have stemmed from the one-sided stress on educational contest mobility. For example, schools in some provinces no longer divide students into fast, medium, and slow classes.(104) Beginning in autumn 1982, key-point elementary schools have been recruiting on a neighborhood basis, rather than citywide or districtwide, with no examination given.(105) In Guangdong, students who have distinguished themselves in one of a variety of ways will be allotted an extra ten points toward their secondary school entrance examination score. Students receiving such benefits will include those acclaimed at county level or above as "3-good" students in junior high (good in academics, morality, and physical ability), those who have received at least a third place in individual athletic competition at the district level or above, and the top players on certain athletic teams.(106)

Although structural adjustment may well encourage students to engage in activities other than examination preparation, they have the potential at the same time to widen the gap between the model citizen and the secondary school student. Surveys have shown that students (and, by implication, their parents) clearly rank occupations.(107) For the foreseeable future, access to higher education and employment in state enterprises will remain at the top of the scale and agricultural and service work will be at the bottom. To convince school administrators, teachers, and students to pay sufficient attention to moral-political ideology, such ideological training will have to be made relevant to student values. In the end, it seems more likely that the gap between the model citizen and the Chinese students will only be reduced by altering the characteristics of the former and accepting the desires of the latter.

NOTES

(1)   Daily Report – CHINA, U.S. Foreign Broadcast Information Service, herafter Daily Report, November 9, 1981, p. K 4, from Renmin Ribao, November 3, 1981. Other reports on the problems of advanced elements and model workers can be found inter alia in Daily Report, September 21, 1981, pp. K 11-13, from Renmin Ribao, September 7, 1981; Daily Report, July 2, 1981, pp. K 6-7, from Renmin Ribao, June 19, 1981; Daily Report, October 2, 1981, pp. K 2-3, from New China News Agency (NCNA), September 18, 1981; Daily Report, August 12, 1981, pp. T 4-6, from Shanxi Ribao, July 22, 1981. See also the forum on this subject in Zhongguo Qingnian, nos. 16, 19, 20, 21, 22, 23-24 (1981).

(2)   Daily Report, October 14, 1981, pp. K 20-21, from Beijing Ribao, September 23, 1981. See also Zhongguo Qingnian, no. 10 (May 26, 1981), pp. 2-4, for a talk on the generation gap (daigou) problem given by the first party secretary of Anhui province. Hong Kong magazines have given publicity abroad to the debate. See Zhengming, no. 48 (October 1, 1981), p. 75, for a talk on the generation gap by Ye Jianying's daughter and Qishi Niandai, December 1979, translated in JPRS, no. 75291, March 12, 1980.

(3)   Daily Report, March 30, 1981, from Gongren Ribao, March 27, 1981; Inside China Mainland (Taiwan), January 1981, pp. 8-11, from Renmin Ribao, November 11, 1980.

(4)   Daily Report, March 31, 1981, pp. L 1-8, from Hongqi, no. 5 (March 1, 1981); Daily Report, March 20, 1981, pp. L 5-7, from Jiefang Ribao, March 12, 1981; Daily Report, February 23, 1981, pp. L 27-30, from Zhongguo Qingnian Bao, February 7, 1981.

(5)   Zhongguo Qingnian, no. 16 (August 26, 1981), p. 21; Zhongxuesheng, no. 11 (1980), p. 10; Hubei Qingnian, no. 6 (1981), p. 10.

(6)   Jieban Ren (Tianjin), no. 3 (1981), pp. 3-5; Huangjin Shidai (Guangdong), no. 8 (1981), p. 15; Zhongguo Qingnian Bao, August 23, 1980, p. 2.

(7)   A debate on the meaning of life was carried out in Zhongguo Qingnian over a ten-month period from May 1980 to March 1981. The debate was initiated by a letter from Pan Xiao, a youth disillusioned by events in society and in her personal life during the ten years of the GPCR. Over 60,000 letters were received by the journal. Zhongguo Qingnian Bao also provided a forum for the debate. The newspaper received 70,000 letters between July 1980 and February 1981 on the issue, with over 300 letters published. For reports on the debate see, in addition to the relevant issues of Zhongguo Qingnian and Zhongguo Qingnian Bao, Daily Report, March 27, 1981, p. L 18, from NCNA, March 25; Daily Report, February 25, 1981, from NCNA, February 24; Zhonggong Wenti Ziliao (Taiwan), no. 076 (March 23, 1981), pp. 1-7; Chinese Education 16, no. 1 (Spring 1981), in which Pan Xiao's letter is translated. Provincial youth magazines also sponsored a debate on the topic. See, for example, Sichuan Qingnian, no. 2 (1981), pp. 16-17.

(8)   Useful bibliographies can be found in Stanley Allen Renshon, Handbook of Political Socialization: Theory and Research (Riverside, N.J.: Macmillan, The Free Press, 1977), pp. 468-528; and Jack Dennis, Socialization to Politics: A Reader (New York: Wiley, 1973), pp. 503-27. A summary of developments in this field can be found in David O. Sears, "Political Socialization," in Handbook of Political Science, vol. 2: Micropolitical Theory, ed. Fred I. Greenstein and Nelson W. Polsby (Menlo Park, Calif.: Addison-Wesley, 1975), pp. 93-153. It should be pointed out that while the term political socialization is new, the concerns with which it deals go back to classical political theory.

(9)   Fred I. Greenstein, "Political Socialization," in International Encyclopedia of the Social Sciences, vol. 14, ed. David L. Sills (Riverside, N.J.: Macmillan, The Free Press, 1968), pp. 551-55.

(10)   A fine summary of Maoist ideas about socialization that synthesizes much of the scholarly literature on the subject is provided in James R. Townsend, Politics in China, 2d. ed. (Boston: Little, Brown, 1980), pp. 177-86.

(11)   John Bryan Starr, Continuing the Revolution: The Political Thought of Mao (Princeton, N.J.: Princeton University Press, 1979), pp. 235-41. For a general study of Mao's ideas on education, see John N. Hawkins, Mao Tse-tung and Education (Hamden, Conn.: Shoestring Press, 1974).

(12)   Starr, Continuing the Revolution, pp. 239-40.

(13)   Parris H. Chang, "Children's Literature and Political Socialization," in Moving a Mountain: Cultural Change in China, ed. Godwin C. Chu and Francis L.K. Hsu (Honolulu: University of Hawaii Press, 1979), pp. 237-56.

(14)   For a detailed analysis of themes in primary school readers published from 1957-64 in Beijing and Shanghai, see Charles P. Ridley, Paul H.B. Godwin, and Dennis J. Doolin, The Making of a Model Citizen in Communist China (Stanford, Calif.: Hoover Institution Press, 1971). These textbooks are compared to textbooks used on Taiwan by Roberta Martin in "The Socialization of Children in China and on Taiwan: An Analysis of Elementary School Textbooks," China Quarterly 62 (June 1975): pp.   242-62. For an analysis of primary school readers published and used during the GPCR years, see Jonathan Unger, ed., "Post-Cultural Revolution Primary-School Education: Selected Texts," in Chinese Education 10, no. 2 (Summer 1977). My own examination of primary school textbooks published between 1979-81 and my discussion of these textbooks with students who had attended primary schools before and during the GPCR confirms this point. Unger (p. 10) makes the point for the GPCR years.

(15)   The ideological content of schooling and the political themes appearing in primary school textbooks are well analyzed in Jonathan Unger, Education Under Mao: Class and Competition in Canton Schools, 1960-1980 (New York: Columbia University Press, 1982), chap. 5. Ridley, Godwin, and Doolin, The Making of a Model Citizen distills 19 separate political themes from the readers they analyze (see pp. 99-135). Recent primary school textbooks seem much more circumspect in identifying the enemy by name. Quite often one finds stories that obviously deal with the Second World War or the Korean War but only the expression "enemy" (diren) is used. There are, however, some stories that specifically refer to "Japanese devils" (Riben guizi) and the "reactionary Guomindang," but these terms seem to be used less frequently than previously. In the six recent primary school readers and one politics reader I have examined, the Soviets and the Americans were not mentioned by name.   Nor was class struggle and landlord exploitation of the peasantry stressed. The readers covered the first two years and the last year of primary school.   These readers were also shown to individuals who had attended primary school in the 1960s and my comments above reflect their opinions as well.

(16)   These are the four most frequent of the 17 behavioral themes identified in Ridley, Godwin, and Doolin, Making of a Model Citizen, pp. 135-61.

(17)   Martin, "Socialization of Children," p. 253.

(18)   The Red versus Expert controversy in Chinese politics has been much commented upon. See, for example, Ann Kent, "Red and Expert: The Revolution in Education at Shanghai Teachers' University, 1975-76," China Quarterly 86 (June 1981): pp. 304-21; Martin King Whyte, " 'Red and Expert': Peking's Changing Policy," Problems of Communism (November-December 1972): 18-27; Dennis Ray, " 'Red and Expert' and China's Cultural Revolution," Pacific Affairs (Spring 1970): 22-33; Richard Baum, " 'Red and Expert': The Politico-

Ideological Foundations of China's Great Leap Forward," <u>Asian Survey</u> (September 1964): 1048-57.

(19)   The use of models as teaching devices throughout Chinese society, in traditional times as well as more recently, has been a frequent subject for analysis. See, for example, Donald J. Munro, <u>The Concept of Man in Contemporary China</u> (Ann Arbor: University of Michigan Press, 1977), pp. 135-57; Richard H. Solomon, <u>Mao's Revolution and the Chinese Political Culture</u> (Berkeley: University of California Press, 1971); Betty B. Burch, "Models as Agents of Change in China," in <u>Value Change in Chinese Society</u>, ed. Richard W. Wilson, Amy Auerbacher Wilson, and Sidney L. Greenblatt (New York: Praeger, 1979), pp. 122-37; Ruth Gamberg, <u>Red and Expert: Education in The People's Republic of China</u> (New York: Schocken Books, 1977), pp. 167-72 and passim.

(20)   The most famous individual of this type was Dong Jiageng. His case is described in Stanley Rosen, <u>The Role of Sent-Down Youth in the Chinese Cultural Revolution: The Case of Guangzhou</u> (Berkeley: Center for Chinese Studies Publication, University of California, 1981), pp. 41-45.

(21)   A number of recent books have described the informal classroom culture in Chinese secondary schools before the GPCR. See Susan Shirk, <u>Competitive Comrades: Career Incentives and Student Strategies in China</u> (Berkeley: University of California Press, 1982) for the most extensive account. Also see Unger, <u>Education Under Mao</u>, chap. 5; Anita Chan, <u>Children of Mao</u> (forthcoming); Stanley Rosen, <u>Red Guard Factionalism and the Cultural Revolution in Guangzhou</u> (Boulder, Colo.: Westview Press, 1982), chap. 2.

(22)   This paragraph draws from the insights provided in Shirk, <u>Competitive Comrades</u>, chap. 2. For the Soviet method of upbringing in collective settings, see Urie Bronfenbrenner, <u>Two Worlds of Childhood</u> (New York, N.Y.: Basic Books, Russell Sage Foundation, 1970), pp. 15-69.

(23)   Although there is no full-length book on the CYL, much useful material is provided in Ronald N. Montaperto, "The Chinese Communist Youth League and the Political Socialization of Chinese Youth" (Ph.D. diss., University of Michigan, 1977).

(24)   For 156 questions and answers regarding various aspects of the CYL and its tasks, see <u>Gongqingtuan jiben zhishi wenda</u> (China Youth League, 1979).

(25)   These recent studies include Anita Chan, Stanley Rosen, and Jonathan Unger, "Students and Class Warfare: The Social Roots of the Red Guard Conflict in Guangzhou," <u>China Quarterly</u>, no. 83 (September 1980), pp. 397-446; and the works of Shirk, <u>Competitive Comrades</u>; Unger, <u>Education Under Mao</u>; Chan, <u>Children Under Mao</u>; and Rosen, <u>Red Guard Factionalism</u>.

(26)   Rosen, <u>Red Guard Factionalism</u>, chaps. 1 and 2.

(27)   Ridley, Godwin, and Doolin, Making of a Model Citizen, pp. 195-97. John Lewis, in his study on teachers' manuals for Jiangsu kindergartens from 1956 emphasizes this contradiction even more strongly. Lewis contrasts child education, "which takes its cue primarily from the priorities of economic development," to the education of political cadres, in which revolutionary political priorities are stressed. Lewis sees "a preschool educational policy designed to foster skilled, self-motivated individuals," and a school system in which "the curriculum is overwhelmingly geared to the cultivation of advanced 'intellectuals' in all fields." In arguing back in 1964 that a rapidly aging elite must now transfer power to a new generation trained to value science, technique, and individual contribution, Lewis is, in fact, echoing some of the concerns that led Mao to launch the GPCR shortly afterward. See John Wilson Lewis, "Party Cadres in Communist China," in Education and Political Development, ed. James S. Coleman (Princeton, N.J.: Princeton University Press, 1965), pp. 408-36.

(28)   Ridley et al., Making of a Model Citizen, pp. 197-98. Other examples of conflicting values are also provided, pp. 198-208.

(29)   Chan, Rosen, and Unger, "Students and Class Warfare," pp. 399-401; Stanley Rosen, "Obstacles to Educational Reform in China," Modern China (January 1982): 5-11.

(30)   For the functioning of one of these specialist schools see Gordon A. Bennett and Ronald N. Montaperto, Red Guard: The Political Biography of Dai Hsiao-ai (Garden City, N.Y.: Doubleday, 1971). Also see Ronald N. Montaperto, "From Revolutionary Successors to Revolutionaries: Chinese Students in the Early Stages of the Cultural Revolution," in Elites in the People's Republic of China, ed. Robert Scalapino (Seattle, Wash.: University of Washington Press, 1972), pp. 575-605; Martin King Whyte, Small Groups and Political Rituals in China (Berkeley, Calif.: University of California Press, 1974), pp. 96-134. The same informant Dai Hsiao-ai, was a major source for the above studies. Further information on Dai's school is provided in interview protocols of Jonathan Unger and Stanley Rosen. Also see Shirk, Competitive Comrades, chap. 2, who found a similar situation at the specialist schools by interviewing someone other than Dai!

(31)   Some details on the vocational schools are provided in Rosen, interview protocols. In 1964, 600 students were expelled from Guangzhou's work-study vocational schools (about 10 percent of the total) for having bad class origin and/or poor political manifestation. For the incident of the "600 work-study students" and their protest in the GPCR, see Rosen, The Role of Sent-Down Youth.

(32)   Perhaps the most deviant behavior, from the standpoint of the state, was exhibited by those in urban minban schools, which ranked lowest in the educational hierarchy. Students in these schools were considered failures. There was little reward to be gained from activist behavior or by studying hard. Ironically, cooperation was

rather high in these schools; students, expecting little from the state, sought the approval of their peers, which often led to a delinquent counterculture. See Shirk, Competitive Comrades, chap. 2.

(33)   The arguments in this section are dealt with in greater detail in Rosen, Red Guard Factionalism, chaps. 1 and 2.

(34)   Shirk, Competitive Comrades, chap. 6; Chan, Rosen, and Unger, "Students and Class Warfare," pp. 406-20.

(35)   For details on the reforms introduced into education during the GPCR see Suzanne Pepper, "Education and Revolution: The 'Chinese Model' Revisited," Asian Survey 18, no. 9 (September 1978): 847-90. Because of the decentralized environment in which the GPCR reforms were implemented, there were many variations from the basic guidelines. As one example, only the larger cities were able to universalize senior high education.

(36)   The specialist schools were something of an exception. Although course work had been reduced from three years to two, in general these schools were not greatly changed during the GPCR years. See Pepper, "Education and Revolution," p. 864.

(37)   Pepper, "Education and Revolution," p. 854. See also Andrew Watson, Living in China (Totowa: Littlefield, Adams, 1977), pp. 131-42.

(38)   Ronald N. Montaperto, "The Chinese Communist Youth League, 1970-1974: A Study of Adaptive Behavior," in Sidney L. Greenblatt, Richard W. Wilson, and Amy Auerbacher Wilson, eds., Organizational Behavior in Chinese Society (New York: Praeger, 1981), pp. 209-30. In the early 1970s a mass organization called the Red Guards (not to be confused with their more destructive namesakes of the late 1960s), seems to have replaced the CYL. In primary schools the Young Pioneers was replaced by a similar organization called the Little Red Soldiers. Like the Pioneers, the new organization included most of the students in a class. There is some disagreement on just how universal the Red Guard organization was in secondary schools in the 1970s. Although most of my informants claimed that membership was virtually universal, in the schools visited by Ruth Gamberg in 1973, membership ranged from 25 to 40 percent. See Red and Expert, p. 205.   Unger, Education Under Mao, chap. 9, argues that by 1974 membership in the Red Guards had become obligatory for all students of senior-high age. One of Montaperto's interviewees claims that the CYL had basically replaced the Red Guards as early as 1972.

(39)   It should be noted that this characterization of student behavior is in keeping with the current assessment of the "ten wasted years" of the GPCR. Many visitors to Chinese schools in this period had nothing but praise for China's "revolution in education." See, for example, Gamberg, Red and Expert. On the other hand, refugee informants had provided a picture rather similar to the current one. See, for example, Unger, Education Under Mao, chaps. 7 and 9.

(40)   Details of the Huang Shuai case and its repercussions can be found in China Reconstructs (August 1974), pp. 2-5.

(41)   This process is described in Unger, Education Under Mao, chap. 5. Also see Rosen, Red Guard Factionalism, chap. 2.

(42)   Unger, Education Under Mao, chap. 9. For a full discussion of the operation of small groups in Chinese schools in the 1950s and 1960s, see Whyte, Small Groups and Political Rituals in China, pp. 96-134.

(43)   Montaperto, "Youth League, 1970-74," p. 219.

(44)   The Huang Shuai and Zhang Tiesheng cases come to mind in this regard. Zhang was a production team cadre who was nominated in 1973 to go to a university. Unable to answer the science and mathematics questions on the written examination, he used the reverse side of the exam paper to protest such discrimination against those too busy doing productive labor to study these subjects. His objections were given nationwide attention, just as Huang Shuai's had been. See Unger, Education Under Mao, p. 198.

(45)   Renmin Jiaoyu, no. 2 (1977), pp. 3-13.

(46)   The anguished cries were from those who complained that the new policy departed from the "class line," would widen the "three great differences" (mental and manual labor, worker and peasant, city and countryside), emphasized only intellectual training, and so forth. See Susan Shirk, "Educational Reform and Political Backlash: Recent Changes in Chinese Educational Policy," Comparative Education Review 23, no. 2 (June 1979): 183-217.

(47)   A number of points treated in this section are discussed in more detail in Rosen, "Obstacles to Educational Reform," pp. 3-40.

(48)   Xuexi yu tansuo (Heilongjiang), no. 4 (1980), pp. 31-36, argues that China's best university students were produced in these years.

(49)   Guangming Ribao, July 21, 1980, p. 2; Joint Publications Research Service (JPRS), no. 76710, October 18, 1980, p. 78, from Tianjin Ribao, July 11.

(50)   BBC Summary of World Broadcasts, FE/6467/BII/15, London, July 10, 1980.

(51)   For criticisms of the stress on putting moral education in first place, see Shehui Kexue Zhanxian (Jilin), no. 2 (1980), pp. 229-35; Jiaoyu Yanjiu, no. 4 (1980), pp. 33-35.

(52)   One who acknowledged her mistake was Huang Shuai, the primary school student who had gained national fame for standing up to her teacher. One model who fell along with the gang was Zhang Tiesheng, who had won praise for turning in a blank examination paper. Criticism of Zhang appears in Renmin Jiaoyu, no. 1 (1978), pp. 19-23.

(53)   Renmin Jiaoyu, no. 1 (1982), p. 5; Zhongguo baike nianjian 1980, p. 536. In 1965 there had been only 360,000 senior high graduates.

(54)   Guangming Ribao (Peking), December 4, 1981; January 17, 1982.

(55)   Zhongguo Qingnian Bao (Peking), July 1, 1980, p. 3.

(56)   JPRS, no. 77861, April 17, 1981, pp. 40-41, from Liaoning Ribao, January 5, 1981.

(57)   Beijing shifan daxue xuebao (Social Science Edition), no. 1 (1982), pp. 7-13. Results of this survey were brought to my attention by David Chu of the Department of Sociology, University of California, Berkeley.

(58)   Xinli kexue tongxun, no. 4 (1981), pp. 26-31. This survey has been translated into English by David Chu and will appear in a forthcoming issue of Chinese Sociology and Anthropology, edited by Chu. I am grateful to him for making this survey available to me.

(59)   Interviewees who had been CYL activists and league branch secretaries in the 1970s particularly emphasize their concern with politics at that time in contrast to the cynicism and utter lack of interest in politics youth of today evince. The materialism, cynicism, and strong attraction to Western ideas of post-GPCR students is also brought up in John Hersey, "A Reporter at Large: Homecoming, Part III," New Yorker, May 24, 1982, p. 62.

(60)   JPRS, no. 78576, July 22, 1981, pp. 20-22, from Tianjin Ribao, May 4, 1981.

(61)   Richard Solomon, "On Activism and Activists: Maoist Conceptions of Motivation and Political Role Linking State to Society," China Quarterly, no. 39, July-September 1969, pp. 76-114.

(62)   Huangjin shidai (Guangdong), no. 8 (1981), p. 15. This letter to the editor was published with no response. Huangjin Shidai, no. 11 (1981), p. 18, carries a letter from a reader reporting on an investigation by the Municipal CYL Committee, which discovered that the large majority of "advanced elements" and "those publicly praised by the leadership" had similar problems. While this reflects the perpetual dilemma faced by all activists caught between their peers and the leadership, the post-GPCR denunciation of "phony activism" under the Gang of Four has greatly exacerbated this problem.

(63)   See Mingbao yuekan (Hong Kong) 15, no. 12 (December 1980): 116; the results of the survey were posted on a bulletin board at the school, but were later torn down. They can also be found in the New York Times, December 30, 1980, pp. A 1-2. Zhonggong Wenti Ziliao (Taiwan), 065, December 29, 1980, pp. 23-24, claims 500 students took part in the survey, with the results originally appearing in a Fudan university publication.

(64)   Daily Report, March 31, 1981, pp. L 19-20, from Kyodo, March 29, 1981.

(65)   Cited in Shirk, Competitive Comrades, chap. 1 (p. 2 of draft manuscript).

(66)   For the more positive polling results see JPRS, no. 77764, April 7, 1981, pp. 32-41, from Renmin Ribao, February 24, 1981;

Beijing Review, no. 30, July 27, 1981, pp. 18-19; JPRS, no. 76474, September 23, 1980, from Jiefang Ribao, July 8, 1980; Daily Report, October 15, 1980, p. L 8, from NCNA, October 15, 1980.

(67)   Guangming ribao, November 3, 1980, p. 3, based on a survey conducted in April and May 1980 in Hunan, Guangdong, and Fujian. Renmin Ribao, November 11, 1980, translated in Inside China Mainland (Taiwan: January 1981), pp. 8-11.

(68)   Daily Report, August 4, 1981, pp. K 3-5, from NCNA, August 2 and 3.

(69)   Renmin Ribao, November 11, 1980.

(70)   Daily Report, February 19, 1981, pp. L 1-3, from NCNA, February 18; Beijing Review, December 8, 1980, p. 6.

(71)   Daily Report, November 4, 1981, pp. 0 1-2, from Fujian Ribao, October 20, 1981.

(72)   Daily Report, January 30, 1981, pp. L 11-12, from NCNA, January 28, 1981; Renmin Jiaoyu, no. 11 (1980), pp. 29-33.

(73)   Beijing Review, no. 49 (December 7, 1981), pp. 21-28.

(74)   Between May and December 1980, Zhongguo Qingnian Bao sponsored a debate on how to handle the relationship between learning and politics. The newspaper received over 4,000 articles; 39 were published. See Daily Report, December 19, 1980, p. L 15, from NCNA, December 18, 1980; Hubei Qingnian, no. 5 (1980), p. 31.

(75)   For comparisons between Lei Feng and Chen Jingrun, see Shanxi Qingnian, no. 5 (1981), p. 6; Chinese Sociology and Anthropology 14, no. 1 (Fall 1981): pp. 32-41; Changjiang Ribao, June 12, 1981, p. 4; Xinhua Ribao, May 26, 1981, p. 3.

(76)   Daily Report, October 15, 1981, pp. K 15-21, from Hongqi, no. 17, September 1; Daily Report, September 10, 1981, p. K 3, from NCNA, September 8; Daily Report, September 25, 1981, p. 0 2, from Radio Nanjing, September 23.

(77)   Daily Report, December 1, 1981, pp. P 1-5, from Hubei Ribao November 9. Also see Jiaoyu Yanjiu, no. 11 (1981), p. 11.

(78)   Daily Report, May 14, 1981, pp. T 1-3, from Renmin Ribao, May 5, 1981.

(79)   Daily Report, April 1, 1981, pp. K 5-6, from Radio Beijing, March 27; Daily Report, February 19, 1981, pp. L 1-3, from NCNA, February 18, 1981.

(80)   Shanghai Jiaoyu, no. 4 (1982), p. 12. There have been many articles in education magazines about the general neglect of students in the second year of junior high, with concentration placed on first-year classes and graduating classes. For examples, see the investigation reports in Shanghai Jiaoyu, nos. 2 and 4 (1982).

(81)   Zhongguo Qingnian, no. 16 (August 26, 1981), p. 21; Hubei Qingnian, no. 6 (1981), p. 10.

(82)   China trip notes, anonymous visitor (spring 1980); Suzanne Pepper, China trip notes, April 29, 1980. Aggregated data tend to mask these differences.   For example, a CYL leader recently announced that 25 percent of Chinese youths aged 15-25 are CYL

members. See JPRS, no. 79889 (January 19, 1982), p. 129, from NCNA, December 21, 1981.

(83)   Some of the criticisms made by those rejecting the Lei Feng spirit include Lei's "slavishness," and lack of independence and individuality; his life-style, which resembled that of an "ascetic monk"; his irrelevance for a modernizing society engaged in scaling the heights of science and technology; his "left-leaning" tendencies. See JPRS, no. 77945 (April 28, 1981), pp. 27-34, from Beijing Ribao, March 4 and 6; Daily Report, March 6, 1981, pp. L 4-8, from NCNA, March 5.

(84)   Jilin Qingnian, no. 8 (1982), p. 36. Also see Zhongxue-sheng, no. 4 (1982), pp. 22-23, and Zhongbao yuekan (Hong Kong), no. 20 (September 1981), pp. 45-47.

(85)   Daily Report, August 25, 1981, pp. K 2-3, from Radio Beijing, August 24; Daily Report, October 1, 1981, pp. K 5-6, from Renmin Ribao, September 25.

(86)   Jieban Ren (Tianjin), no. 3 (1981), pp. 3-5.

(87)   Jiaoyu Yanjiu, no. 1 (1981), pp. 45-50.

(88)   Xinli Kexue Tongxun, no. 4 (1981), pp. 26-31, translated by David Chu.

(89)   Jiaoyu Yanjiu, no. 11 (1981), pp. 6-12.

(90)   Jiaoyu Yanjiu, no. 4 (1981), pp. 36-40.

(91)   Jiaoyu Yanjiu, no. 4 (1981), p. 36.

(92)   Renmin Jiaoyu, no. 3 (1982), pp. 29-31.

(93)   For reports on the exodus of village youths to Hong Kong, see Steven Mosher, "The Lure of the Big City," Far Eastern Economic Review, October 31, 1980, pp. 12-13; Anita Chan, Richard Madsen, and Jonathan Unger, "Epilogue," Chen Village (Berkeley: University of California Press, forthcoming).

(94)   For the first phenomenon, see the report from Bolo county, Guangdong, in Xuexi yu xuanchuan, no. 1 (1982), p. 42; the second phenomenon is reported in Jiaoyu Yanjiu, no. 5 (1981), pp. 61-63.

(95)   Renmin Jiaoyu, no. 3 (1982), pp. 29-31.

(96)   Jiaoyu Yanjiu, no. 4 (1981), pp. 39-40. A survey of schools in Hangzhou also found most students unconcerned with politics. See Zhengzhi Jiaoyu, no. 5 (1981), pp. 36-38.

(97)   Beijing Review, no. 48 (November 30, 1981), p. 15.

(98)   Zhongguo Qingnian, no. 16 (August 26, 1981), p. 21.

(99)   Shanxi Qingnian, no. 8 (1980), p. 46.

(100) Sichuan Qingnian, no. 7 (1981), p. 17. There are also reports of counties and communes that do compensate those involved in league work. See Sichuan Qingnian, no. 7 (1981); Hubei Qingnian, no. 12 (1980), pp. 18-19.

(101) Huangjin Shidai, no. 5 (1981), p. 16.

(102) Gansu Qingnian, no. 3 (1981), pp. 10-11. For rather similar reports, see Shanxi Qingnian, no. 12 (1980), p. 17; and Zhongguo Qingnian, no. 3 (1980), p. 24.

(103) Daily Report, January 6, 1982, p. K 11, from Tanjug, January 5.

(104) Guangming Ribao, November 4, 5, 7, and 14, 1981, all p. 1. This is by no means universal. The Ministry of Education still has decidedly mixed feelings about such classroom divisions. Interview conducted at the Ministry of Education, Beijing, August 15, 1982.

(105) Beijing Ribao, April 13, 1982, p. 1; Yangcheng Wanbao, May 20, 1982, p. 1.

(106) Yangcheng Wanbao, May 20, 1982, p. 1.

(107) For a ranking of 38 occupations by students at three secondary schools in Shanghai, see Shehui (Shanghai), no. 2 (May 1982), pp. 22-25.

6

WORKER EDUCATION: REVOLUTION AND REFORM

Nat J. Colletta

INTRODUCTION

Since the 1920s, China has relied heavily on adult education to effect desired changes in political ideology, socioeconomic relations, and human productive capabilities. The belief in the power of education in general, and adult education in particular, to create a new socialist man and construct a new social order has at times reached religious proportions. The cyclical shifts in ideological fervor and accompanying socioeconomic development strategies have been mirrored in the relative emphasis placed on agricultural versus industrial development, quantitative versus qualitative orientations, mass versus elite education, and more specifically,

I would like to take this opportunity to thank the International Council for Adult Education (ICAE), particularly Budd Hall, director general of ICAE, and the late Roby Kidd, former head of the China-ICAE project; Aklilu Habte of the World Bank Education Department; R. Stern, E.V.K. Jaycox, and C. Koch-Weser of the East Asia Pacific Programs Department, World Bank; and Zang Boping, vice-minister of education, and Yao Zhongda, deputy director, Bureau of Worker and Peasant Education, Ministry of Education, for making my participation in the first ICAE study of worker-peasant education in China possible. I would especially like to thank my colleagues on the study team and those "front-liners" working in the area of adult education in China, particularly Wang Jiantiang and Wang Yianwei for their human and intellectual support throughout our visit.

adult versus formal school education. Even within a particular educational mode such as adult education, the focus has continually shifted between peasant and worker education.(1)

The purpose of this chapter is twofold: first, to examine briefly the changing face of urban adult education in relation to the larger political-economic transformations that have taken place in China over the past three decades; and second, to describe and draw lessons from the present policy, programs, and objectives of worker education in the People's Republic of China (PRC) today. For the purposes of this chapter the terms "adult education" and "worker education" will be used interchangeably.(2)

THE 1949 ANTECEDENTS TO WORKER EDUCATION

Though Chinese civilization developed written language over 4,000 years ago, it remained, along with other forms of specialized knowledge, the sole property of a small ruling class. The Confucian period of traditional education exemplified the elitist nature of education in its selection and ideological preparation of future governing elites. Theory ruled supreme over application as there was a general disdain for manual labor and natural science. Up until the time of the first revolutionary activities of the early 1900s, the traditional education system remained an unchallenged mechanism for reproducing the stratified semifeudalistic society characteristic of ancient China.(3)

In the early 1920s, at least two major challenges to the traditional elitist system of Chinese education were launched by mass-oriented adult education programs. One was led by antigovernment Communist Party leadership and the other by nongovernmental Chinese Christian leadership.

Borrowing heavily from the revolutionary experience of the Soviet Union, the Communist Party established the first worker continuing education school in January 1922 at Wufuxiang, Anyuan county, in Jiangxi province. This was fundamentally a continuing education program held in the evening for railway workers. Jiangxi was one of the first central Soviets or so called liberated areas set up under the leadership of the Chinese Communist Party. In 1923, Mao Zedong established a self-study university in Changsha, Hunan province. Reflecting his personal criticism of formal university study, the university took as its motto "read by oneself; ponder by oneself; mutually discuss and study" and required no entrance examination.(4)

A few years later, Mao revealed his now famous Report of an Inspection of the Hunan Peasant Movement, which noted the opening of a number of village peasant schools. These early Communist-led efforts at mass education focused on raising the cultural or literacy level of the masses combined with providing ideological training.

The success of these early Communist-inspired mass educational activities has been described as follows:

> According to partial statistics from the Central Soviet areas in Jiangxi, Fujian and Guangdong for 1933, some 6,462 continuing education night schools were being operated in 2,932 villages, with an enrollment of 94,517. There were also 32,388 literacy classes being held with an attendance of 155,371. Of these, according to statistics from Xingguo County, women accounted for 69% of the enrollment in the continuing education schools and 60% in the literacy classes.(5)

From the mid-1930s to the point of liberation in 1949, the Communist efforts at mass adult education centered and flourished in Mao's revolutionary retreat of Yan'an. As Peter Seybolt and Mark Seldon, among others, point out, there was a variety of educational programs introduced during the Yan'an period, e.g., the Chinese People's Anti-Japanese Military and Political College (Kangda), the Lu Xun Academy of Literature and Arts, the Bethune Medical School, the Chinese Women's University, informal reading circles, and study criticism groups, among other "mass line" oriented education that created an important legacy of ideas and innovative practices destined for subsequent revival.(6)

In Yan'an, early efforts at popular education and ideological training, primarily through evening general literacy classes, were soon integrated with social and economic innovations, such as cooperatives, into a comprehensive program to build new socioeconomic structures and inculcate appropriate collectivist values among the masses in the newly liberated areas. Evening schools for workers and peasant, half-day schools, winter schools, among other activities of adult education, emerged as early institutional forms. Undergirded by the concept of minban or minban gongzhu (management by the people with government assistance), these early revolutionary mass education programs were the roots of many of the worker-peasant education programs of the Great Leap Forward and Great Proletarian Cultural Revolution (GPCR) eras.

During the anti-Japanese period (1936-45), adult education reached its highest point. At that time, in the liberated areas the general education policy was that "cadre education was more important than mass education and adult education was more important than children's education."(7)

While the Communist Party-led attempts of mass-oriented adult education were being developed in the central Soviets, at Yan'an and in other emerging liberated areas under the guidance of Mao Zedong (with broader influence from the earlier Soviet revolutionary mass education model), a separate but parallel experiment in mass adult education was evolving in Dingxian, Hobei province. Known as the

Mass Education Movement, this movement was guided by the ideas of Tao Xingzhi, an eminent Chinese educational philosopher, and James Yen, a Western-educated, Christian-influenced Chinese who, like his Communist-Marxist-Leninist influenced counterpart Mao Zedong, sought to release the masses from the shackles of ignorance and impoverishment. In 1923, the Chinese National Association of the Mass Education Movement was organized based on the previous experimental Mass Education Movement activities. Its stated purpose was "to explore the potentialities of the masses, and find a way of educating them, not merely for life, but to remake life."(8)

For both Communist and Christian-led mass adult education experiments in revolutionary China, adult education was viewed as an instrument of socioeconomic transformation. Its goal was not only to raise the literacy level of the masses, but also to change the role of the educational structure itself from one that reconstructed the existing social order of oppression and inequality to one that "dared construct a new social order." However, the degree to which these movements actually challenged the existing structure varies considerably with Mao's efforts manifested in armed struggle, while Yen's approach basically supported the existing status quo, albeit from a critical posture.

It is hard to say just how much these two major early movements of Chinese adult education were in direct communication. There is no record of personal exchanges between Mao and Yen. However, Stuart R. Schram, commenting on "Mao's genius for exploiting respectable people and institutions for radical ends," observed that Mao guided the Hunan program of the Mass Education Movement but "instead of using the textbooks employed elsewhere, Mao had a special set prepared."(9) These texts stressed class conflict and communism.

In 1947, when the Mass Education Movement had turned for support to the Chiang Kai-shek Nationalist Government and was clearly associated with "negative" foreign missionary and American aid influences, Yen was forced to flee the mainland, first operating on Taiwan and later internationalizing the mass education program in the present day International Rural Reconstruction Movement headquartered in the Philippines.

This early experience in worker education, although limited, provided the Chinese Communist Party (CCP) with a model that with the establishment of the People's Republic of China in 1949 was extended on a nationwide scale.

POLICY VARIATIONS IN WORKER EDUCATION: 1950-82

The first National Conference of the People's Republic Period on Workers' and Peasants' Education convened in September 1950. Soon after, in coordination with land reform and production efforts, short-term middle schools for workers and winter schools for peasants were institutionalized as major programs to eliminate illiteracy. During the early 1950s, eradicating illiteracy or raising the cultural level of the masses dominated the adult education scene. While mass campaigns were launched earlier in some parts of the country, they only began to spread throughout the country during the 1950s. In the beginning of the mass literacy campaigns in 1952, the so-called quick method was developed (probably based on Yen's earlier literacy technique) in an attempt to reduce the learning period from three years to 300 hours by focusing on phonetic symbols. Literacy became an important tool for realizing revolutionary and ideological consolidation.

In 1953, with the adoption of a Stalinist-type economic development strategy of the first Five-Year Plan (1953-57) in which priority was placed on capital-intensive industrial development, the concept of spare-time education to upgrade the skill level of workers took precedence over mass peasant education. Spare-time education was designed to provide the requisite skilled labor pool for the shifting emphasis to urban industrialization. Much of the worker education programming that is now emerging under the Four Modernizations program had its roots in this early period of adult education for rapid industrial development (1955-58). We will return to discuss this era in greater detail under enterprise education.

The 1949-58 period of adult education was notably expansionary. By 1958, upon the dawning of the Great Leap Forward, the results found in Table 6.1 were proclaimed.

Despite its positive results in the adult education area, the first Five-Year Plan led to a number of imbalances and contradictions, e.g., industry versus agriculture, capital-intensive versus labor-intensive modes of production, large-scale versus small-scale development strategies culminating in the Great Leap Forward of 1958-61. Initially, the Great Leap Forward endeavored to rectify these imbalances through industrial decentralization and the transformation of the cooperative movement into the commune movement, e.g., consolidation of cooperatives into larger scale communes that could support sideline or rural industries producing for local consumption.

Mismanagement and poor weather, coupled with the worsening of Soviet-Chinese relations, opened a larger ideological debate of Redness versus Expertness. The failures of the first Five-Year Plan and the ensuing attempts at instant remedy through the Great Leap Forward laid the foundation for a paralyzing Chinese self-doubt that contributed to the launching of the GPCR.

From the stress on ideological consolidation via literacy promotion among the masses of the early 1950s to the emphasis on more specialized skill-oriented spare-time education for workers in factories and scientific agriculturalists on communes of the mid-1950s and early 1960s, the Chinese came full circle back to a revolutionary and ideological emphasis on adult education during the GPCR (1966-76) period. The GPCR represented a radical approach to worker education as China sought to thoroughly implement slogans that had been voiced earlier: combine theory and practice, bridge the gap between mental and manual labor, become both Red and Expert. Factory spare-time schools became July 21 Workers Universities and commune spare-time agro-technical schools became May 7 Peasant Agricultural Colleges with ideological training prevailing over the transmission of technical and scientific skills (see Chapter 7 for details on May 7 Peasant Agricultural Colleges).

TABLE 6.1
Spare-Time and Illiterate Students, 1949-58
(in thousands)

Year	In Spare-Time High Schools	In Spare-Time Secon-dary All Schools	In Spare-Time Secon-dary Schools	In Spare-Time Pri-mary Schools	In Anti-illiteracy Classes
1949	0.1	0.1	-*	-	657.07
1950	0.4	0.1	-	-	1,372.0
1951	1.6	0.3	-	-	1,375.0
1952	4.2	0.7	249.0	1,375.0	656.0
1953	9.7	1.1	404.0	1,523.0	2,954.0
1954	13.2	186.0	760.0	2,088.0	2,637.0
1955	15.9	195.0	1,167.0	4,538.0	3,678.0
1956	63.8	563.0	2,236.0	5,195.0	7,434.0
1957	75.9	588.0	2,714.0	6,267.0	7,208.0
1958	150.0	-	5,000.0	26,000.0	40,000.0

*Data not available.
Source: Ten Great Years (Peking: State Statistical Bureau, 1960).

As Robert D. Barendson summarized,

thus the main thrust of his (Mao's) educational policy since 1949 has been to produce a new type of intelligentsia by making the necessary general and specialized education available to politically reliable working class elements and insisting that all students be required to receive regular political education in schools and participate regularly in manual labor as part of the school program.(10)

The major directive for May 7 schools of various types linking education in the army, factories, and communes to that of formal schools emanates from Mao's May 7, 1966, letter to Lin Piao, which is summarized by Theodore Hsi-en Chen as follows:

> The letter [from Mao] to Lin Piao was concerned with the army and instructed that the PLA "should be a great school" in which "the armymen should learn politics, military affairs, and agriculture," and "take part in the socialist education movement in the factories and villages." The army should engage in three major tasks: "agriculture, industry, and mass work." After these specific instructions for the army, Mao's letter went on to apply his ideas to education in general stressing the importance of "learning other things." Workers and peasants should study "military affairs, politics, and culture" and engage in criticizing the bourgeoisie. Students should "learn other things, that is, industrial work, farming, and military affairs. They should also criticize the bourgeoisie." The same principle holds for government and Party personnel and for people in trade and commerce. The section on students includes Mao's often repeated statements on the need to shorten the school term and terminate the domination of the schools by bourgeois intellectuals.(11)

As for the July 21 Workers Universities, the experience at the Shanghai Machine Tool Plant, where technicians and workers were trained in workshops and classes by veteran workers and equated to university graduates, formed the basis of Mao's July 21, 1968, directive:

> It is still necessary to have universities; here I refer mainly to colleges of science and engineering. However, it is essential to shorten the length of schooling, revolutionize education, put proletarian politics in command, and follow the road of the Shanghai Machine Tool Plant in training technicians from among the workers. Students should be selected from among workers and peasants with practical experience and they should return to production work after a few years of study.(12)

The July 21 Workers Universities and May 7 schools were complemented by a "rustification" program that involved the transfer (sometimes forced) of students and intellectuals to the countryside to expose those with "revisionist" ideas to the ideological tenets of the socialist state through reeducation and manual labor.(13) As the issue of succession to Mao's leadership gained prominence over the earlier debate of the choice of an appropriate development strategy, adult education, particularly in the above-mentioned forms of the GPCR became a messianic movement for the ideological purification of earlier intellectual and technocratic sinners.

Finally, with the downfall of the Gang of Four, the official end to the GPCR (1976), and the inauguration of the Four Modernizations Movement, the Chinese were left in a state referred to as the "three lows and one lack," i.e., low cultural level, low technical standard, low ability of management, and a lack of engineers and technicians. An economic development strategy is now emerging that has swung the ideological pendulum toward the right in an attempt to balance scientific agriculture with industry, to have a mixture of scale, to create a complementarity of socialist and capitalist incentive systems, and ultimately, to blend the development of worker and peasant education, and formal and adult education, into a unified centralized system of education and training with equivalent standards, quality, certification, incentives, and legitimacy. However, many China scholars would claim that the new swing right has merely ushered back an elitist, urban-biased intellectual and cadre class.

As ideological conditions have changed, so too have the socio-economic development strategies and attendant educational modes, content emphasis, administrative control, and nomenclatures. In many parts of the country, functional substitutes for July 21 Workers Universities, May 7 Peasant Agricultural Colleges, and other innovative adult education programs of the GPCR are now beginning to revert to their earlier GPCR names of Workers Sparetime Universities and Agrotechnical Sparetime Schools.

Ideologically-oriented adult educational programs, such as the May 7 Cadre Schools and the student and intellectual rustification programs, have been either abolished and/or are rapidly winding down. Literacy efforts, which generally were largely dormant during the GPCR, are now being reconstituted mainly through spare-time upper-primary schools and evening classes for adults. From parallel and competing systems, the formal school and adult education programs of the GPCR period are now being viewed as integrated and complementary programs under a single education and training system. As can be seen from Figure 6.1, both worker and peasant education programs are now centralized under the Ministry of Education with definite line and staff relationships down to the provincial level. Relationships exist at the subprovincial level, as well, down to the production brigades of the commune, but are not shown in Figure 6.1. This organization chart is in clear contrast to the decentralized ad hoc administration and management of worker and peasant education during the GPCR. The government's goal is to institutionalize and systematize "all education to serve the National Development Goals of the Four Modernizations — Industry, Agriculture, the Army, Science and Technology."(14)

The above brief policy overview sets the stage for a discussion of those major institutions and programs for worker education that have characterized this unique element of Chinese education, particularly during the GPCR and Four Modernizations movement.

Figure 6.1   Organization Chart: Worker-Peasant Education

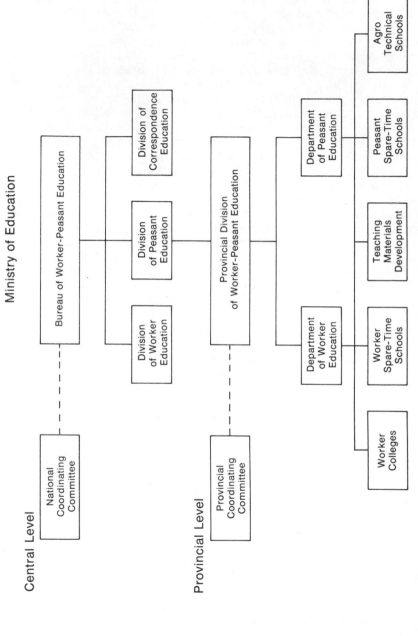

Source: Constructed by the author from various interviews.

WORKER EDUCATION: RED OR EXPERT?

A main effort of the Chinese Revolution has been an attempt to eliminate the distinction between worker performance tasks and management administrative functions, between manual labor and intellectual labor, and ultimately between town and countryside. The key concepts of worker management, production-linked education, and sideline or small-scale industrial development in the context of communes have been directly aimed at blending and, ultimately, eliminating these distinctions. Most factories or enterprises have at one time or another organized schools where workers could obtain new skills and knowledge, upgrade existing skills, and prepare for new roles and functions.

As indicated previously, accompanying the first five-year industrial-oriented plan, efforts were made to introduce a variety of training schemes for workers within factories. The concept of workers' spare-time schools had its strongest roots during this industrialization drive of the middle and late 1950s. As historically acknowledged by the director of the Beijing Second Cotton Mill: "with the development of production, we opened a staff and workers' sparetime school since the operation started in 1955. At that time, there were over 5,000 workers. Most of them only went to primary school. Some were illiterate or semi-literate so the task of staff and workers' education was focused on popularizing junior middle schooling and eliminating illiteracy." In the mid-1950s as progress was being made on the literacy front, emphasis shifted more and more to technical training and the acquisition of specific expertise.

With the Great Leap Forward, and the attempt to reduce disparities between worker and management, city and farm, and industry and agriculture, came the "two participations," whereby workers participated in management and managers took part in line production. Emanating from the Anshan Constitution (1960), this plan expanded worker education from the literacy training of the early 1950s, through the skill-training emphasis of the mid-1950s, to the world of worker control of the 1960s as "politics took command" during the GPCR.(15)

At the advent of the GPCR, spare-time factory schools became July 21 Workers Universities as "serving the people" replaced the goal of professional advancement, ideology replaced scientific competence, and adult education became highly politicized. In sum, political goals replaced production targets as politics, being Red, indeed, took command.

To address the distinction between manual and intellectual work during the GPCR the "three in one" concept was introduced; joint management teams of workers, technicians, and cadres (managers) were formed to break down the existing division of labor and to reorganize work relations in factories. Such teams primarily provided ideological training, but experiences were also created that exposed engineers to manual work and technicians to engineering and manual labor and placed workers in direct management or leadership roles. In addition, May 7 Cadre Schools were established in the countryside. These schools served the dual function of manifestly providing an institutional arrangement for the ideological purification of factory management and leadership (cadre with revisionist tendencies) through manual labor, while latently providing managerial and technical skills for industrializing the rural areas, thus bridging the gap between town and countryside. In effect, the development of many sideline commune industries was stimulated in this fashion. However, even earlier, during the Great Leap Forward era (1958-59), industries with spare-time schools were "directed to train personnel in the many small or newly established commune industries. The industrial plants complied by sending teachers to classes organized in the new or smaller factories, or by arranging for the scattered workers to attend expanded classes in the major plants."(16)

Factory Extension

In addition to creating the July 21 Workers Universities within enterprises and the May 7 Cadre Schools — latently linked to the emergence of rural industry, there was a general effort to decentralize industry in the urban areas by encouraging neighborhood committees to set up collective small-scale enterprises or "street factories." Most of these industries were started by women seeking more liberating roles and additional family incomes by producing for the local consumer, e.g., soap, sewing, shoe, and other repair operations.(17)

This effort to restructure social and productive relationships led to the development of rural industry as a system of simple networks emerged to link large-scale urban factories to small-scale urban "street factories" and rural commune "sideline industries." In effect, enterprises became an industrial version of American Land Grant agricultural colleges or some American community colleges as they extended their expertise and technical assistance to neighborhoods and communes to help establish small-scale industry. As communes developed the capacity to produce goods that they had previously imported from urban areas, they could better realize their goal of total self-reliance. It was hoped that the gradual urbanization of the communes and the ruralization of the large factories through such factory extension education and technical extension programs would hasten the breakdown of distinctions between industry and agriculture, city and countryside. (A detailed discussion of the rural component is found in Chapter 7).

The role of some factories serving as extension agents, and the process by which a factory might perform this role, were succinctly described by the director of the Hunan Rubber Factory:

First we sent several technicians and workers out to Taijing commune to discuss plans for setting up a small workshop to produce rubber boots, We then invited several persons from the commune to come and train by working in our boot production unit. While they were here, our staff brought some of our extra equipment to the commune and established a small workshop. Their trainees in our factory then returned and our technical staff stayed on to help them get going. This whole process took about six months to a year. After an additional few months, our staff were able to return to the main factory. As they faced problems in the commune workshop, they would call on us and we would help them solve them. When their commune workshop production was at a level whereby they could meet our previous market demand, we totally stopped producing that particular line of boot and, in fact, turned our market over to them and our attention to producing new items.(18)

It is not clear how the new administration views such learning networks. There is some evidence that the process described above is now considered inefficient, time-consuming, and unplanned, yet it continues to operate. However, it is being eclipsed by a more formalized and centrally planned program of in-plant spare-time education.

In-plant Spare-time Education

Currently major urban enterprises and rural sideline industries that incorporate contemporary adult education activities offer three general modes of training and education: full-time relief from production with full pay and benefits; part-time relief from production with full pay and benefits; and spare-time schooling usually after working hours.

Those studying full-time are typically studying through the media of television lectures, correspondence courses, and/or classroom work within the plant in university degree equivalent programs. Full-time programs such as these are geared toward moving technicians to engineer levels. The part-time training mode is usually offered from four to six hours per week but can be up to half time. This program combines classroom training and on-the-job apprenticeships and is focused on technical content to move workers up to the technician level or upgrade technical skills through in-service training. Leadership and management training is also usually conducted in the part-time mode. In some cases, technicians and/or managers are released half time, up to six months, for more intensive in-service training. The third major mode is spare-time education, which is typically provided in-plant but after working hours (three evenings per week for two or three hours each). This is generally a middle or upper secondary school equivalency program. Language studies and other specialized courses may also be offered in this mode, but the factory only covers the costs of those spare-time studies directly related to the production process of the plant.

In addition to the above in-plant programs, many enterprises have sent employees to full-time regular state universities and spare-time colleges run by the local government. For example, at Guangzhou Heavy Machinery Plant, 22 persons have recently been sent to study in regular universities and 155 persons have been enrolled in provincial and municipal spare-time colleges.

Administratively, there is a "lead" education committee in each enterprise composed of representatives from the CCP, plant administration, Workers' Union, Youth League, Women's Federation, and technical departments. They make all first-line decisions regarding educational goals, plans, enrollments, staffing, time schedule, finance, equipment, and so on. A director and staff for factory spare-time education is appointed to oversee the implementation of their decision.

Workshop Apprenticeship Training and Basic Education

Another program being stressed during the Four Modernizations Movement utilized a more traditional apprenticeship model. While the dominant instructional-learning modes, content focus, and target populations of apprenticeship training and basic education activities fall under the general guidance of the plant and, in particular, the Sparetime College Educational Committee, in some plants individual workshops frequently have worker education committees and offer their own spare-time courses. Each workshop has a deputy director in charge of adult education and one technician responsible for specific tutorial activities. The workshop classes comprise mainly literacy or basic education courses. They are provided six hours per week in two-hour sessions three days per week.

Also, lectures by workshop technicians that focus on specific technical and production-related problems are offered for all employees. New workers within the various workshops are usually assigned to "lead" (master) workers under an apprenticeship arrangement. There are frequent workers' assemblies to air major concerns and plans. Workshops and workshop technicians are heavily involved in on-the-job and apprenticeship training, providing lab facilities and instructional staff, respectively. For example, to illustrate the scope of the efforts conducted by workshop units, at Beijing First Cotton Mill primary technical education has developed greatly over the years. According to 1979 statistics, "study classes, technical training in rotation classes, technical practice and operation competitions organized by different workshops have been held more than 980 times, and joined by 260,000 persons.(19)

Many of the instructional staff come from neighboring normal colleges or universities or enterprise-administered formal primary and secondary schools. As mentioned before, technical-course staff are regular factory technicians who double as adult education instructors. All instructors are either paid about 6 yuan ($4) per instructional hour or are paid in kind, e.g., they are given release time from normal production activities or extra work points.

One must remember that most large-scale urban enterprises are, in effect, cradle-to-grave communities providing all services (including formal schools) and goods to their staff and their families. Food provision may be the only exception to this self-sufficient, self-constrained aspect of urban enterprises; however, some even cultivate small land areas to provide for partial food requirements.

The facilities of the plant itself, e.g., workshops that may be idle, primary and secondary school classrooms within the plant compound, and, in some cases, specially constructed community and/or spare-time education centers, are utilized for adult education. Equipment, e.g., televisions, lab instruments, and so on, is either that of the workshops or directly purchased by the plant. Instructional materials are now centrally produced regular school and university texts provided by the Bureau of Worker-Peasant Education, supplemented by local enterprise produced manuals, handbooks, and the like. All plants visited by the author had small libraries and/or reading rooms with very modest holdings.

WORKER EDUCATION: FINANCING, PLANNING,
AND THE FUTURE

The adult education activities of enterprises are financed from four major sources: labor union contributions from worker wages; direct reinvestment of profits, varying from enterprise to enterprise; a modest state contribution for books and equipment; and direct student fees.(20) The latter category is only for those courses that the factory deems not directly related to the production processes of the plant. Actual unit costs for instruction are difficult to obtain and where such data is available costs are not uniform from one enterprise to another. For example, in the Hunan Power Machinery Plant the cost given is 600 yuan ($400) per student per year (32 weeks, 24 hours per week) for technical courses and secondary equivalence, and 700 yuan ($466) per student per year (20 weeks, 24 hours per week) for T.V. University equivalency courses. The opportunity cost of student labor for the T.V. University equivalency courses is about 40 yuan ($27) (wages) per month, while the opportunity cost of secondary school equivalency is given as zero since students in this program are not on the payroll of the plant. The T.V. University cost only includes the cost to the factory and not of the Central T.V. and Broadcast University. Broadcast costs for Beijing T.V. University, for example, are calculated at approximately 20 yuan ($13) per student per semester. Table 6.2 presents enrollments, staffing, and cost estimates (where available) in the several factories visited by the author.

In line with the new Four Modernization emphasis on centralized planning and education for expertise, enterprises are now required to develop spare-time education plans. Such plans are expected to set specific targets in line with meeting the broader goals and objectives set out for worker education in the five-year plan. The organizational structure of worker-peasant education can be seen in Figure 6.1. For example, the Chengdu Rolling Stock Plant has established a plan with the following specific goals: "By the year 1985, 80 percent of the workers less than 35 years old and with schooling of junior middle school level will be brought up to the equivalent level of that of secondary technical school graduates; also by 1985, all staff member and workers less than 35 will receive a junior middle school education."(21)

It is estimated that by 1985, more than half of the needs for middle-level technicians and lower level professionals will be met by workers' universities. Table 6.3 provides a picture of recent Worker University enrollment trends.

While it is difficult to sort out the differential impact of the numerous variables, e.g., technology, training, finance, organization, impacting on the production function of factories, the Chinese usually attribute marked changes in productivity to the adult education program. For example, at the Foshan Silk Textile Factory, they attribute a 15 percent excess of planned production, an increase in quality (fewer rejects) of five percent, and profit of 66 percent in excess of that planned to training. At Beijing First Cotton Mill, the director has stated that,

> the development of the staff workers' education has raised their cultural and technical level, and has brought about the advance in production. Now 120,000 cotton yarns are produced each year, which is double that produced in the beginning years of the factory.(22)

Research assessing the comparative cost-benefit analysis of worker education schemes is sorely needed and would likely at this time be welcomed by the Chinese themselves.

In conclusion, the Chinese, especially through the activities of the Bureau of Worker-Peasant Education, are now trying to "emulate" or standardize course content exams and certification among enterprises. As the Director of the Hunan Rubber Plant has stated, "the classes emulate each other in activities of study, in the size of enrollment, in the rate of attendance, in consolidation

TABLE 6.2
Enrollments and Staffing of Select Enterprise Worker
Education Programs

Enterprise	No. Employees	Enrollment	Staff Permanent	Invited	Cost Capital	Operating
					Yuan	Yuan
Beijing Internal combustion engine factory	10,200	3,600	57	100	300,000	280,000
Beijing Textile Plant	-	-	50	100	-	-
Chengdu Rolling Stock Plant	4,500	4,380	39	83	36,000	200,000
Hunan Power Machinery Plant	2,144	906	-	-	-	-
Hunan Rubber Plant	-	1,145	-	-	- T.V. University 700 yuan/year Worker University 3,000 yuan/year Spare-time 2,400 yuan/year	
Guangzchou Heavy Machine Plant	6,300	731	29	35	-	-
Foshan "Wai Man" Silk Textile Plant	1,500	1,420	3	32	-	-
Peking Second Cotton Mill	7,600	2,259	40	-	-	-

*Data not available.

Notes: Recurrent costs of 2% of 25% of annual workers wages allocated to union
activities plus variable amount from factory profits.
Operating costs include books and salary of instructor and workers being paid.
Admission upon recommendation of unit plus exam.
Entitlement of each worker to six hours of education per week.
Fees are paid individually by workers for those courses not related to
enterprise production.

Source: Constructed by the author from various interviews.

TABLE 6.3
July 21 Worker Colleges

Years	Number of Colleges	Number of Students Enrolled
1975 (June)	1,200[a]	90,000
1975 (December)	5,160[b]	250,000
1976 (March)	6,000[b]	460,000
1977 (July)	15,000[a]	780,000

Sources: [a]Beijing Review, no. 31, 1976; and Current Scene, no. 8, 1976, quoted from New China News Agency, July 21, 1976, p. 21.

[b]Beijing Review, no. 13, 1976, p. 23.

work, in the passing of exams, and so on." There is little doubt that the ultimate goal is to raise the quality of worker education through academic standardization while keeping financing, administrative control, and accountability in the hands of the local enterprises. The concepts of educational quality and school certification have finally come to the work place in China, and the quest for "expertise" has clearly outstripped the drive to "politics in command."

ISSUES AND LESSONS FROM CHINESE EXPERIENCE

Despite the periods of political turmoil and unrest and the radical shifts between ideological/educational foci that have characterized China's recent history, the results of its efforts at adult education over the past 30 years (1950-80) have been most impressive in absolute, if not, relative terms. It is reported that from 1978-81 alone over 130 million new literates have been generated and over 38 million semiliterates have been raised to primary school equivalency level. An additional 3.3 million workers and peasants have obtained secondary school equivalency and 200,000 have reached the level of higher education equivalency through adult education programs. About 80 percent of the participants of adult education programs have been promoted to ranks of technician, engineer, or other leading positions and now form the "backbone" of China's development effort.(23) About 1 million workers are currently enrolled in factory-run universities and in spare-time colleges sponsored by provinces and municipalities. In addition, there are approximately 68 million students in spare-time schools run by enterprises, communes, production brigades, worker and youth palaces, local government, and regular universities, among other institutions.(24)

There is little doubt that, from the Chinese viewpoint, the most important functions of adult education have been political socialization (value change), the solving of practical problems in industry and agriculture, and the raising of the basic education (cultural) level of the masses. Relative priority on these three aspects of adult education has shifted over the past three decades as ideological forces have struggled for, and have exchanged power, but all three aspects have always been evident.

As of 1982, the priority of adult education efforts was placed on worker and cadre (leadership-management) training in support of achieving the goals of the Four Modernizations. As one plant director of spare-time education stated: "Most students are from factories and have over 10 years experience, so their goals are clear. Apart from theory, they wish to bring up their ability to deal with practical problems they encounter in their daily work." Commenting on the recent National Conference on Adult Education, Heng Wei, director of the Bureau of Education, Shanghai municipality, and deputy director of the National Committee of Worker-Peasant Education, told the author that the Central Committee recently submitted a document on adult education that outlines the priority tasks:

> We shall formalize adult education step by step, the preliminary concept is to achieve a systematic and preliminary formalized adult education system. The first task is to enlighten leaders of all enterprises to the fact that adult education is closely related to productivity. In order to increase productivity, we must go for adult education. We must coordinate short term and long term planning. We must organize national coordinating committees in each province, city, county, and commune to coordinate work and to plan adult education across bureaus of varying ministries.(25)

He further added that increasing financing, upgrading teaching, generating student places, and improving instructional materials would be the operational targets.

While adult education is applied and production linked wherever possible, it is currently being pursued as an equivalent to formal education in quality, certification, social status, and financial remuneration. It supplements and builds upon any previous formal education of participants. Hawkins accurately summarized this tendency toward equivalency and institutionization: "the message here seems to be that these kinds of programs (alternative adult education) are allowable provided students reach comparable levels with students in the more conventional formal colleges and universities."(26)

The above outlined parameters set for adult education, in turn, guide the design of adult education programs. They must focus on quality, not only on quantity; must have an immediate application and an identifiable economic payoff, and, therefore, must directly relate to increasing unit production; and should be in accordance with concrete conditions, and thus, meet identified local needs. The current administration is now attempting to develop a more systematic and institutionalized adult education network with committees and worker-peasant education at all levels of the political hierarchy from the national to the communal level. This measure will be supplemented by the design of courses to upgrade the leadership skills of cadre and instructors and by the coordination of instructional materials development. A series of national and provincial materials development conferences, at which guiding principles for instructional materials and actual texts, worksheets, and activities in accordance with these principles are produced, are now under way. Research activities to assess learning needs, identify appropriate teaching methods and strategies, compile syllabuses, and generally review the experience in adult education over the past 30 years are now being planned as tasks of adult education committees at the provincial level.

The Chinese clearly view the current era of adult education and development as a period of restoring, restructuring, and consolidating the better elements of earlier programs, particularly those of the 1950-58 and 1961-65 periods. Consequently, the fear that the baby may be thrown out with the bath water, regarding the abandonment of adult education innovations introduced during the Great Leap Forward and GPCR periods, may be premature. For example, attempts recently to discredit Harbin Workers' Sparetime University were thwarted when its spare-time college graduates were tested and scored on a par with the graduates of regular universities who had pursued similar industrial architectural curricula. Also Jiangxi Communist Labor University has recently been held up as a model for spare-time colleges because of its effectiveness in offering short-term training and correspondence courses and using traveling teachers.(27)

Nevertheless, the educational pendulum is swinging toward the institutionalization of an adult education program that emphasizes quality and legitimacy over equality and access, expertise over redness. Historically, the first Five-Year Plan stressed production linked with training; the Great Leap Forward's pendulum swung toward production linked to ideology; the post-Leap marked a return to the production-training nexus; and the GPCR's swing reinstated the supremacy of ideology over training. Today training is linked to production and certification; politically speaking, industrial and economic readjustment has led to educational readjustment. "Learn from Dazhai" (a successful agricultural commune), "Emulate Jiangxi Labor University," among other such quotes, are visibly being replaced throughout the countryside on schools, houses, and factory walls by others more akin to the Four Modernizations.

What are some of the major lessons one might draw from the Chinese experience in urban adult education to date? First and foremost is that the mobilization of a political will, the creation of a strong bureaucratic organization, and the establishment of a definitive planning process that endeavors to coordinate demand with available delivery services are sine qua non of China's adult education success despite periods of extreme decentralization. The Chinese educational bureaucracy not only penetrates vertically to the lowest level through the CCP, the army, and the government cadre — but it also spreads horizontally — through key mass organizations such as the Communist Youth League, All China Federation of Workers, National Federation of Women, and mass media. It is a broadly based and participatory organizational mode that serves the double function of promoting communication and of standing ready to serve as a mechanism for exercising political social control. As Paul T.K. Lin succinctly stated, "putting planning and coordination back in the hands of the local authorities has the effect of enhancing self-reliance within the overall framework of national planning.(28)

A second key lesson lies in the Chinese use of modeling, meetings, on-spot conferences, and other ad hoc group arrangements in a decentralized but controlled system for promoting the exchange of experiences and the summing up of lessons. China has a built-in organizational learning capacity by continuously encouraging the sharing of experiences and the critical analysis of how the lessons of a given experience might be applied in varying conditions. Such a systematic means for applying new and old knowledge in various settings makes China look like one large "learning exchange." E.M. Rogers and Chen Bizhao refer to this process as summarized in the Chinese slogan "Grasp both ends and move the middle forward," meaning the most advanced units should provide models for others on a widespread basis, as a means of "horizontal diffusion."(29)

A third important lesson lies in the Chinese ability to mobilize unused and underutilized material and human resources, integrating the two to make for a balanced or ecosystem approach to development. Factory and school staffs and facilities provide educational services to both adults and youth. Traditional herbalists become front-line health care workers. Those who have lost their jobs due to the introduction of mechanized agriculture are often gradually integrated into a commune's developing sideline agro-industry. One might say that the Chinese see the forest as well as the trees in every development endeavor.

A fourth lesson concerns the realm of motivation. "Popularization" is a key Chinese educational concept. User demand regarding government policy and the functional use of ensuing adult education programs is created through "preeducation" or "consciousness-raising." For example, during the literacy campaigns, propaganda teams were sent to communes to publicize relevant documents and instructions of the State Council among the peasants. Peer pressure, exercised through the praising of models and the criticism of failures by the mass media and mass organizations, is instrumental in further motivating potential users to the advantage of available programs. Wall posters, billboards, chalkboards, public meetings, among other media, are highly visible methods of reward and sanction in China. China's models of educational extension may provide a fifth lesson. Their three extension models — program extension, exemplified by factory workshop extension to build sideline industries in the countryside and street industries in the urban neighborhoods; the institutional extension model, for example, moving agricultural college faculties from urban environments to the rural communes; and the information extension model, as demonstrated by the mass campaign approach for health, literacy, and family planning — all have many elements that could be replicated in other development settings. However, according to the author's findings, the Chinese are now downplaying these innovative extension models.(30) It is questionable as to whether or not innovative programs of previous eras have been adequately evaluated before decisions to abandon them have been hastily taken solely because of their previous ideological associations.

Many problems and questions abound when one gazes into China's adult education and development future. As Susan Shirk has noted, "It is ironic that today, when elements of the Chinese model have become incorporated in development criteria and the politics of some Third World countries, the Chinese themselves seem to be abandoning the model."(31) In a way, Chinese educational theory and practice, like that of Western countries, are concentrating on a "back to the basic movement," while the third world is left with their respective hand-me-downs (the overimplementation of political content, open classrooms, and new math). There is a critical need for the Chinese to scrutinize their past efforts closely in order to avoid overlooking the good aspects of the adult educational innovations of earlier periods including the GPCR, just as there is a need for Western educators to analyze the results of past innovative educational strategies before their wholesale abandonment. Especially in China, it is difficult to access empirical evidence on just how effective and efficient such innovations were.

Though a review (such as this one) of worker education in China tends to leave the reader with a feeling of "qualified optimism" about the future of such programs there, many questions remain unanswered. Will formalizing adult education reduce its ability to respond to changing local/individual needs? Or rather will equivalency and certification efforts serve to legitimize adult education and put it on a par with more traditionally accepted forms of schooling? Does the current system of Chinese adult education lead to the development of critical thinking skills or does it merely endeavor to create a disciplined work force? How do policies and educational offerings simultaneously accommodate the needs of those in rural and urban settings? Of young and old? Of men and women? What efforts need to be made to provide educational and cultural activities for those who were too old to work? As the rapid pace of technology and mechanization eliminate jobs, will there be a need to totally reeducate workers rather than merely upgrade them? Should career counseling/education be made a standard part of educational curricula? How can relevant textbooks be functionally improved? How can they be produced and distributed on a mass scale? Should more energy be placed on developing a variety of teaching media (e.g., films, filmstrips, transparencies) that can be widely distributed? How can formal universities be mobilized to play a more important role in providing continuing adult education? What can China teach the rest of the world about adult education, or vice versa? And how can such an exchange of information best be implemented?

The time is ripe for China to evaluate its rich experience in adult education and to share the lessons gleaned from such evaluations with the rest of the world. Clearly, on both sides, there is much to be learned and gained.

NOTES

(1)   Various sources are available that chronicle this shifting emphasis, see Suzanne Pepper, "Education After Mao," China Quarterly 81 (March 1980): 1-65; Suzanne Pepper, "Education and Revolution: The 'Chinese Model' Revisited," Asian Survey 18, no. 9 (September 1978): 847-90. Jan-Inguar Lofstedt, Chinese Educational Policy (Atlantic Highlands, N.J.: Humanities Press, 1980); Theodore Hsi-en Chen, The Maoist Educational Revolution (New York: Praeger, 1974); Theodore Hsi-en Chen, "Chinese Education after Mao: More Revolutionary or More Academic," Teachers College Record 79 (February 1978): 365-88; Susan Shirk, "Educational Reform and Political Backlash: Recent Changes in Chinese Educational Policy," Comparative Education Review 23, no. 2 (June 1979): 183-217.

(2)   The primary data for this paper emanates from participation on the first study team visiting China under the auspices of the China-International Council for Adult Education Cooperation Project. The visit took place from March 15-April 14, 1981. The study team was hosted by the Bureau of Worker-Peasant Education, Ministry of Education. The study team members were: Kasama Varavanr, literacy and adult education specialist, Thailand; John Whitehouse, labor education specialist, International Labor Organization, Canada; and Nat Colletta, nonformal-adult education

specialist, East Asia Pacific Projects Department, World Bank. The visit was part of a three-year effort to promote the exchange of persons and knowledge on adult education between the People's Republic of China and the 60 plus national adult education associations of the International Council for Adult Education.

(3)   Lofstedt, Chinese Educational Policy.

(4)   John N. Hawkins, "Deschooling Society Chinese Style: Alternative Forms of Nonformal Education," Educational Studies 4 (1973): 113.

(5)   Yao Zhongda, "Adult Education in the People's Republic of China," personal correspondence to J.R. Kidd, China-ICAE Project, Toronto, Ontario, 1980.

(6)   Christopher Lucas, "Adult Education in the People's Republic of China," Adult Education 26 (1976): 144-45.

(7)   Yao Zhongda, "Introductory Comments on Adult Education in the People's Republic of China," Beijing Symposium on Adult Education, March 1981, Beijing, PRC, transcribed notes.

(8)   Quoted in James Yen, The Ting Hsien Experiment in 1934 (New York: International Institute of Rural Reconstruction, 1934), p. 47. For underlying educational philosophy, see Tao Hsing-Chih's translated papers in Chinese Education 7, no. 4 (Winter 1974-75).

(9)   Stuart R. Schram, Mao Tse-tung (Harmondsworth: Penguin Books, 1966), p. 68.

(10)   Robert D. Barendsen, The Educational Revolution in China (Washington, D.C.: Government Printing Office, 1975), p. 3.

(11)   Chen, The Maoist Educational Revolution, p. 113.

(12)   Robert D. Barendsen, The Educational Revolution in China, p. 13.

(13)   At least in form, rustification was tried under the Mass Education Movement in 1929. The leading Peking newspaper reported at that time: "It was the most magnificent exodus of the intelligentsia into the country that had taken place in Chinese history to date. Holders of old imperial degrees, professors of national universities, a college president and a number of Ph.Ds and M.D.s from leading American Universities had left their positions and comfortable homes in cities to go to the backwood of Tinghsun to find ways and means to revitalize the life of an ancient, backward people, and to build democracy from the bottom up" (Mass Education Movement Report, 1944). However, it should be noted that this was a "voluntary" program of rural service.

(14)   Yao, "Introductory Comments," transcribed notes.

(15)   For a Marxist interpretation of this period, see Charles Bettelheim, Cultural Revolution and Industrial Organization in China - Changes in Management and The Division of Labor (New York: Monthly Review Press, 1974).

(16)   Paul Harper, Spare-Time Education for Workers in Communist China (Washington, D.C.: Government Printing Office, 1964), p. 15.

(17) Bettelheim, Cultural Revolution.

(18) From transcribed interview notes taken in Hunan, April 1981.

(19) From transcribed notes of plant brief, Beijing First Cotton Mill, April 1981.

(20) Trade unions collect 2 percent of the total enterprise employee wages to finance all their activities; e.g., recreation, education, and so on. The Central Committee stipulates that 25 to 30 percent of that 2 percent of total wages be spent on education.

(21) From transcribed notes of plant brief, Chengdu Rolling Stock Plant, April 1981.

(22) From transcribed notes, Beijing First Cotton Mill, April 1981.

(23) Yao, "Introductory Comments," transcribed notes.

(24) Da Gong Bao, 1980.

(25) From transcribed notes, Shanghai Bureau of Education, April 1981.

(26) John N. Hawkins, "Educational Change in China: The Post Gang of Four Era," Educational Perspectives 18 (May 1979): 13.

(27) Hawkins, ibid; Victor Kobayashi and Jin Dongro, "Education in the People's Republic of China, An Update," mimeographed (Ann Arbor, Mich.: School of Education, University of Michigan, 1980).

(28) Paul T.K. Lin, "Development Guided by Values: Comments on China's Road and its Implications," International Development Review 17 (1975): 3.

(29) E.M. Rogers and Chen Bizhao, "Diffusion of Health and Birth Planning Innovations in the People's Republic of China," in Report of the Rural Health System Delegation to the People's Republic of China, (1978), pp. 1-40.

(30) ICAE trip notes, 1981.

(31) Susan Shirk, "Educational Reform and Political Backlash," p. 183.

7

RURAL EDUCATION AND TECHNIQUE TRANSFORMATION

J.N. Hawkins

China's rural sector continues to present China's educational leadership with an enormous challenge. Roughly 80 percent of the population resides in the countryside and is engaged in both agricultural and industrial development projects. The modernization of agriculture has been a consistent priority since 1949 and the role of education in this transformation has been preeminent. An analysis of Chinese developmental policy will be presented in this chapter, with specific reference to post-Great Proletarian Cultural Revolution (GPCR) and Four Modernizations programs focused on interior marginal regions designed to transform and diffuse techniques and skills necessary to implement appropriate developmental activities.(1)

Educational programs such as these have been an important factor in Chinese efforts to transform the interior rural regions in terms of both agricultural and industrial technology. Key aspects of China's developmental programs geared toward rural regions have been capital construction, development of fertilizer plants and complementary inputs such as water acquisition and control, and the development of high-yield seed varieties.(2) Parallel forms and nonformal educational programs either to transfer or transform the necessary skills and techniques to adequately manage these development programs have proceeded at an uneven pace. Prior to the 1960s, this learning network stressed quality to such a degree that students were learning the latest techniques and technologies far beyond China's means to implement. The current debate in developmental education over quality and quantity might better be framed in terms of appropriate or inappropriate.

It is significant that the emphasis placed upon development programs in rural regions in China goes back to the early 1950s and is even reflected in reports filed by Soviet advisors praising Chinese decisions to transform small-scale, low-cost industry in the interior, albeit to provide the infrastructure for the eventual development of a heavy industrial base.(3) The Chinese, for their part, were concerned with physical and economic geography and man-land relationships, specifically in rural regions, and from the outset assigned priorities to land survives and studies in rural areas.(4)

While there appears to be general agreement among Chinese leaders and decision makers regarding the necessity to focus development efforts on rural areas (or at least not ignore this facet of development), there were, of course, significant policy disputes during the past 33 years of the People's Republic (and these will be discussed briefly below). However, it is safe to say that despite periodic disagreement over development direction and thrust, there has been a consistent commitment to some form of integrated approach to agricultural and industrial sectors of the economy, especially the information diffusion network concept accompanying such programs. Even the most current dispute over the policies and practices of the GPCR period does not involve significant disagreement over the issue of an integrated web of agricultural extension and research and emphasis on small and medium-scale appropriate techniques and technologies for rural development.(5)

These two concepts – technique and technology – are thus seen as intimately linked with broader development policies and plans. Technology is defined as a system of knowledge that combines certain specific factors and inputs in production in a specific manner. Technique is defined as know-how, knowledge pertaining to individual components of technology transmitted or transformed through some educative process or mechanism. The learning networks that were in place during the GPCR and the adaptations that have been made since 1976 are the focal point of this chapter and will be analyzed in the context of the complex of political and institutional linkages at various levels in Chinese society.

A. Donnithorne's study of the Chinese economy was one of the first to establish the critical nature of China's productive capabilities in interior rural regions.(6) Goods produced under the rubric "handicraft workshop" (gongchang shougongye) are found primarily in marginal rural areas and in 1962 formed 67 percent of everyday consumer goods. Nearly 80 percent of small farm tools were reported to be made by workers in this category.(7)

Other commodities produced in this category include: textiles and clothing, plastic ware, agricultural tools, agricultural processing plants, spare parts workshops, repair services, traditional arts and crafts, and land improvement projects. Ten years later reports indicated that extensive mechanization had occurred in many of China's rural areas.

Following the completion of the third and fourth Five-Year Plan (FYP), it was reported that 24 of China's 26 provinces and autonomous regions were able to produce walking tractors and that the total number of all tractors (including the larger ones) was 4.7 times the number produced in 1965; rural power consumption rose 4.5 times since 1965; small chemical works accounted for 69 percent of total output of chemical fertilizer and small coal pits accounted for 30 percent of the total coal output.(8)

More recent reports since 1976 confirm this trend.(9) While the usefulness of such figures is hindered by the absence of total aggregate production data, they do serve to focus attention on the importance the Chinese have attached to integrated rural development and mechanization, especially of small and medium agricultural supporting industries. Moreover, observations by Western economists buttress Chinese claims in this area reinforcing officially stated goals to directly capitalize on the demonstration effect of rural exposure to industry, the diffusion of local industry to marginal areas, and the corresponding need to transform the quality of factors of production, including human resources.(10)

In summary, the Chinese have been encouraging rural counties to continue farmland capital construction, further mechanize, develop technical training for rural personnel, encourage the continuation of sideline production and occupations, and increase individual farmer participation. Additionally, while internal self-sufficiency is an obvious plus (pursued more during the GPCR than now), the Chinese have not ruled out importation of foreign techniques, and technologies, but rather have stressed that appropriate measures be taken to assure that it is done critically.(11)

During the mid-1970s, the programmatic outline for development projects in rural China focused on: soil improvement, rational application of fertilizer, water conservancy, improved seed strain, rational close-planting, plant production, field management, and innovation of farm implements.(12) In 1979 the emphasis had shifted somewhat toward more technology-intensive and foreign import strategies combined with increased centralization of control over agricultural development. The previous policy of "agriculture first" may be yielding to "industry first" as the Chinese attempt to rapidly mechanize the rural sector. However, as Reynolds cautions in his article: "It is important to remember that policy reversals are not always as earth shattering as the rhetoric of the Chinese media might suggest."(13) However, the Chinese continue to emphasize appropriate development in rural regions, and the unique and innovative technique transformational learning networks that have been established over the past two decades may have broad implications for many other nations currently reassessing previous development strategies.

Comparative research has indicated that environmental conditions in several areas are important preconditions to development, but more specifically educational linkages and output are perhaps an essential key, both a cause and effect of overall development.(14) Chinese efforts to mechanize the rural sector, increase levels of technological efficiency, and scale-up traditional agricultural technology have depended to a large degree on such educational linkages. This complex web of information flow will be examined below to reveal the diffusion of learning networks in rural regions, their skill transformation capabilities, and their linkages to technology transformation projects and other educational agencies.

R & D, FORMAL AND NONFORMAL, SHORT-CYCLE EDUCATION, AND NONSCHOOL ACTIVITIES: EDUCATIONAL TECHNIQUE TRANSFORMATION IN RURAL CHINA

It has been noted that the successful transformation of technology for agricultural production depends to a large degree on the sophistication and efficiency of the linkages between research and development, overall training and education of agro-technicians, and popularizations and diffusion of agricultural technical skills to the broader rural population through a program of agricultural extension: in short, the transformation of technique and skill levels.(15)

While this triad seems logical and a standard formula for agricultural development and education, and provides the broad strategic goals, it says little about the variety of tactical means possible to implement such a program. What kind of Research and Development (R & D) should receive priority and in what setting? Does "education" mean formal agricultural secondary and tertiary institutions, short-term nonformal configurations, correspondence education, or some mix of these and other educational alternatives? Is extension one-way, as implied in the concept (extending modern techniques from R & D centers, through agricultural colleges to the farmer in the field), or can important information, skills, and techniques be extended from the field to the R & D centers? What are the means to extend information in a nonschool, noninstitutional mode? It is clear that the technique component of rural development, especially for marginal regions, is a complex, practical, as well as a conceptual matter, and perhaps is even more perplexing in the case of China, where educational and developmental strategies have shifted over the years.

Despite the enormous material and human resources devoted to education in general, and agricultural education in particular, since 1949, it has only been since 1970 that it is estimated that agricultural production and the transformation of techniques and technologies have begun to benefit from this investment in a recognizable manner.(16) Particularly important for rural regions has been the thrust to establish a variety of learning personnel in rural regions (although this program has recently been trimmed). A GPCR program to resettle literally millions of educated, semiskilled young people to China's interior provinces has been called into serious question and met with limited success. However, the idea of young people being actively involved in rural development has not been rejected by the new leadership.(17)

It has also recognized that the Chinese have successfully tapped into indigenous, traditional, cellular, organized networks to establish transformed learning networks.(18) The small farm market of 100 to 200 people equals the commune production team; the larger market village serves as the headquarters of the production brigade; the old administrative town serves as the headquarters for the commune. While this model varies, especially in the more developed core regions, it is especially applicable to interior, marginal areas with dispersed heterogeneous, labor-intensive populations.

Much in the same manner as the industrial sector has developed an elaborate linkage system for transfer and transformation of techniques and technologies (see Chapter 6), the rural agricultural sector has evolved a set of relationships and linkages between the four educational levels mentioned above to provide appropriate and adequate information flow and generation to support the numerous technology transformation projects now underway in interior rural regions. It is important to remember that these two processes — technique and technology transformation — are designed to be integrative, supportive, and mutually dependent upon each other. Here we are focusing on the educational component in its broadest sense in order to more fully comprehend the dimensions of China's information network for technique transformation for rural regions.

Four levels of information flow appear to be important in the Chinese case. We will look at each of these in turn. They are: first, research and development; second, formal and nonformal agricultural universities and colleges; third, short-cycle training classes and activities; and fourth, nonschool information dissemination activities. As we shall see, these are not discrete distinctions, each containing within the category a variety of means and methods, and each interacting under certain conditions with another category. Yet these interactions are not random. In concluding, we shall attempt to make some sense of the patterns that emerge.

RESEARCH AND DEVELOPMENT

Research and development activities to transform agricultural techniques have been carried on at virtually every level of society in China, from the central, governmental institute and academy level to provincial institutes and colleges, through xian (county) governmental bureaus, and at each of the three commune levels —

commune, production brigade, production team. Post-1970 policies have focused on a mix between basic and applied research, although the GPCR period (down to 1976) favored applied and the current Four Modernizations Movement is emphasizing restoration of basic research. In both cases, the emphasis is on working on-site as much as possible.

Examples of on-site R & D activities during the GPCR abound. Recently the Chinese Association of Science and Technology sponsored a symposium to encourage scientists to "Take On-the-Job Training of Science and Technology Personnel as a Primary Task."(19) The Association specified that multiple levels should be employed in conducting R & D while training scientific and technical personnel: first, short-term training of a special type; second, advanced studies on a single topic; third, a series of lectures on a single topic; and fourth, systematic professional training. Each activity should either yield research results or disseminate findings. This reaffirmation of GPCR policies corresponds to the complex linkage system established in the early and mid-1970s, which, although modified, is still being utilized.

For example, drought-prone areas such as the Jiangxi Autonomous Region were the site of joint R & D activities in 1976 as government hydrogeologists from Beijing were sent to link up — or form a hookup (guogou) — with local researchers and residents of the region to conduct an extensive survey and carry out experiments to determine the optimum method of obtaining underground water. The results of the study provided a data base for the implementation of an action program, and in addition, returned to the institute in Beijing data for further consideration.(20)

Central level academies and institutes also have had the capacity to form links with local production brigades and production teams, bypassing provincial and county research institutes. These linkages are less for the immediate solution of technical problems than for the mobilization and training of local residents in data collection techniques and projects. In rural regions this activity, for example, has focused primarily on seed selection projects and insect control.(21) There is less evidence recently of the continuation of this form of linkup, but it is clear that the emphasis at this level is essentially geared for a mix of applied and basic research and for the reaching out into the rural community for data collection activities.

The next R & D level focuses on the province. This pattern emerged during the GPCR and has carried over into the Four Modernizations period. Each of China's provinces has one or more specialized agricultural research institutes.(22) In some rural regions branch agricultural science institutes were established, as well as experimental organizations at the commune and production brigade levels.(23) Provincial institutes were somewhat more specialized and generally geared their research projects to critical agricultural problems in the region. Once a problem was identified, the institute established a research base and branching centers (at the <u>xian</u> and production brigade levels, often bypassing the commune administrative structure) to carry out both long- and short-term experiments in such areas as plant disease, insect control, cross-hybridization, fertilizer production, and so on.

Once the stage of testing and refinements was reached, a project generated at the institute level was quickly transferred to local research bases. Personnel were trained locally and in general, the research emphasis focused on applied problems and linking up more often and for longer periods with local levels. In addition, efforts were made during the early phases of the Four Modernizations period to dovetail the research tasks and problems of several different provincial level institutes and focus them on one specific task.(24)

A by-product of working and training local residents is that some are recruited into the institute through short-term training classes and become students working on research topics of specific concern to their <u>xian</u> and commune. Their studies are conducted in the region and results are written in colloquial language to be circulated to commune members and researchers alike.(25)

Scientific agricultural research on a mass mobilization base, however, begins at the <u>xian</u> level and extends to the production team. The Chinese employ what is called the "four level scientific research network," which consists of a more applied research institute at the <u>xian</u> level, a series of commune research <u>stations</u>, corresponding research <u>teams</u> at the brigade level, and highly specialized research <u>groups</u> at the production team level.(26)

An example of how this network functioned during the GPCR can be found in Huanan <u>xian</u> Heilungjiang. This network consisted of over 8,000 individuals and concentrated on regional specific agricultural concerns such as seed improvement, plant protection, soil and fertilizer research, meteorology, and farm implement transformation. Contractual agreements were arranged with local commune stations and production brigade research teams that jointly established and operated as appropriate the "three fields system" – harvest field, experimental field, and seed field.

Research plans were jointly formulated by the <u>xian</u> institute and the commune and subcommune stations, teams, and groups. Needed human and material resources, such as skilled labor, veteran peasants, seed, fertilizer, and other inputs, were provided by the commune and production brigade. Higher level technical expertise was provided by the <u>xian</u> institute involving research design specialists, laboratory facilities, and specialized hardware. Thus the research conducted was geared to the local, utilized local resources, and corresponded to seasonal fluctuations. Three-in-one combinations of technicians, students, and peasants allowed for integrated research and effective demonstration of the results. As progress was made and results verified, reports were compiled in simplified language and a parallel set of horizontal linkages between xian in the region was operationalized for cross-region sharing and demonstration of research results. This popularization diffusion drive depended heavily on the "three-in-one teacher corps," which was formed following successful experimentation and research in a specific area. A multiplier effect began to operate involving ever-increasing numbers of technicians, students, and farmers, as trainees became trainers with the responsibility of spreading the word to other xian and communes.(27)

With the arrival of the Four Modernizations Movement, this pattern has been downplayed but not abandoned. Terminology associated with the GPCR (e.g., "three-in-one") has not been dropped, but efforts to link research institutes with local communes and involve commune and brigade cadres in training are continuing. The recent reorganization of Jiangxi Communist Labor University is one such example. The university has been given the major responsibility for training agricultural technicians and conducting on-site research. Prefectural branch schools and xian schools have been transformed into secondary technical schools and brought under the state plan and the authority of the xian Chinese Communist Party (CCP) education departments, but they will continue to train commune and brigade personnel and involve them in research, and to conduct rotational training for commune and brigade cadres, linking them with ongoing research projects.(28)

By employing a multilayered research and development strategy, as described above, the Chinese are increasingly able to make maximum use of the rather limited research and technical resources currently available. While the research emphasis in agriculture for rural regions has shifted between basic and applied, both administrations (the GPCR and Four Modernizations) recognized the need for local participation and involvement.

EDUCATION/TECHNIQUE TRANSFORMATION

Tales in developing countries bemoaning the critical shortage of technically skilled personnel are legion. The shortage is used as a scapegoat for virtually every developmental problem facing many Asian, African, and Latin American nations, and solutions are sought wherever they might be found. While the debates continue as to how best to approach this problem, perhaps the most interesting trend is that which recognizes that highly skilled technical personnel in whatever number do not necessarily augur a solution to the variety of technical and technological problems a given society faces.

A more important consideration focuses attention on the appropriateness of the techniques being imparted and the manner in which they are communicated. During the GPCR, a multifaceted approach to this question emerged as a variety of education/technique transformation strategies were utilized to train technical personnel in specific skill areas and at the same time efforts were made to scale up existing indigenous techniques and skills for individuals in interior rural areas. Since the advent of the Four Modernizations Movement, many of these efforts have been criticized for lacking quality and not fitting closely enough with national plans. In this section, the model prevalent during the GPCR will be detailed with comments as to changes that have occurred during the past five years of the Four Modernizations.

For over a decade technique transformation activities in rural China have relied heavily on a mix of formal and nonformal peasant and agricultural colleges. Agricultural colleges may either be located at the provincial level or the regional level. Surrounding prefectures will often have clusters of specialized secondary agricultural technical schools to serve as feeders to more advanced study. Graduates of these colleges are allocated according to state and regional plans to work at the provincial, prefectural, and xian levels, but rarely at the commune or subcommune levels. As we have seen, xian R & D institutes perform a training function providing limited numbers of agricultural technicians for the communes, production brigades, and production teams, but the gap in the training programs at this level is filled primarily by a series of alternative spare-time institutions (to be discussed in the next section of this chapter).

Agricultural colleges then focus their attention on more extended, middle-level training of agricultural specialists. During the GPCR, Zhaoyang Agricultural College emerged as a model for training institutions located primarily in rural regions. Students were recruited from the surrounding community who had generally worked at the commune level for two or more years, were considered model peasants, and had the equivalent of a middle school education often having graduated from one of the contiguous secondary agricultural technical schools. The course of study was three years and the curriculum was geared to the growing season so that students could study full time during slack periods and assist in production research activities during the growing season.

In addition to basic courses in seed culture, plant protection, herbal medicine, soil fertility, water conservancy, and fertilizer, the students worked with local communes and production brigades to draw up long-term plans directed toward solving a specific agricultural problem in that region. Research was conducted on experimental plots, and results were compiled and disseminated regionwide. The research projects were also the final evaluation of the student's performance. Following graduation the students were expected to return to their commune and to begin carrying out three tasks: first, organize scientific experiment groups at the production team level; second, establish technical training classes on various subjects for the local inhabitants; and third, promote interdepartmental and interinstitutional links with other provincial agricultural colleges for information diffusion.(29)

Graduates of these institutions thus formed the core of a contingent of middle-level agricultural technicians trained in basic skills and specialities and with intimate knowledge of the rural regions in which they worked. They also provided the backbone of technical personnel to staff the widespread mass technique transformation apparatus termed May 7 Peasant Colleges. With the emergence of the Four Modernizations program, the Zhaoyang model and Zhaoyang in particular were criticized for their lack of quality and expertise in training middle-level technicians. Yet when tested, their graduates performed at least as well as graduates of more standard agricultural colleges. It remains to be seen if the current administration will completely abandon this model of rural education or simply perform minor adaptions.(30) At this time it is reported that Chinese officials are considering "deruralizing" some of the model agricultural universities such as Zhaoyang.

As has been noted above, the agricultural learning network had thus far only extended to the xian level and the broad base of commune and subcommune level had not been reached. The May 7 Peasant Colleges, a post-1970 phenomenon, were designed to complete this tertiary level network. The colleges have since been renamed according to their district, e.g., the Zhengzhou May 7 Peasant College has been renamed the Zhengzhou Agricultural Secondary School and has been downgraded from college status to that of Agricultural Secondary School.

The persistent but slowly increasing mechanization and industrialization of rural China, and the parallel transformation of agricultural technique and technology, has created a significant demand for basic level technical skills from a population with little or no experience in this area. The May 7 Peasant Colleges were perhaps the most flexible link in the information/training chain we have been tracing. They were physically located at either the xian or commune (production brigade) levels. Generally small in size, they enrolled at any one time 100 to 200 students. The course of study ranged from two to three months to three years. Training was very intensive and specialized. A two- to three-month course focused on training of tractor drivers, electricians, or paramedical personnel. Five- to seven-month courses were given for machinery repair, basic veterinary science, and water conservancy practices. More extended study of one to two years would provide training in more technical matters, such as plant protection, insect control, microbiology, animal husbandry, and teacher education.(31)

Management responsibilities for these colleges were lodged with the xian CCP committees, in cooperation with commune revolutionary committees linked horizontally with xian and provincial agricultural departments. Graduates of the agricultural colleges provided the basic corps of professional faculty and were augmented by agro-technicians, veteran peasants, "experienced people from concerned departments," and CCP cadre.(32)

At the county level, enrollment was generally around 200 students per college, and at the commune level, closer to 100 students.(33) Students were enrolled without age or educational restrictions. Once admitted, they were not required to finish the entire curriculum but could leave when they felt they had mastered the material. In addition, they could return when they needed a refresher course, or ran into an unanticipated technical problem. Students continued to be paid in work points by their production brigade and could work out their course of study so as to be able to continue some level of work in the brigade during their study. Students were recommended by the commune/production brigade level and were often chosen from among educated youth who had returned to the countryside and veteran peasants.(34)

Links between the peasant colleges, secondary agricultural technical schools, and provincial agricultural colleges were strong, but the flow of information and training was directed between the mass base at the commune level and the technique transformation institutions at the xian commune levels. In terms of the more formal, tertiary-level technical training institutions, the May 7 Peasant Colleges performed the basic function of disseminating technical information and training agro-technicians in substantial numbers. It should be remembered that all levels of training − national, provincial, xian, and commune − are increasingly becoming inseparable links in an information chain and learning network that extends into the most remote regions of China. It should also be stressed that in each level of institution, each component of technique transformation extension and demonstration capabilities is present and becomes operational, as students, both during and following their course of study, hook up (guogou) with other departments and institutions to offer a staggering variety of short-term training classes, thus completing the formal and nonformal technique transformation network in rural China.

EXTENSION AND DISSEMINATION: SHORT-TERM TRAINING CLASSES

In order for rural technology, scientific farming, and technique transformation activities to really take hold among marginal and rural populations, two ingredients are absolutely essential: first, basic level of literacy and consciousness among the peasantry (in the Freire sense of conscientizacao; and second, an effective agricultural extension and demonstration program. While literacy has been an educational priority since 1950, and consciousness raising has occurred within the parameters of ideology and mobilization strategies, it appears that literacy rates have not been keeping pace.(35)

A 1971 study indicated that in rural regions adult illiteracy was on the increase and had risen to the 20 percent level.(36) Ten years later there still appears to be a problem in maintaining literacy levels.(37) This phenomenon was attributed during the GPCR to the decline of rural spare-time schools in the 1960s and consequently special senior spare-time primary schools were established to cope with this problem. The specific stated purpose of the GPCR literacy drive was to "meet the needs of production and mechanization."(38)

During the current Four Modernizations Movement, declining literacy rates are attributed to policies carried out under the GPCR.(39) In any case, the challenge is formidable and the Chinese have been responding with a variety of approaches.

The bulk of extension and dissemination activities conducted through short-term training classes, however, has focused on either agro-industrial skills or those directly associated with agricultural production. The basic goal of the first focus has been to demonstrate innovative technical practices to peasants and workers unfamiliar with the various processes identified as targets for technique transformation. Often the industrial component of training classes in this area were organized by urban trade union councils that formed special task forces of workers, veteran peasants, and official cadre to initiate the establishment of technical exchange stations. Serving primarily as demonstration and consulting agencies, the exchange stations worked in specialized groups, e.g., lathe turning, benchwork, foundry work, heat treatment, welding, and so on, and operated short-term training classes at the station or on-site in rural industries. The exchange station also published a variety of technical data, sponsored forums, and held exhibitions of new and innovative techniques and technologies.(40) When a light industrialization program was initiated in a rural area, the prototype plant was considered a pilot-demonstration plant. It served as a transition institution to gradually transform peasant agricultural skills to more industrial skills. Production was normally slow and of uneven quality in the early stages and indigenous methods were utilized as much as possible (a practice now criticized as being wasteful and of poor quality). Gradually the techniques and technologies were scaled up and appropriate expansion of industrial activity proceeded.(41)

More agriculturally related extension and demonstration projects were initiated directly in the communes and took the form of adult evening schools. In some communes it was reported that 90 percent of the adult cohort was studying and attending evening classes.(42) These demonstration classes were run at the production brigade and production team levels and focused on specific agricultural techniques, e.g., seed selection, water conservancy, fertilizer, farm implement production and use. The classes and demonstrations were for two- to three-hour periods and conducted by graduates from the peasant colleges, other professional teachers from institutes and agricultural colleges, and by veteran peasants who had mastered the technique.

As individual knowledge and skill levels rose, commune members were recruited into experimental teams and groups at the production brigade and team levels.(43) The effort here was threefold: first, to demonstrate new and innovative agro-technical skills; second, to transform existing indigenous technical skill levels; and third, to broaden the overall base of R & D by recruiting peasants who had mastered the skills into one of the four levels of R & D at the subprovincial level xian institutes, commune stations, brigade teams, and team groups. Thus a two-way flow of information and personnel was effected as R & D institutes, agricultural and peasant colleges, and demonstration short-team training classes interacted in a dynamic manner for technique and technology transformation.(44)

Current policy has centralized spare-time peasant education under the Bureau of Worker and Peasant Education. Spare-time agricultural efforts are now more integrated and follow a state plan. Each commune must draw up its own strategy for meeting the plan and submit it to regional and central authorities. The Agricultural Secondary School continues to be the primary adult education institution, and is followed by agro-mechanic workshops at the commune level and agricultural stations at the production brigade level.

It is not clear whether the changes that have been made in the 1980s are more form than substance. The emphasis has clearly shifted from decentralized to centralized, agriculture to industry, but despite these priorities, peasant education – both formal and nonformal – remains of considerable importance.(45)

NONSCHOOL INFORMATION DISSEMINATION

A less emphasized but significant technique transformation method for rural regions is the variety of educational nonschool mechanisms being utilized to transmit agricultural technical information to masses of people. Perhaps the most innovative example of this activity occurred during the GPCR and was called the personal demonstration method. Model peasants in rural regions who had conducted innovative research, mastered certain agro-technical skills, or otherwise caught the attention of local leaders were picked up by the xian level research and educational institutions and sponsored for a series of individual demonstrations of their skills and techniques. They toured provinces and focused on selected production teams and brigades.(46) If the individual was especially adept in coping with certain technical difficulties and promoting innovations, then the possibility of annual funding for more long-term research and demonstration activities emerged.(47)

Film and radio media represent another nonschool dissemination activity currently in use. The Shanghai Scientific and Educational Film Studio was among the first to announce its programs for producing technique transformation films for widespread diffusion to rural regions.(48) Since then, television has played an increasing role and a national level T.V. University has been created.(49) With the current modernization drive, credentials can be earned for course work via the media and the entire nonschool approach to technique transformation has been brought under national control. The infrastructure for such a media blitz is clearly evident; as early as 1974, 90 percent of all production brigades and production teams had loudspeaker systems and 63 percent of all rural households reportedly had radio receivers.(50) Increasingly, media programming is focused on transmitting agro-technical information for China's rural population.

Finally, the increased publication and availability of books and magazines containing technical information is another source of information contributing to the technique transformation goals and objectives. Popular and specialized magazines are widely disseminated to rural regions and are edited for such use by the Chinese Academy of Sciences. Since 1976 several new series have appeared that focus on scientific experiments, geographical knowledge, plant genetics, animal husbandry, and botany.(51) Libraries are open in the evening and during rest hours and are operated by youth league personnel and educated young people. Discussions and forums around technical subjects are also part of the village library program, especially during the GPCR.(52)

These activities are not priority focus for technique transformation, either during the GPCR or currently. Rather, as we have seen, the Chinese have sought to rely much more on the multilayered learning network described above. However, these nonschool activities may increase in importance in the future, and at this time clearly serve as an important adjunct to the more formalized information and research chain detailed in the previous sections.

CONCLUSION

China's technique and technology transformation programs for interior rural regions have over the years assumed a distinctive pattern. While changes in direction and thrust have occurred (and the debates continue today), some tentative conclusions can be advanced here. Technique transformation educational programs designed to provide the skilled human resources for technological transformation projects have clearly been an important component of Chinese developmental strategy. The regional focus during the past ten years, and especially since 1970, has been on interior, "marginal" regions as described in the beginning of this chapter.

The boundary surrounding the policy and planning mechanism discussed above and defining the parameters within which technique and technology transformation must occur is the political dimension characterized by ideology and mass mobilization. The ideological components of authority allocation and participation were expanded during the GPCR to involve increasing numbers of middle and lower level decision makers (within the small group context) and mass mobilization tactics were employed, thus adding the dynamic necessary to begin an implementation program of the techniques and technologies chosen as essential.

More recently, there has been a contraction of this involvement and a more centralized, hierarchical structure has replaced mass mobilization techniques. The ideological boundary now framing rural education stresses "modernization and industrialization," and tends to be more pragmatic than visionary.

While the Chinese have arrived at this point in a process manner (a mix of trial and error and sustained planning), the major features of the system are similar to conclusions reached by other writers concerned with appropriate technology, planning, training of change agents, and development strategy in general for rural regions. The introduction of innovative practices (techniques) and agrotechnology in regions with less-developed methods involves a series of discrete stages that can be grouped in two clusters: diagnosing the intervention, and diagnosing the potential for change in the system.(53)

With regard to the first cluster, planners and policymakers need to be cognizant of the possible outcomes of the proposed innovation, what kind of backup features might be necessary, the cost and durability of the innovation, the social and political costs and benefits, and other risk factors. The second cluster would focus on defining the system to be affected (the dimensions of the region, degree of marginality, the local decision-making structure, and so on), the functional roles played by participants in the system (inside advocates, opinion leaders, official and unofficial legitimizers), the job-related roles played by participants (officials who link the local system with the wider social system, interest groups, and so on), the occasion and timing of the introduction of the innovation, and the overall communication and planning strategies (learning networks, participatory planning mechanisms, and so on). All of these factors appear to be component parts of the Chinese technique transformation process in rural regions.

Continued success in promoting technique and technology transformation efforts in rural regions in China will depend to a large degree on the sociopolitical environment in which such programs are conducted.

A final conclusion regarding the future commitment of the Chinese to appropriate technology and techniques for rural development is not possible here. Recent changes in leadership and the lure of rapid mechanized development in the agricultural sector may demand an eventual reassessment. Past experience, however, provides an interesting and thought-provoking model for rural education and development, the study of which is deserving of serious attention.

NOTES

(1) Technology transformation refers to an approach that focuses on scaling up existing techniques gradually and with high levels of participation, as opposed to the transfer of techniques from one sector to another. In China, this transformation process is carried out through the rural education system, utilizing both formal and nonformal means. In this chapter Chinese efforts to introduce a learning network in the rural sector to assist in the transformation of agricultural and industrial technology will be explored. Specific reference will be made to China's marginal regions, highlighting the variety of educational networks aimed at transforming the techniques deemed essential for promoting agricultural and small-scale industry.

(2) For GPCR policy, see A.L. Erisman, "China's Agricultural Development," in People's Republic of China: An Economic Reassessment (Washington, D.C.: Government Printing Office, 1974-75). For a comparative assessment of the two periods (GPCR-Four Modernizations), see Bruce L. Reynolds, "Two Models of Agricultural Development: A Context for Current Chinese Policy," China Quarterly 76 (December 1978), pp. 842-72.

(3) I. Ovdiyenko, "The New Geography of Industry in China," Soviet Geography 4 (1961): 39-56.

(4) C. Hsieh, "The Status of Geography in Communist China," Geographical Review 49 (1959): 323-41.

(5) For GPCR period, see F. Chao, "Shehuizhuyi nongye jinbu fazhan de shinian," Hongqi 6 (1976): 56-60. For the current period, see "Jiji kaizhan nongmin jiaoyu," Renmin Jiaoyu 1 (1981): 9-10.

(6) A. Donnithorne, China's Economic System (London: George Allen and Unwin, 1967).

(7) Ibid.

(8) Xinhua (Beijing), June 29, 1976.

(9) Reynolds, "Two Models of Agricultural Development," pp. 867-68.

(10) Carl Riskin, "Local Industry and the Choice of Techniques in the Planning of Industrial Development in Mainland China," Planning for Advanced Skills and Technologies 3 (1969): 171-81; China: Socialist Economic Development (New York: World Bank, 1981).

(11) Y. Lo, "Self-Reliance and Making Foreign Things Serve China," Renmin Ribao, May 5, 1977; see also Reynolds, "Two Models of Agricultural Development," p. 868.

(12) Beijing Review, January 12, 1977.

(13) Reynolds, "Two Models of Agricultural Development," p. 868.

(14) Barry Richman, Industrial Society in Communist China (New York: Random House, 1969); L. Orleans, Manpower for Science and Engineering in the People's Republic of China, Background Study no. 4 (Washington, D.C.: Government Printing Office, 1980).

(15) L.T.C. Kuo, The Technical Transformation of Agriculture in Communist China (New York: Praeger, 1972).

(16) A.G. Ashbrook, "Economic Overview," in People's Republic of China: An Economic Reassessment (Washington, D.C.: Government Printing Office, 1974-75).

(17) H. Zuo, "China's Education: The Type of People It Brings Up," Beijing Review, January 17, 1980.

(18) A.G. Ashbrook, "Economic Overview."

(19) Guangming Ribao, August 19, 1980.

(20) Xinhua (Nanning), August 6, 1976.

(21) Xinhua (Shanghai), April 22, 1974; Xinhua (Tianjin), March 11, 1975.

(22) For example, in 1975 Kirin province had 14 such institutes with roughly 60 full-time agronomists each; Xinhua (Changchun), February 6, 1975.

(23) Xinhua (Changchun), February 6, 1975.

(24) Xinhua (Shenyang), May 14, 1976; Xinhua (Chengdu), April 21, 1977.

(25) Xinhua (Shenyang), April 13, 1973; Xinhua (Shijiazhuang), March 3, 1976; FBIS, June 9, 1980.

(26) Xinhua (Herbin), May 5, 1976; Xinhua, (Lhasa), August 25, 1976.

(27) Bring the Agricultural University Down to the Country-side," Chinese Education 22-23 (Spring 1975); originally from Hongqi, no. 5, (1974), pp. 73-77.

(28) FBIS, June 9, 1980; Nat J. Colletta, "Worker-Peasant Education in the People's Republic of China: A Study of Adult Education in Post-Revolutionary China," manuscript, June 1981.

(29) Xinhua (Shenyang), January 26, 1976; Y. Cheng, "Make Further Efforts to Foster New Socialist Things," Hongqi, no. 8, (1976).

(30) At this time it is reported that Chinese officials are considering "deruralizing" some of the model agricultural universities such as Zhaoyang. See Colletta, "Worker-Peasant Education," pp. 50-51. However, there does appear to be some confusion as certain agricultural secondary schools have been identified since the Four Modernizations Movement as key schools and have since used that designation as a justification to have their status raised to that of a university. (China trip notes, 1980).

(31) Xinhua (Changchun), June 22, 1973; Xinhua (Hangzhou), September 22, 1975; Xinhua (Shijiazhuang), April 12, 1976.

(32) Xinhua (Changchun), April 17, 1975.

(33) Xinhua (Shijiazhuang), April 12, 1976; Xinhua (Daiyuan), February 23, 1976.

(34) Xinhua (Hangzhou), December 12, 1974.

(35) Cheng, "Make Further Efforts"; Colletta, "Worker Peasant Education," pp. 38-44.

(36) Xinhua (Nanjing), November 2, 1975.

(37) Colletta, "Worker-Peasant Education," p. 43.

(38) Xinhua (Nanjing), November 2, 1975.

(39) Colletta, "Worker-Peasant Education," p. 44.

(40) Xinhua (Hofei), February 4, 1976; Xinhua (Shijiazhuang), August 11, 1976.

(41) J. Sigurdson, "Rural Industry — A Traveler's View," China Quarterly 50 (1972); Donnithorne, China's Economic System.

(42) Xinhua (Changsha), February 24, 1973.

(43) Xinhua (Fuzhou), February 2, 1974; Xinhua (Wuhan), August 22, 1973.

(44) Xinhua (Harbin), November 25, 1975; Xinhua (Hangzhou), July 4, 1975; Xinhua (Changsha), February 24, 1973; Xinhua (Shenyang), April 25, 1974.

(45) Colletta, "Worker-Peasant Education," p. 38.

(46) Xinhua (Changchun), September 24, 1976.

(47) Xinhua (Zhengzhou), July 11, 1974.

(48) Xinhua (Beijing), May 24, 1975.

(49) Colletta, "Worker-Peasant Education," p. 69.

(50) Xinhua (Beijing), October 8, 1974.

(51) Xinhua (Beijing), August 23, 1976.

(52) Xinhua (Changsha), April 12, 1974.

(53) J. Becker and C. Hahn, Wingspread Workbook for Educational Change (Boulder, Colo.: Social Science Education Consortium, 1975).

8

EDUCATIONAL POLICY AND NATIONAL MINORITIES IN THE PEOPLE'S REPUBLIC OF CHINA: THE POLITICS OF INTERGROUP RELATIONS

J.N. Hawkins

Chinese education has been widely recognized as existing in one of the more highly charged political environments among the nations of the world. Indeed, since 1949, China's educational system, personnel, and policymakers have been embroiled directly in every major political campaign launched during that period.(1) At times, both the system and those associated with it have benefited by the political changes that have taken place among China's leaders. At other times, the system has been totally shut down and faculty, students, and the society as a whole have suffered as a result; the faculty through rigid restrictions on their professional activities and outright persecution, and the students due to lost time, and lack of skills, making at least one group a lost generation (e.g., Red Guards). Of the many groups that interact with the educational system, one that has not been sufficiently studied is the group that comprises China's minorities. This chapter will focus on the politics of China's educational policy and intergroup relations contrasting the two most recent political campaigns: the Great Proletarian Cultural Revolution (GPCR) and the current Four Modernizations campaign. In each case the issues of political-educational philosophy, educational goals and objectives, recruitment of personnel, and curriculum (primarily language and culture) will be examined, within the political and historical context of China's education and intergroup relations environment.

This chapter is a revised version of a chapter published in R. Murray Thomas, Politics & Education (Oxford: Pergamon Press, 1983), pp. 125-48.

176

Recent research concerning intergroup relations has revealed the existence of a variety of methodological contexts in which to frame comparative ethnic relations. Traditional race relations cycles have given way to approaches that seek to provide explanation through consensus, interdependence, symbolic interactions, structural functionalism, and power-conflict theories.(2) Each of these approaches, drawing heavily from both political science and sociology, are not to be considered mutually exclusive. Usually, however, they are employed in an effort to order our thinking regarding intergroup relations after they have been assigned either to the systems (structural-functionalist) side of the continuum or to the side of the power-conflict theorists. In the case of China's minorities, a more appropriate approach utilizes a dialectical model such as that suggested by R.A. Schermerhorn.(3) Briefly, the dialectical approach allows one to account for change and movement in a total social situation, to recognize the interrelationships between groups, to focus on the problematic aspects of stability and structure, and to acknowledge the inherent duality of most social actions.(4) This approach is not incompatible with either systems theory or power-conflict theory. The former accounts for the functional aspects of ethnic groups in the total society, ethnic groups as subsystems of the whole, and the latter reminds us of the obvious antagonism that underlies subordinate-superordinate relations. This duality is recognized by Chinese scholars as well reflected in the title of a recent study of the subject by Fan Wenlan.(5) China's national minorities and the majority Han population have been intertwined historically, sometimes "fusing" or assimilating and at other times in antagonistic conflict. The cluster of political variables that have been most significant have been those associated with power differentials, cultural congruity (or incongruity), questions of authority, legitimacy, and centripetal versus centrifugal tendencies.(6) The schooling network, cadre training programs, and human resource development programs in general all have direct bearing on the political issues raised above. The degree to which these interactions undergo change and transformation as a result of educational policy and practice during the two periods discussed in this chapter will shed light on the process of minority group interactions in a political-economic context such as that which has prevailed in China for the past three decades.

CHINA'S NATIONAL MINORITIES: THE CONTEXT

Ethnic identification has been a consistently difficult task for China's political leaders. Officially, the State Council of the Central People's Government has declared that there are 56 distinct ethnic groups, although as recently as 1979 the number was 54 (see Table 8.1). Geographically they are distributed over 50 to 60 percent of the total land area and numerically account for about 6 percent of the total population (See Map 8.1). The situation is much more complex, however. When the People's Republic was first established in 1949, it is reported that over 400 groups registered themselves as national minorities. By 1957 the government had determined that there were only 11; further field work and research has resulted in the current figure of 56. As is reported in the article by Fei Xiaotong, ethnic identification continues to this day and the number of ethnic groups will undoubtedly change in the years to come.(7) Regardless of the number of ethnic groups or their percent of the total population (which appears quite small when viewed in a comparative context), the outstanding political fact is related to the "frontier" character of China's minorities. The majority of ethnic groups in China live in marginal regions, sparsely populated, but in the case of Yunnan and Xinjiang provinces they reside in strategic border regions, thus raising the issue of political and military reliability. Xinjiang province, for example, borders the Soviet Union, Tibet, and India. Minorities in this region have been of special interest to the Chinese since they first began formulating policy toward the region during the Qing dynasty (1644-1911). At least 13 minority ethnic groups reside in this vast area and at times have been at the center of international tension in the region. The end result of all of this complexity is that overall policy formulation toward China's national minorities has been a difficult and conflict-ridden task.

TABLE 8.1
Major Ethnolinquistic Groups in the PRC

National Minorities	Major Areas of Distribution	Population 1978 (000)	Religious Belief	Language/Script
Tibetan	Xizang (Tibet), Qinghai, Sichuan, Gansu, Yunnan	3,450	Lamaism	Tibetan language/script
Uygur (Uighur)	Xinjiang	5,480	Islam	Uighur language/script
Monggol (Mongolian)	Nei Monggol, Jilin, Liaoning, Heilongjiang, Xinjiang, Gansu, Qinghai, Hebei, Henan, Yunnan	2,660	Lamaism	Mongolian language/script
Hui	Ningxia, Gansu, Henan, Hebei, Qinghai, Shandong, Yunnan, Anhui, Xinjiang, Liaoning	6,490	Islam	Han language/script

TABLE 8.1
(Cont.)

National Minorities	Major Areas of Distribution	Population 1978 (000)	Religious Belief	Language/Script
Miao	Guangdong, Guizhou, Hunan, Yunnan, Guangxi, Sichuan	3,920		Miao language/script
Yi	Yunnan, Sichuan, Guizhou, Guangxi	4,850		Yi language/script
Zhuang	Guangxi, Yunnan, Guangdong, Guizhou, Hunan	12,090		Zhuang language/script
Bouyei (Puyi)	Guizhou	1,720		Bouyei language/script
Korean	Jilin, Heilongjiang, Liaoning	1,680		Korean language/script
Man (Manchu)	Liaoning, Heilongjiang, Jilin, Hebei, Nei Monggol, Beijing	2,650		Han language/script
Dong (Tung)	Guizhou, Hunan, Guangxi	1,110		Dong language/script
Yao	Guangxi, Hunan, Yunnan, Guangdong, Guizhou, Yunnan	1,240		Yao language
Bai	Yunnan	1,050		Bai language
Tujia	Hunan, Hubei	770		Tujia & Han languages
Kazak (Kazakh)	Xinjiang, Gansu, Qinghai	800	Islam	Kazak language/script
Hani	Yunnan	960		Hani language/script
Dai (Tai)	Yunnan	760		Dai language/script
Li	Guangdong	680		Li language/script
Lisu	Yunnan	470		Lisu language/script
Va (Wa)	Yunnan	260		Va language/script
She	Fujian, Zhejiang	330		She & Han languages
Gaoshan (Kaoshan)		--*		Gaoshan language
Dongxiang (Tunghsiang)	Gansu	190	Islam	Dongxiang language
Naxi	Yunnan	230		Naxi language/script
Lahu	Yunnan	270		Lahu language/script
Shui	Guizhou	230		Shui language
Jingpo (Chingpo)	Yunnan	83		Jingpo language/script
Kirigiz (Khalkhas)	Xinjiang	97	Islam	Kirgiz language/Uighur script
Tu	Qinghai	120	Lamaism	Tu language

TABLE 8.1
(Cont.)

National Minorities	Major Areas of Distribution	Population 1978 (000)	Religious Belief	Language/Script
Daur (Tahur)	Heilongjiang, Xinjiang, Nei Monggol	78		Daur language
Mulam (Mulao)	Guangxi	73		Mulam language
Qiang (Chiang)	Sichuan	85		Qiang language
Ulang (Pulang)	Yunnan	52		Ulang language
Salar (Sala)	Qinghai	56	Islam	Salar language
Russian	Xinjiang	0.6	Orthodox	Russian language/script
Gelo (Kelao)	Guizhou, Yunnan	26		Gelo language
Xibe (Sibo)	Xinjiang, Liaoning, Jilin	44		Xibe language
Maonan	Guangxi	31		Maonan language
Achang	Yunnan	18		Achang language
Tajik	Xinjiang	22	Islam	Tajik language/ Uighur script
Ozbek (Uzbek)	Xinjiang	75	Islam	Ozbek language/ Uighur script
Nu	Yunnan	19		Nu language
Tatar	Xinjiang	29	Islam	Tatar language/ Uighur script
Ewenki (Owenk)	Heilongjiang, Nei Monggol	13	Shamanism	Ewenki language
Bonan (Paoan)	Gansu	68	Islam	Bonan language
Jing (Ching)	Guangxi	54		Jing & Han languages/scripts
Yugur	Gansu	88		Yugur language
Benglong (Penglung)	Yunnan	10	Buddhism	Benglong language
Drung (Tulung)	Yunnan	41		Drung language
Oroqen (Olunchun)	Heilongjiang	32	Shamanism	Manchu language
Hezhen (Hoche)	Heilongjiang	0.8		Manchu language
Moinba (Monba)	Xizang (Tibet)	40		Moinba language
Lhoba (Lopa)	Xizang (Tibet)	200		
Jinuo	Yunnan	10		Jinuo language
Kucong	Yunnan	--		
Deng	Xizang (Tibet)	--		Han & Tibetan script
Lebu	Xizang (Tibet)	--		

*Data not available.
Source: China Handbook (Hong Kong: Kingsway Press, 1980).

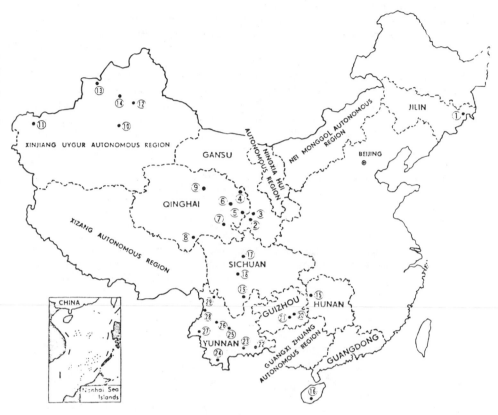

Map 8.1. Distribution of National Minorities

1. Yanbian Korean Autonomous Prefecture
2. Gannon Tibetan Autonomous Prefecture
3. Linxia Hui Autonomous Prefecture
4. Haibei Tibetan Autonomous Prefecture
5. Huangnan Tibetan Autonomous Prefecture
6. Hainan Tibetan Autonomous Prefecture
7. Guoluo Tibetan Autonomous Prefecture
8. Yushu Tibetan Autonomous Prefecture
9. Haixi Mongolian, Tibetan, Kazakh Autonomous Prefecture
10. Bayingolin Mongolian Autonomous Prefecture
11. Kizilsu Khalkhas Autonomous Prefecture
12. Changji Hui Autonomous Prefecture
13. Bartala Mongolian Autonomous Prefecture
14. Ili Kazakh Autonomous Prefecture
15. Xiangxi Tujia, Miao Autonomous Prefecture
16. Hainan Li, Miao Autonomous Prefecture
17. Aba (Ngawa) Tibetan Autonomous Prefecture
18. Garze Tibetan Autonomous Prefecture
19. Liangshan Yi Autonomous Prefecture
20. Qiandongnan Miao, Dong Autonomous Prefecture
21. Qiannan Bouyei, Miao Autonomous Prefecture
22. Wenshan Zhuang, Miao Autonomous Prefecture
23. Honghe Hani, Yi Autonomous Prefecture
24. Xishuangbanna Dai Autonomous Prefecture
25. Chuxiong Yi Autonomous Prefecture
26. Dali Bai Autonomous Prefecture
27. Dehong Dai, Jingpo Autonomous Prefecture
28. Nujiang Lisu Autonomous Prefecture
29. Degen Tibetan Autonomous Prefecture

<u>Source</u>: <u>Beijing Review</u>, no. 6, February 9, 1979.

The Chinese Communist Party (CCP) began this task as early as 1922 when a manifest emerged from the Second Chinese Communist Party Congress held in Shanghai. References were made to the concept of autonomy and federalism specifically toward the Mongols, Tibetans, and Turkic Moslems of Xinjiang. The concept of federalism particularly was an adaption of minority policies that had been expressed by Soviet leaders and had little to do with actual conditions in China. By 1935 China's Communist leaders began to abandon this notion and instead developed an approach characterized as "regional autonomy" that was legitimized in 1949 and came to be defined as: "an area where a certain minority people have formed themselves into compact communities shall be constituted as a national autonomous district, along with the right of electing local government and the power of issuing ordinances and regulations not contrary to the provincial constitution."(8) In practice it meant that while selected minority areas would enjoy autonomy with respect to "local conditions and needs" (such as education, culture, language), they would remain an indivisible portion of China combining to form a multinational unitary state.(9)

For convenience, the period from the establishment of the People's Republic in 1949 to the outbreak of the GPCR in 1966 will be divided into two subperiods. The first subperiod (1950-57) can be characterized as the initial formulation of a national level policy for minorities. During this period, Chinese official policy identified two broad goals: first, unification of China proper and consolidation of disputed borders; second, promotion of interethnic solidarity.(10) It became clear that while the Chinese government was prepared to grant limited autonomy, they were also going to maintain political and economic control until a certain degree of stability among and between minorities was achieved. For example, while class struggle was a major priority in China's relationships with its own upper classes, the government moved very cautiously (in Xingjiang for example) and took pains not to alienate minority elites. Rather, their power was gradually reduced through such reforms as the cooperativization program introduced in 1956.(11) In the field of education specifically, a "national minorities educational conference" was held in Beijing (June 1956) to map out a 12-year plan and to rank order educational priorities. Several broad goals were detailed: increased training of minority cadres by improving academic institutes; emphasis on adult literacy classes; universalize primary education and develop middle schools; establish more teacher education institutes; improve quality of language and translation capabilities.(12) By 1968 it was hoped that China's minorities would achieve parity at all educational levels with the national average.

The second subperiod (1958-65) was dominated by two major political-economic events: the Great Leap Forward and the Sino-Soviet split. With the inauguration of the Great Leap Forward political and economic policies (renewed emphasis on class struggle and a massive economic drive, including the introduction of rural communes) and the corresponding deterioration of relations with the Soviet Union, minority affairs also experienced a period of stress and difficulty. One example would be the situation of Xinjiang, an especially strategic region because of border alignments with the Soviet Union. In 1958, the commune movement was launched in the pastoral areas, and in 1960 urban people's communes were established in the cities. The various minority elites in the region sensed the impending divergence between Soviet and Chinese policies and began to increase demands for the establishment of separate nations. The Han Chinese and some minority leaders responded with an attack on "local nationalism" and for four years an intense political struggle was waged on several fronts simultaneously. First, there was an effort to bring the commune concept to the minority areas and adapt it in practice to local conditions. Second, a political struggle emerged to replace nationalist-minded and/or pro-Soviet minority elites with cadre more committed to CCP policy and practice. Finally, an educational program was initiated corresponding to Great Leap Forward national educational reforms with the addition of some measures aimed specifically at the minority areas (e.g., increased use of the Chinese language in the schools, more emphasis on class struggle and assimilation than on autonomy). The situation finally erupted into a large-scale exodus of at least one minority group in the area (Kazakhs) across the border to the Soviet Union. While Soviet interference was clearly a factor, Chinese and minority leaders throughout China realized that several problems existed with regard to a policy focused on class conflict and assimilation. With the downfall of Great Leap Forward policies and the criticism of the movement as a whole, national minority policy underwent a revision more in the direction of cultural autonomy. In the years immediately preceding the GPCR, increased emphasis was placed on minority languages, expansion of educational facilities in minority regions, recruitment of minority teachers, and advancement and popularization of minority cultural forms.(13) Cooperation and harmony were stressed instead of conflict and an attitude was present in Beijing that Han Chinese should treat minorities like "little brothers."

In summary then, the dialectical relationship between the Han majority and China's various minorities (conflict and unity) is revealed during the two periods discussed above. The period up to the GPCR sets the stage for the most dramatic policy debate since 1949: the GPCR and Four Modernizations approaches to majority-minority educational relations.

GREAT PROLETARIAN CULTURAL REVOLUTION

The outbreak of the GPCR in 1966 dramatically altered educational priorities for national minorities by shifting the emphasis from training for economic development to turning (minority areas) into a "big classroom of living study and application to Mao Zedong thought."(14) The overall emphasis was placed on political education, nationalities' unity through class struggle, and carrying out revolution in the schools.(15) Toward the latter part of the active phase of the GPCR (1968), statements in the official press began to appear directing educational goals for national minorities toward the overall national goal of increasing production, and promoting social and economic development. What this meant for education will be examined below, focusing on political philosophy and educational goals and objectives, the educational system, access to it, training and recruitment of national minorities, and particularly the language issue.

Political Philosophy and Educational Goals
and Objectives

The cornerstone of GPCR political philosophy toward national minorities can be summed up in the phrase: "the nationality struggle is a question of class struggle."(16) In a variety of news releases minority leaders stressed the need to distinguish between class enemies and friends regardless of nationality. Struggle-criticism-transformation sessions were organized and extensive criticism of previous minority policy (1962-66) dominated these discussions. Certain policy statements associated with the previous Liu Shaoqi government came under particularly harsh attack. Such policies stated that "conditions are too difficult" for minorities and therefore "special attention" must be paid to minority problems.(17) In the field of education, it was said that there was a "special character to the frontier regions," and therefore educational development would be slow and require much aid and assistance from outside. To all of this, GPCR critics responded that minorities, like everyone else in China, would simply have to practice "self reliance" and experiment with new, different forms of education in order to achieve national goals. Results would be obtained through "hard work."(18) Minority leaders criticized previous national minority policy for being paternalistic and exploitative. Han leaders, it was charged, had teamed up with the reactionary upper classes of the various minority groups to exploit both Han and minority workers and peasants. As one leader in Xinjiang pointed out: "the essence of national oppression in Xinjiang was the ruthless political oppression and economic exploitation of the working people of various nationalities (Han people included) by the exploiting classes of the minority nationalities in collusion with the reactionary Han rulers."(19) Although this extreme form of oppression ended with the establishment of the People's Republic in 1949, the writer continues: "Although in the main socialist transformation has been completed in the system of ownership, there is still the struggle between restoration and counter-restoration. The overthrown landlords, herders and other reactionaries have made use of their political, economic, and cultural influences to try to undermine national unity.(20) This critique was repeated in numerous publications and presents a position that was characteristic of the GPCR period, a position that emphasized class struggle and conflict, among and between minorities and the Han majority.(21)

A major educational implication of this political philosophy is the critique that previous educational policy toward national minorities emphasized the theory of "innate intelligence," which was interpreted to mean that minorities needed special assistance because of their backward conditions. It was charged that previous leaders had been influenced by Confucian thought and had proposed that only they (the Han leaders) were "sages" and "geniuses" and minorities were "born low."(22) While it is unlikely that Liu Shaoqi, Lin Biao, or any other leaders actually used such terminology, the critique is consistent with the position taken during the GPCR that social class is a more politically correct distinction to make than ethnicity when analyzing intergroup relations. Educational goals then stressed the need for minorities to use their own resources (self-reliance) to expand primary and secondary school oppor- tunities, further develop a variety of nonformal educational means to reach marginal populations, extend the use of minority languages as the medium of instruction, recruit more minority teachers, and expand colleges and technical institutes.(23) The major difference in both the political philosophy and the educational goals, when compared with previous policies, was the focus on class struggle and self-reliance.

The System and Access

The fundamental point made during the GPCR regarding access of minorities to education revolved around a class analysis that stated priority in education should go to "poor and lower middle level peasants, workers, and herdsmen."(24)

It was charged that during the previous ten years both Han and minority elites essentially served their own interests at the expense of expanding, through experimentation and alternative education, learning opportunities for lower class minorities. More specifically, in such areas as Tibet, it was reported that the CCP should lead emancipated serfs to develop "proletarian culture and customs" (as opposed to Han or ethnic Tibetan) and that the new culture and customs would be developed through political-culture evening schools operated two evenings per week. In such schools the curriculum would consist of revolutionary theory, and formation of theoretical study groups to popularize such works as Karl Marx's Communist Manifesto, The Critique of the Gotha Programme, and so on. The works of Mao Zedong would also be studied and popularized through traveling study groups. Other measures to assure the development of proletarian culture and customs were the development of photographic and journal exhibitions of class education (recalling the suffering of the past), spare-time art propaganda teams, newspaper reading groups in the fields, special radio broadcasts, and film presentations, all focused on the theme of class conflict and revolution. Once such revolutionary political ideas had been grasped by young people, they would then be full participants in the society's educational system.(25) In other areas, such as Xinjiang, Guangxi, and Yunnan, reports were similar. A correct class understanding was a prerequisite for access to resources such as education and the assumption was that young people from among the poor and lower middle peasant, worker, and herdsmen groups by their very nature possessed such an understanding; others less fortunate would have to acquire it through special classes.(26) By focusing on social class as the primary determinant of access, such factors as enrollment emerged (in some areas it was reported to have trebled since 1965), management of schools (shifted from professionals to newly trained lower class cadres), and cadre training.(27) In order to increase access for lower class minorities, nonformal education was introduced as a major mechanism in the form of spare-time schools, "roving" schools, and tent schools (for China's seminomadic populations).(28) The rationale for these changes continued to be grounded in the notion of conflict and struggle as the sine qua non for a correct approach to Han-minority relations. A leading figure in Xinjiang province expressed this concept most clearly by suggesting that minorities and Han Chinese must "fight shoulder to shoulder" against class enemies and exploiters in both their ranks.(29) Finally, regarding the argument that expanding access to education for lower class minorities was unfair since they were unqualified, minority and CCP leaders countered by stating that success would be achieved through "the initiative of the Han and [minority] poor and lower middle peasants . . . in revolutionary spirit of self-reliance, industry, and thrift."(30)

One major obstacle, of course, to the program of expanding educational opportunities for minorities was the critical shortage of teachers; a problem that was national in scope but especially severe in minority areas. A crash program was thus embarked upon to expand the teacher corps by establishing special teacher education programs specifically designed to train minority teachers from among the lower class groups. It was charged that the previous policy had sought to alleviate the teacher shortage by importing Han teachers and only training those minority teachers who had the proper "qualifications and credentials." GPCR officials, both in Beijing and in the minority areas criticized this approach for its cultural imperialism, social class bias in favor of the upper classes, and for the continuation of the teacher shortage. In Tibet, Xinjiang, Nei Mongolia, and Yunnan, special teacher education schools were started beginning in 1972 and by 1974 dramatic results were reported. In Yunnan, minority teachers of the Lisu, Nu, Tulung, Yi, Naxi, and Pai nationalities were reported to have increased four-fold.(31) And in Nei Mongolia, the number of Mongolian teachers were said to have more than doubled.(32) It is, of course, necessary to remind ourselves that these figures are unsubstantiated and little comparative data are available. Yet it illustrates the efforts that were being made to implement the ideology of class analysis, the perception that some leaders had of majority-minority relations, and the institutional solutions that were being experimented with. What may be more significant is the fact that educational officials in China today do not dispute such claims, preferring to comment only on the quality of minority teachers trained during this period.(33)

The educational system itself during the period consisted of a formal educational component similar in many respects to the formal system in China as a whole.(34) The nonformal network was tailored to the specific needs of each minority region.(35) However, the policy dispute that was waged during the GPCR regarding the system concentrated on the question of quality. At both the elementary and secondary levels, it was charged that minority attempts to manage their own affairs, expand facilities and revise the curriculum to suit minority needs were consistently stifled by the Beijing government in the early 1960s (Liu Shaoqi is specifically singled out in this respect). In Xinjiang for example, a model elementary school established in 1958 and popularized in the press (the Hongyen school) was criticized during the early 1960s for not following "conventional" patterns. As a result the curriculum was revised to focus on quality and only 13 percent of the school-age cohort were admitted, and this group represented children of the former bourgeoisie and CCP officials.(36) During the GPCR this particular school was reorganized into three mobile tent schools that moved with the herdsmen in order to provide some form of education for children of seminomadic families. The curriculum was also reorganized to eliminate course material that did not directly relate to the lives of the minority groups involved (Kazakhs and Uighurs). School terms were geared toward local conditions of production and a day care program established to release older children from this responsibility.(37) Similar reports were received from other minority regions. For example, in Changqihui autonomous zhou schools were reorganized to stress "flexibility" instead of "regularity," thus increasing enrollment and attendance from 75 to 95 percent over a six-year period.(38) Similar results were reported from the Guangxi Autonomous Region.(39) Graduates of secondary schools were expected to return to their local communes to engage in development work rather than think of moving to urban centers for higher education. The focus was on training for middle level vocational-technical skills under the policy of "from the commune, back to the commune."(40) Moreover, students who had graduated from the middle school level or had left to return to production were encouraged to return to school from 6 months to 1½ years for further study and enrichment. They could be admitted anytime during the year and recalled if needed for production. The curriculum at the middle school level concentrated on bookkeeping, public health, veterinary science, agricultural machinery repair, and agro-technical skills of various sorts — all areas deemed important for rural development in minority regions.(41)

Minority student graduates from middle schools were also influenced by the political movement to send educated young people to the countryside. It did not matter that they already lived in some of the most remote regions of China, under the policy that "minorities should struggle like everyone in China" they were assigned to even more marginal regions in order to receive "reeducation by poor and lower middle peasants."(42) Again, the emphasis was on social class, ideological struggle, and practical application of knowledge obtained in school rather than on any specific ethnic characteristics. For those minority students fortunate enough to attend institutions of higher education, the choices were primarily limited to two types of institutions. The first were colleges and universities operated and located in minority areas and enrolling principally minority students, and the second were the local and central level nationalities institutes. With respect to the former, priority for enrollment was given to "worker-peasant-soldier students" who had been recommended by their supervisors on the work site. The first classes of students in this category graduated in 1974 (having been admitted in 1971) and were reported to have been trained in a "practical" manner, in middle level skills specifically tailored to the developmental needs of the various minority areas.(43) The curriculum was designed specifically for each institution by the teachers and students, and colleges and universities of this type were operated in a "self-reliant" manner. Higher education thus followed the same pattern of access according to social class, training according to the "local needs," and management and administration according to the principle of self-reliance.

Finally, the various nationalities institutes, which are the major mechanism for recruiting minority cadres and increasing their participation in the decision-making process in China, also underwent change and reform during the GPCR. Both the Central Institute of Nationalities in Beijing (started in 1951) and various local nationalities institutes located in the autonomous regions began in 1971 to enroll students directly from the ranks of poor and lower-middle peasants and herdsmen. In all cases enrollment was reported to have increased and the curriculum was designed for political and practical study.(44) Enrollment procedures were so dominated by social class consideration that it was reported that in the case of the South Guangxi Nationalities Institute, one student of the Yao nationality was enrolled even though she only had three years of formal schooling (compared with the previous policy of only enrolling those with the equivalent of a middle school education). Despite her poor preparation she was expected to succeed because of her innate ability as a member of the poor and lower middle peasants to "overcome all difficulties, with a strong will and to make rapid progress." According to this policy, social class background and "will" were more important predictors of success than examination results and years of schooling.(45)

The Language Issue

A critical factor in intergroup relations characterized by cultural incongruity is the issue of language as a form of cultural transmission and means of communicating social and political messages. In China most minority languages are significantly different from the Han dialect. Altogether there are more than 50 distinct ethnolinguistic groups. China's various constitutions have generally stated that minority groups residing in autonomous regions have the freedom to use the spoken and written languages of their group in public proceedings, the press, and in the school.(46) However, during the GPCR it was also stated that minorities "need to learn Han spoken and written language in addition to mastering their own."(47) For their part, Han personnel working in minority areas were urged to learn local dialects and languages as part of their training.

More important than this rather vague language policy, however, has been the effort by the central government since 1949 to increase minority publications, reform written scripts where ·they existed and create written languages where they were lacking. As a result, up to 1966 information of dialect differences and grammar was collected, glossaries compiled, folklore recorded, and local poetry and other literary efforts studied.(48) By the 1970s the emphasis had shifted somewhat to encouraging minority groups to learn Han Chinese and at a conference held in Qingdao it was suggested that national minorities learn the standard Chinese dialect (putonghua) and no less a figure than former premier Zhou Enlai sanctioned minority languages conforming "as much as possible to Han Chinese."(49)

The period of the GPCR saw two major changes in language policy. First, it was suggested that minority written languages be reformed to conform to the written script used in Han Chinese (pinyin). The rationale for this reform was a statement attributed to Mao to the effect that, "The written language must be reformed, and it is necessary to take the orientation of phonetic spelling in common with the written languages of the world."(50) The emphasis, however, was not on mastering the alphabet to increase further the penetration of Han Chinese, but, rather, increasing literacy in the minority languages. This policy was especially critical in areas where an alternative script had existed and was tied closely to the culture of the minority group. (e.g., Xinjiang where the Arabic script was in widespread use among Kazakhs and Uighurs). Such reform was heralded as part of the class conflict between the old and the new, between the traditional minded and the revolutionary minded; more specifically, it was stated that "language reform work is a revolution to throw out the old and usher in the new and the realm of culture."(51) However, implementing the policy was not all smooth sailing. As in other educational areas, phoneticizing minority languages and discarding scripts that had been closely associated with the culture of the ethnic groups in question created conflict among and between Han and the minority elites. The GPCR leadership thus recruited their support from among "the workers, peasants, soldiers, the revolutionary intellectuals, and revolutionary cadres," in order to "smash the interference and sabotage of the class enemies at home and abroad."(52)

Obviously, there was resistance to abandoning the older scripts. The argument to phoneticize minority languages was couched in terms of expanded access to education and other resources. It was stated that it would assist minority-Han communication since the scripts were almost identical; would facilitate the struggle to increase literacy and accelerate the universalization of education; would create improved conditions for modernizing communications through the use of typewriters, printing, and telegraphic equipment; and would strengthen the unity of the various nationalities through improved cross-cultural communications.(53) Most important, the move toward a more standardized script among the various nationalities would be an important component in promoting class struggle and strengthening the base of the poor and lower middle peasants and herdsmen.

The second major change focused on the content of written materials in the new scripts developed for selected national minorities. Newspapers, journals, educational materials, and literary works written in the new script also were urged to "revolutionize the content" of the various publications. Translators concentrated on translating works by Marx, Engels, Lenin, Stalin, and Mao as well as revolutionary poems and songs by local minority writers. In addition, revolutionary Han literature, such as that written by Lu Xun, was translated into the reformed minority languages.(54) The reform of written script for minority languages was thus seen as basically a political matter: "Language reform is not a technical matter but primarily a political task. . . . "(55) The goal was to expand ideological education, increase access of minorities to revolutionary works of both local and Han writers, raise literacy rates, expand educational opportunities for poor and lower middle peasants and herdsmen, and through all of this promote class struggle and nationalities' unity. Although the official policy suggested that traditional minority languages and literature would be preserved for future research the message was clear the new policy was to lay a foundation "for the abolition of the old written languages and the all-round use of the new written languages" with a content that would ensure that "class struggle is the key link and everything else hinges on it."(56)

Summary

During the GPCR, government and educational officials, both Han and minority, viewed intraethnic and interethnic educational relations from a decidedly conflict perspective. Nationalities' unity was always part of the slogans emanating from both minority officials and central officials in Beijing; but the literature and documentation from this period as well as interview data clearly illustrate the conflict orientation. Educational goals and objectives focused on the educational need of minorities in much the same light as of the Han majority; both were to struggle hard and practice "self-reliance." Social class was a more important variable in the educational process than ethnicity. Regarding the system and access to it, again, social class was the determining factor and political-ideological correctness the only measure of a student's worth. Education was to promote "proletarian culture and customs" and traditional ethnic culture was relegated to archaic historical study. Language and literature likewise were reformed both in form and content to be politically correct, more efficient (e.g., linked to Han developments such as the use of a phonetic script), and to promote the educational interests primarily of lower class minorities. Nationalities' unity was the goal but the primary mechanism for achieving this goal focused on class conflict and struggle.

THE FOUR MODERNIZATIONS MOVEMENT

The era of the Great Proletarian Cultural Revolution came to an abrupt halt on October 6, 1976, when four of the major leaders of the movement (collectively known as the Gang of Four — Jiang Qing, Wang Hongwen, Zhang Chunqiao, and Yao Wenyuan) were arrested, incarcerated, eventually tried, and convicted. Prior to this event, China's veteran leadership contingent had all but disappeared with the deaths of Premier Zhou Enlai, Zhu De, and Chairman Mao

Zedong, all in 1976. The new leadership initially led by Hua Guofeng and now by Deng Xiaoping (twice purged during the GPCR), began the task of redirecting China's domestic and foreign policies toward the goal of modernizing industry, agriculture, science and technology, and the military establishment. The overall domestic goal was to reach a level of industrial and agricultural productivity, military preparedness, and scientific progress equal to that of other major world powers by the year 2000. To accomplish this rather ambitious objective would require a degree of order and stability lacking during the turbulent years of the GPCR. It would also require a highly trained and professional work force at all levels but especially among those most educated. Thus, the educational system began to be restructured to emphasize quality and promote high achievers, regardless of social class background. It is in this general context that China's new leaders began to formulate a revised educational policy toward China's national minorities.

Minority Policy Restated

The transition from the policies of the GPCR to those of the Four Modernizations Movement was not accomplished in a clear-cut manner. Shortly after the arrest of the Gang of Four, articles began appearing in the Chinese press critical of minority policy during the GPCR. In the first few articles an almost equal emphasis was placed on the question of class versus ethnicity. Mao's Ten Great Relationships were discussed in terms of the conflict between Han chauvinism and local nationalism. With an emphasis on unity between the majority and minorities, Mao had stated that, "the key to the question lies in overcoming Han chauvinism and local nationalism."(57) In another article in Hongqi, Mao is again quoted to the effect, "in the final analysis, nationality struggle is a matter of class struggle."(58)

Having paid homage to Mao and the concept of class struggle, both articles go on to concentrate on the various ways policy should be formulated to achieve "unity." The Gang of Four was roundly criticized for putting undue emphasis on class struggle; while Mao did indeed himself stress class struggle, he also stated that, "the question of minority nationalities has both its generality and its particularity."(59) The authors of these two articles go on to state that only by combining a kind of two-pronged analysis can the CCP arrive at a correct party line. The gang is charged with either placing too much emphasis on class struggle or on the notion of nationality, thus creating splits between nationalities and within ethnic groups. The Hongqi article concludes by pointing out that with respect to the issue of Han chauvinism versus local nationalism the emphasis must be on opposing Han chauvinism. The burden, in other words, for redressing problems between the Han majority and the various nationalities must be placed on the majority. The distinction based on ethnicity was thus clearly made.

With the adoption of a new constitution, we are able to see some important language and content changes. The previous constitution (1975) contained a very general statement regarding the notion of a unitary multinational state, regional autonomy and the question of chauvinism. It also stressed the critical role of "class dictatorship" and the class nature of intergroup relations.(60) The new document is slightly more codified. The basic principle for minority relations is "equality, and unity, mutual aid and cooperation and common development." Article Four, which deals specifically with the minority issue, states:

> All nationalities are equal. There should be unity and fraternal love among the nationalities and they should help and learn from each other. Discrimination against or oppression of any nationality and acts which undermine the unity of the nationalities are prohibited. Big nationality chauvinism and local-nationality chauvinism must be opposed.(61)

The areas underlined represent new language inserted by the new administration. Of special interest are the clauses referring to "acts which undermine the unity of nationalities," for it is precisely in this area that the previous administration has been most severely criticized. It was their emphasis on class struggle that led to the lack of unity among nationalities, or so it is charged. The other clause, on mutual help and learning from one another, is further discussed below.

The current administration has repeatedly emphasized the need for Han assistance to minority areas: "It is a principle of national policy in this multinational state that every support in manpower, material, and financial resources must be given to the minority regions to promote their economic and cultural growth."(62) This particular report goes on to comment on all the industrial and scientific progress that has been made in minority areas. Criticism is made of the lack of such progress during the GPCR period largely because of the lack of an affirmative action policy on the part of the Han majority. While the article discusses the need for major assistance efforts on the part of the central government, there is virtually no discussion on politics, class struggle, or the issue of nationality versus the class struggle. Another article goes further still.(63) While upholding the integrity of the concept of national regional autonomy and additional policies for training large numbers of minority cadres, the article goes into detail to explain these concepts. Essentially it states that areas that are impacted sufficiently by minority populations may establish organs of self government "as long as it constitutes an administrative unit" and "operates within the law." More legalistic regulations are stated for such minority areas that wish to ask for special privileges in the areas of cultural affairs or political organization. Proposals must be submitted to the National People's Congress in Beijing and the emphasis now is clearly on the central government (Beijing) to help the "less developed" areas culturally, economically, technically, and linguistically (assistance with "underdeveloped languages").

These new policy statements seemed aimed at tightening up central control of the minority regions on the one hand, and adopting a more liberal attitude toward cultural differences on the other. This dual posture is expressed by a somewhat condescending approach to "assistance to underdeveloped areas" similar to deprivation theory, with which we are more familiar. Minorities are viewed as in need of help, special consideration, and advanced training from their more sophisticated and cultured Han brethren. Politics plays a very little role as does social class, as minorities are viewed as a special group in need of special treatment. Thus, the emphasis on unity, Han assistance to minority regions, increasing productivity, furthering quality education, and drawing ethnic distinctions rather than social class came to characterize post-GPCR policy toward national minorities. It has been elaborated upon further during the past four years and implemented in both the educational system and with respect to the language issue.

The System and Access

The most obvious difference in current minority educational policy, with respect to the purpose of education and the accessibility for minorities as compared with the GPCR period, is the relationship between education and production. Previously the emphasis was almost exclusively on "education for class struggle and revolution." For the past four years, the emphasis has gradually shifted to production first, then education and training.(64) Within schools, the primary function of educational personnel is teaching, with politics and ideological education a distant second (it has been reported that teachers should devote 5/6 of all their time to teaching and the remainder to "other activities," including political education).(65) National minority groups are now viewed as a composite and distinguishable from the Han majority primarily because of their ethnicity, culture, and language rather than social class background. Minority leaders, such as the Vice Chairman of the Tibetan CCP committee, Mr. Gyancan, have stated that national minorities should view the Han majority as "elder brothers" and realize that they are part of the Chinese motherland: "Elder brothers must care for and love their little ones, who must in turn respect and be concerned for their elder brothers."(66)

For education this rather "familial" policy has meant that the central government has initiated a policy of granting special funds for minority areas to assist in their "economic and cultural development," the obvious implication being that they are underdeveloped in both areas. In more detail the policy states that, "it is the principle of national policy in this multinational state that every support in manpower, material and functional resources be given to the minority nationality regions to promote their economic and cultural growth."(67) The emphasis on the educational system is directed toward human resource development for economic growth through a subsidized program of educational assistance; little mention is made of political education or social class.

The educational system itself has been restructured in line with national efforts to increase the number of years of elementary and secondary schooling from 9 to 12, reintroduce examinations, key schools (special schools for high achievers), and increase enrollments. Most minority areas are reporting increased enrollments since 1977 in regular schools, as opposed to the previous efforts to expand facilities and enrollment through an alternative, nonformal educational program.(68) Minority areas now receive about 8 percent more capital construction funds than do Han areas, in line with the policy of "assisting the backward areas because of their special situation."(69)

The special treatment extends beyond funding to include any educational areas where it can be shown that "minorities' lives were made more difficult."(70) Singled out for special attention are the numerous minority teachers trained during the GPCR who, it is now charged, are substandard and in need of in-service education. Special study classes have been established to upgrade the teaching abilities of minority teachers in order to "meet the new demands of the government."(71) This program was launched in coordination with the new unified set of textbooks published and distributed by the central government in September 1978. Minority teachers are expected to use the new textbooks (published in both Chinese and major minority languages) and in-service education classes have been developed to assist them. The classes are taught by Han Chinese professors from major colleges and universities in the minority areas.

This policy is in contrast with the GPCR decentralized policy of textbook compilation and use. Thus, six major goals relevant to the educational system have been identified by the new administration: first, readjust the system so that it corresponds with the "regular" educational system prevalent throughout China; second, develop new political education among students with an emphasis on unity among nationalities; third, focus on the moral, intellectual, and physical development of minority students (this is the same goal expressed for Han students); fourth, improve minority teachers' teaching quality; fifth, train more minority teachers; and sixth, increase educational and capital construction funds for minority areas.

The previous policy of sending educated minority youth to the more remote areas of minority regions has also been abandoned and minority secondary school graduates are encouraged to take the national examination system along with Han graduates. During the first few years of the new administration, the emphasis was on recruiting able minority students for higher education through the various nationalities institutes. Rigorous entrance examinations were held and the better students were sent to Beijing for cadre training in the Central Institute for Nationalities. The stated goal of this training was to "upgrade the backwardness of the various nationalities."(72) Two years later in 1980, problems emerged with this program and it was charged that the educational level of minority students was too low and special spare-time classes had to be organized before they could adequately handle the course work of the institutes. Moreover, it was found that their study habits were unsatisfactory – problems all related to the previous ten years.(73)

Regular universities and colleges also revised their policies toward minority students. In the Nei Mongolia region, for example, it has recently been reported that an admissions quota of 20 percent should be established to ensure minority enrollments. Although the articles indicated that this was a CCP policy, it is unclear whether or not it is being implemented nationwide.(74) The Ministry of Education has, however, stated that a new affirmative action program for minorities is being designed and implemented through-out China's colleges and universities. The core of the program is to increase access to higher education for minority applicants by lowering the minimum examination score for students from minority regions; this procedure is followed for both the key and ordinary universities and colleges. Once admitted, minority students will also receive special tutoring in academic areas where their skill levels are "substandard." These special classes are called "preparatory classes" (yuke ban).(75) No similar program has been announced for Han students and it is clear that social class plays little if any role in selecting minority students. A further measure to increase access of minority students to China's colleges and universities is a proposal to establish special "nationalities classes" (minzu ban) in selected secondary schools throughout China's minority regions. Minority students would be admitted through a system of examinations and once admitted would receive free education designed to prepare them for higher education.(76)

Finally, a research and development component of the educational system has also been adjusted to align with the new policy toward national minority education. In keeping with the priorities of the Four Modernizations Movement regarding science and technology research in minority areas, minority researchers will in the future focus their attention on "specialized scientific experimentation."(77) New scientific research organizations, conferences, and laboratory facilities are being developed in minority areas for high-level research and development. This policy is in contrast to the GPCR program, which emphasized "going into the field" to conduct research with workers, peasants, and herdsmen. Reports of efforts to disengage from the GPCR program are widespread.(78)

The Language Issue

As was noted above, during the GPCR period the Chinese government pursued a language policy that gave credence to minority languages, constitutionally protected and promoted their use at the local level, and at the same time, encouraged the adoption of a revised script more in line with the phonetic script used in Han Chinese (pinyin). Up to this point, there is little to distinguish the GPCR language policy from that expressed by the new leadership. There is, however, a significant difference in how both administrations view the functional use of minority languages. The GPCR leadership was opposed to the use of minority languages in any form (traditional or revised) if they were used to promote local, ethnic, or nationalistic attitudes or if they reflected traditional ethnic "feudal or bourgeois attitudes." The debate that has emerged since 1976 in contrast centers on the use of traditional minority language forms precisely for ethnic identity rather than for functional use. This new policy was highlighted at a major meeting in 1978 attended by over 100 specialists representing members and/or representatives from the various minority nationalities. A set of three recommendations emerged from this meeting, all designed to reverse policies initiated and implemented during the GPCR:

1. All ethnic literature societies, disbanded as being "nationalistic" during the GPCR, are to be restored, and a special institute of minority nationalities literature is to be established.
2. The journal Folk Literature, which ceased publication during the GPCR, is to be reestablished and a call was issued for manuscript contributions on literary works and articles by minority authors in their own languages.
3. The collection and compilation of folk history in the oral tradition is to be resumed as well as the continued collection of folk literature in the minority languages from the autonomous regions.(79)

In addition to making the above suggestions, the conference participants utilized the meeting to denounce minority language policy during the GPCR period. It was charged that during this time, the previous government had "wrought havoc" in the field. All collection, compilation, and editing functions of minority language specialists were suspended and several collections already in existence were destroyed as being too traditional, feudal, or bourgeois. Specifically mentioned as being destroyed were original copies of the 12 million word Tibetan epic Jamser and 34 of 40 chapters of the Kazakh narrative poem Forty Branches of Bahetier. These and other examples were cited by participants as examples of the incorrect assessment made by GPCR officials of the relationship between ethnic identity and social class.

Related to the topic of preservation of nationality literature is the question of teaching of traditional literature forms. During the GPCR, scant attention was paid to formal instruction and curriculum in this area and instead educators concentrated on bilingual education of a functional variety. At a recent meeting in Huhehot, however, various minority institutions held a conference on the compilation of textbooks on theories of minority literature and art. It was reported that teachers of Mongolian, Korean, Chang, Miao, Uighur, Hui, and Han literature engaged in "heated" discussion on the topic of bringing forth ethnic distinctions in literature. Here again the emphasis seems to be on the "ethnic identity" question rather than on class divisions within ethnic groups and the implications of this division for language instruction.(80)

On the question of the functional use of minority languages for political and economic affairs to promote class struggle and the revolution, there is at least one significant region in South China where it appears there is a move toward promoting the functional use of putonghua in most communities in the area, at the same time preserving the local languages and literature for "historical" purposes.(81) It is important to recognize that the Guangxi region is the homeland of six ethnic groups – Zhuang, Miao, Yao, Mulao, Maonan, and Gelao – for which the functional development of both written and oral language was an expressed desire during the GPCR period. It is now reported that the people of the region asked to learn putonghua and for this reason all education is now to be carried out in this Han dialect. It is too early to predict whether this experience represents a trend, especially for those groups small in number and lacking in written language, but it clearly represents a departure from the language policy of the period 1966-76.

A final area of contrast between GPCR and current policy toward minority languages is in the area of content. Regardless of which language form is used, traditional, revised phonetic, or Han, GPCR policy focused on the use of language for promoting the class struggle, communicating political ideals and values among and between minorities and majorities, and for generally promoting revolutionary goals and objectives. Current policy views the context issue as being concerned primarily with the use of language to promote the "Four Modernizations." If this can best be done with textbooks published in minority languages, so be it; if not, then minority areas might have to adopt the more "advanced and universal" Han dialect. Whatever language forms are used, minority areas have been assured that "traditional-ethnic" languages will be preserved and studied in an academic environment if not used in a daily, functional context.(82)

CONCLUSION

The major difference between the two periods with respect to minority educational policy has been noted in the sections above. The political economy of China has in many respects determined majority-minority policy, depending upon which interest group is more influential in Beijing and within minority leadership groups. During the GPCR the "political" aspect of China's development program was most emphasized and this was reflected in every aspect of minority educational affairs. It was explicitly stated in educational goals and objectives, it was implemented in programs effecting minority access to the educational system, and politics prevailed with respect to the language issue. Leadership groups within the minorities and in the central leadership in Beijing emerged because they were in agreement with GPCR policy. The duality stated earlier in this chapter between "conflict" and "unity" expressed itself during the GPCR primarily on the side of conflict. Once the leadership groups began to shift in 1976 to the "economic" component of China's political-economy, minority policy followed suit. Minority-majority affairs were discussed against a background of economic need and the goals of the Four Modernizations program. Whether the topic was political philosophy, access to the educational system, or the language issue, the evaluation of progress in these areas centered on whether or not economic advances were likely. Among minorities and between minorities and the Han majority the emphasis is now clearly on "unity"; in fact, the term "melting" is now used to discuss the probable future of minority-majority interaction.(83) All aspects of the educational system have shifted to facilitate economic growth, nationalities' unity, and more harmonious relations between social classes.

During both periods Chinese officials and minority leaders have sought to introduce social change in the border and other minority regions. During the GPCR the approach utilized attempted to maneuver an existing conflict-ridden situation to political advantage in order to eventually eliminate conflict by ridding both groups (minority and Han) of "class enemies," thus creating a unified, change-oriented proletarian mass movement. Since 1976, China's leaders are focusing their efforts on promoting social change through cooperation and assistance, moderate politics, and rational economic programs. Issues related to educational access and equity, revolutionary ideology, and class stratification are rarely read in the press or heard in conversations. Foremost in many people's minds in China is whether or not the pendulum will again swing back to another variant of the "conflict" approach to intergroup relations. As is the case with other nations, this likelihood will increase if the "modernization" approach does not solve real problems of educational and economic inequity between China's majority and numerous minorities.

NOTES

(1)   For a summary of these various educational campaigns see Stewart E. Fraser and John N. Hawkins, "Educational Reform and Revolution in the People's Republic of China," Phi Delta Kappan (April 1972): 1-10.

(2)   The evolution of these approaches can be found in R.E. Park, Race and Culture (Glencoe: Free Press, 1950); N.R. Yetman and C.H. Steel, eds., Majority and Minority (Boston: Allyn and Bacon, 1975).

(3)   R.A. Schermerhorn, Comparative Ethnic Relations (New York: Random House, 1970), p. 48.

(4)   Schermerhorn, Comparative Ethnic Relations, p. 48.

(5)   Fan Wenlan, "Problems of Conflict and Fusion of Nationalities in China," Social Sciences in China I (1980): 71-82.

(6)   Schermerhorn, Comparative Ethnic Relations, p. 72.

(7)   Fei Xiaotong, "Ethnic Identification in China," Social Sciences in China I (1980): 98.

(8)   "Zhongguo renmin zhengzhi xieshang huiyi," Zhongyang zhengfu faling huibien (Beijing: Renmin chuban she, 1952), p. 4; see also B.I. Schwartz, Chinese Communism and the Rise of Mao (Cambridge: Harvard University Press, 1964) for a discussion of early Chinese communist organizational strategies.

(9)   Lee Fu-hsiang, "The Turkic Moslem Problems of Sinkiang," (Ph.D. diss., Rutgers University, 1973), pp. 79-127.

(10)   Saifudin, "Zhongguo renmin ho zhoungguo minze de geming," Renmin Ribao, October 2, 1951, p. 3.

(11)   Lee, "The Turkic-Moslem Problems," p. 245.

(12)   Survey China Mainland Press, no. 1304 (June 4, 1956)(hereafter cited as SCMP).

(13)   SCMP, no. 3364 (December 24, 1964).

(14)   SCMP, no. 4756 (September 28, 1970).

(15)   SCMP, no. 4506 (September 11, 1968).

(16)   SCMP, no. 4498 (September 18, 1969).

(17)   Xinhua, April 21, 1972.

(18)   Xinhua, April 21, 1970.

(19)   Xinhua, October 15, 1975.

(20)   Xinhua, October 15, 1975.

(21)   Xinhua, March 5, 1974; Xinhua, September 17, 1975; Xinhua, February 14, 1976; Xinhua, May 7, 1976.

(22)   Xinhua, February 21, 1974; Xinhua, March 5, 1974.

(23) SCMP, no. 5556 (February 8, 1974).

(24) Xinhua, February 8, 1972; Xinhua, November 27, 1974; Xinhua, December 17, 1974.

(25) Xinhua, November 27, 1974.

(26) Xinhua, February 8, 1972; Xinhua, October 25, 1972; Xinhua, September 2, 1974.

(27) Xinhua, September 26, 1974; Xinhua, September 2, 1974; Xinhua, December 17, 1974.

(28) Xinhua, September 2, 1974.

(29) Xinhua, December 17, 1974.

(30) Xinhua, February 8, 1972.

(31) Xinhua, October 7, 1972.

(32) Xinhua, December 11, 1972.

(33) China trip notes, March 1981.

(34) Fraser and Hawkins, "Educational Reform and Revolution," p. 9.

(35) John N. Hawkins, "National Minority Education in the People's Republic of China," Comparative Education Review 1 (1978): 159.

(36) Xinhua, February 25, 1975.

(37) Xinhua, February 25, 1975.

(38) Xinhua, June 21, 1974.

(39) Xinhua, April 18, 1974.

(40) Xinhua, June 8, 1975.

(41) Xinhua, June 8, 1975.

(42) Xinhua, February 18, 1975.

(43) For information on the Guangxi Autonomous Region see Xinhua, August 24, 1974; for Nei Mongolia see Xinhua, September 12, 1974.

(44) Xinhua, February 13, 1972; Xinhua, February 19, 1975.

(45) Xinhua, January 20, 1974.

(46) The Constitution of the People's Republic of China (Beijing: Foreign Languages Press, 1952); see also "All Nationalities Have the Freedom to Use Their Own Spoken and Written Languages," Beijing Review, no. 23 (1975), pp. 13-15.

(47) "All Nationalities," p. 15.

(48) SCMP, no. 945 (November 28, 1954); SCMP, no. 1177 (November 24, 1955).

(49) Renmin Ribao, February 17, 1972.

(50) Guangming Ribao, August 13, 1976.

(51) Guangming Ribao, August 13, 1976.

(52) Guangming Ribao, August 13, 1976.

(53) Guangming Ribao, August 13, 1976.

(54) Xinhua, November 5, 1973; Xinhua, September 20, 1975; Xinhua, September 5, 1976.

(55) Xinhua, November 5, 1973.

(56) Guangming Ribao, August 13, 1976.

(57) Hongqi, no. 8 (1977), p. 58.

(58)   Hongqi, no. 8 (1977), p. 58.
(59)   Hongqi, no. 8 (1977), p. 59.
(60)   "All Nationalities," p. 13.
(61)   Beijing Review, no. 6 (February 9, 1979), p. 7.
(62)   Xinhua, September 22, 1978.
(63)   Beijing Review, no. 6 (February 9, 1979), p. 6.
(64)   Xinjiang Ribao, February 21, 1980.
(65)   Xinjiang Ribao, February 21, 1981.
(66)   Renmin Ribao, February 25, 1980, p. 3.
(67)   Xinhua, September 22, 1978.
(68)   Xinhua, November 15, 1977; Xinhua, May 21, 1978; Xinhua, February 8, 1979.
(69)   Xinhua, November 15, 1977; Xinhua, February 8, 1979.
(70)   Xinhua, February 8, 1978.
(71)   Xinhua, May 20, 1978.
(72)   Xinhua, March 30, 1978.
(73)   Xizang Ribao, January 22, 1980.
(74)   FBIS, May 8, 1980.
(75)   FBIS, May 9, 1980.
(76)   Guangming Ribao, January 15, 1981.
(77)   Xinhua, August 8, 1978.
(78)   For Xinjiang see Xinhua, August 8, 1978; for Tibet see Xiang, September 4, 1977; for Ningxia Hui see Xinhua, June 18, 1977.
(79)   Xinhua, November 29, 1978.
(80)   Xinhua, May 19, 1978.
(81)   R. Alley, "Minority Languages," Eastern Horizon 17 (1978): 15.
(82)   Guangming Ribao, January 15, 1981.
(83)   Fan, "Problems of Conflict and Fusion," p. 73.

9

TEACHER TRAINING: A VIEW FROM CHINA

Chen Qi

HISTORICAL BACKGROUND

In ancient China, teachers who gave individualized instruction in the private sector did so without benefit of special training. Most of these instructors were intellectuals who had failed the imperial examination or had passed only the lower level. Left over from the older society and respected for their profession, they were rank ordered in the so-called "tian-di-jun-qin-shi" (Heaven, Earth, Monarch, Parent and Teacher). Over time this respect waned and what social position the teacher once had declined further. They became inferior persons. In part this was due to the status of the educational system. While historically and culturally educated persons were respected if they were teachers, they, in practice, were accorded little status and prestige.

The education of teachers in China can be traced to the turn of the twentieth century; from the beginning it has been influenced by Western countries. The first normal school, established in 1902, was the Teachers' Academy in the Nanyang Public School of Shanghai. Established during the same year was the Beijing Normal University. Before the creation of the People's Republic of China (PRC) in 1949, education for teachers was inferior as the government did not consider education a very serious concern. There no longer were any special requirements to becoming a teacher – it was in the province of anyone – the criteria being solely desire and literacy.

Since the government no longer provided or established requirements for training of teachers, the few teachers who did possess superior teaching and training talents and obtained their certification were unable to find suitable positions. Some families viewed the status of teachers as being on the same level as a "knowing" servant. There was an old saying, "If you have five decaliters of grain in your home, you won't have to be a children's monarch." The position of the teacher had reached its lowest ebb.

Traditionally, most students in the normal schools and universities came from the poorer families, primarily because the schools never charged tuition and the students were supplied free meals, albeit of poor quality, but still better than none. Considering their family backgrounds, and because schooling offered them a prestige they normally would not have, they were, as a class, diligent in their studies and aware and sympathetic to the plight of the poor. It was these normal schools and universities they attended, therefore, that later would become the seat of the students' revolutionary movement, and many of the scholars became the future leaders within the movement, like Mao, who had studied at the Hunan First Normal School.

PEOPLE'S REPUBLIC OF CHINA: A NEW ERA OF TEACHER EDUCATION

After 1949, with the birth of the PRC, the government emphasized the importance of improving the status of teachers. Because the basic criteria for the development of the educational undertaking involved the recruitment of a large number of teachers, improvement of teacher training was finally given high priority. On October 1, 1951, the Government Administrative Council of the Central People's Government of the PRC issued the Decision of the Reform of Education Systems, in which the various systems at all levels were reestablished, and guiding principles and clearly defined tasks of teachers' education programs drawn. Later on, regulations for the training of teachers were also reinitiated.

The objective was to have those preschool normal schools, whose purpose it was to train personnel for preschool education, train the teachers for the kindergartens; the regular normal schools were to train teachers for the primary grades. Both types of normal schools were to recruit their trainees from junior high schools and were to prepare them through a three-year course of study. Instructors for junior high schools recruited from senior high schools would be trained over a two to three-year period in the professional teacher schools. Instructors for the senior high grades had to be graduates from senior high schools and would be trained in the normal university or teachers' colleges through a four-year curriculum.

Because there was a great lack of trained faculty or of sufficient number to fill the required positions, during the early 1950s a vast number of graduates from the normal colleges and universities became college instructors as well as becoming research specialists.

In the countryside were a few junior normal schools (equivalent to the junior high level) where elementary school graduates were trained to become elementary school teachers through a three-year program. (See Table 9.1.)

TABLE 9.1.
Teacher Education System

Type of School	Prerequisite	Equivalent Level	Length (in years)	Objective
Normal university	senior high school	university	4-5	high school teacher
Teachers' college	senior high school	university	4-5	high school teacher
Teachers' training institute	senior high school	college	2-3	junior high school teacher
Normal school	junior high school	senior high school	3	primary teacher
Junior normal school	primary school	junior high school	3	primary teacher
Preschool normal school	junior high school	senior high school	3	kindergarten teacher

Source: Constructed by author from various interviews.

Again during the early 1950s, teacher education in China, like other aspects of the educational system, put into practice theories adopted from the Soviet Union. Consequently, a process of reform was initiated similar to that practiced by the Soviet Union, specifically in the areas of teaching programs, in content of the curriculum, in teaching methods and principles, and so on. The teachers colleges and normal universities, in particular, followed the Russian concepts. Soviet experts were invited to present lectures that were to cover various specialities, both at the ministry and university levels. Some of these imported experts were advisors to the Ministry of Education and to the various presidents of the universities.

The curriculum, inaugurated for teachers in higher education, fell into four categories: political theories, educational theories, fundamentals of professional theory, and professional courses. Some students, if they were from families of poorer circumstances, were awarded fellowships. All students were exempted from paying tuition, and received free meals.

In several instances, the teachers' position was elevated. They were recognized as "engineers of the human soul"; their salaries were increased; some, if outstanding, were elected as representatives of the National People's Congress and the local people's congress, and they were designated as model instructors. A trade union for teachers was established that fell under the sphere of the All-China Federation of Trade Unions. These improvements signified that teachers were now to be as respected as others of the working class. Their social and economic status and education as a whole were making great strides forward.

Owing to the fact that the restructuring of teachers' training was comparatively new, a large percentage of the total number of students recruited into the university force were absorbed into the normal universities and colleges, but the quality of their training was relatively low. Many students, still relating to the former status of teachers, did not wish to choose a career in education. It took a few years for a turnaround, after schools, and society as a whole, attempted to educate their students to seek a teaching career. Thereafter, a number of model teachers did emerge and their faithfulness and regard for the new educational process proved advantageous in recruiting the younger student.

THE TWO-SLOGAN DEBATE: NEW DIRECTIONS IN HIGHER TEACHER EDUCATION

China completed its socialist transformation in the system of ownership of the means of production in 1956, which steered the country into the socialist construction period. Since there was now a requirement for improving the quality and quantity of education, and the process needed to be swiftly speeded up, teacher training was involved. During the period of the Great Leap Forward, an important debate occurred regarding teacher training. This was summed up in the two slogans: "Keep up with the comprehensive universities," and "Face toward the high school; emphasize the specific properties of teachers training."

The former argued that if the students spent much time involved in educational and practice teaching courses, they must, of necessity, spend less time in their speciality. If this proved to be true, they would fall behind the university students who were more engrossed in a comprehensive speciality. The latter slogan argued that the objective of teacher education was to train teachers; therefore, the schools for teacher education had to allow more time to teach the student, pedagogy, psychology, and so on. In the context of the Great Leap Forward, the former point of view was the more popular. At the Beijing Normal University, an additional slogan of "Keep our university abreast with the high grades, precision, and the advance" (called "gao-jing-jian") was also offered.

The normal university was extended from four to five years. This reflected the debate in one aspect: because of the shortage of teachers at that time, graduates from regular comprehensive universities were assigned to teaching positions in high schools at an equivalent position with graduates from normal universities and teachers colleges. An investigation into this dilemma revealed that at first the graduates from normal universities were the better teachers, due to their concentrated studies and practices in educational theory and methods; but after a few years of teaching experience, the graduates from the regular comprehensive universities matched or surpassed them. As a result, the former slogan, "Keep up with the comprehensive universities," was considered the more correct approach. In the long run, however, this resulted in a weakening of courses in educational science. Other unfavorable factors involving educational science will be discussed later.

The question remained whether to emphasize educational science or the professional disciplines. Could anyone with but a professional knowledge became a teacher, school administrator, or a higher level educational official? Or, in other words, was specific training in the educational field an advantage? Obviously, the results of the investigation were not analyzed objectively. The differences between the two types of graduates were, in the main, due to that very complicated reasoning. Several aspects of the analysis were neglected. First, there existed between the two types of universities a difference in academic quality. These differences were shaped historically, which could not be immediately erased. The teaching of educational science, as adapted from the Soviet Union, was dogmatic and uninteresting, and there was a lack of true educational research. This was particularly so in the courses of pedagogy and psychology. In other words, the introduction of these courses was quite new and much improvement was required; and many students and some administrators did not like the educational science courses. Furthermore, students at both universities exhibited differences in academic preparation, social background, and overall quality. Teachers, too, had differential career performance records – some highly motivated and competent and others less so.

Even if attention were paid to raising the social, economical, and political status of teachers, the government was unable to realize the importance of an educational science of teacher education and of a long-range strategic viewpoint. However, a smaller portion of the budget was allotted for education. The psychology courses were criticized as being pseudoscience and were withdrawn. These typical actions reflected the shortsighted analysis of the class struggle taking place within the academic area.

During the period following the Great Leap Forward (1960-62), the entire educational system, including teacher education, was readjusted. Several errors were recognized and measures taken to correct them. For example, there had been a too rapid expansion of normal universities and schools, which resulted in a lowering of quality overall. An incorrect analysis had been made of the field of educational science and psychology and this, too, was corrected as psychology was reintroduced into the curriculum. The central government and the Chinese Communist Party (CCP) acknowledged their previous mistakes and engaged in self-criticism. The two-slogan debate, which had disrupted the field of teacher education, was stopped and educators were encouraged to analyze both positive and negative aspects of both types of schools and focus their attention on improving teacher education without choosing sides in the debate. Finally, it was recognized that the 17 years' experience in teacher education prior to the GPCR was an important period in laying the base of a new teacher education program consistent with the new period of the PRC. Even during this period there were some "leftist" defects that left a negative impact; however, they were corrected in 1962. Thus, while teacher education programs developed somewhat slowly before the Cultural Revolution, during the Cultural Revolution they were completely devastated and kept surpressed for the duration (See Table 9.2).

TABLE 9.2.
Development of Normal Schools and Student Teachers

	1946	1950	1956	1958	1962	1965	1970	1971	1976	1980	1981
Schools	902	586	598	1028	558	394	402	636	982	1071	961
Students (in 1,000s)	246	159	273	386	182	155	32	120	304	482	435

Note: 1946 was the highest year before 1949, including Taiwan and overseas Chinese schools.
Source: Constructed by the author from various interviews.

TEACHER EDUCATION: THE CULTURAL REVOLUTION

After a period of stagnation that covered the first five years of the Cultural Revolution (1965-70), most normal schools were demoted to regular high schools. Beginning in 1970 with the heavy demand for primary and secondary schools, their rapid development resulted in a frantic call for teachers, and normal schools began reopening in order to supply the demand.

Although the normal schools were reopened, normal universities and teachers' colleges remained closed. It was not until 1973 that the universities began their recruitment for student teachers. By 1971 the rush for mass education proceeded so rapidly and the demand for teachers was so intense that students were eagerly pressed into teaching services before they had time to graduate from the normal schools. As a consequence, most of the new teachers for the primary and secondary schools were recruited from graduates who had just completed primary and/or high schools.

In the countryside it was the poor and lower middle peasants who managed the schools. A certain number of peasants recruited as teachers had very limited educational background. The purpose of recruiting this social class into the educational ranks was to strengthen their class consciousness and overall class education. These teachers, in the main, composed the later components of the minban (people-managed) teachers' group and helped to fill to overflowing the teaching ranks with an even greater percentage of unqualified teachers. Students recruited for normal schools during the so-called class struggle were eliminated from any chance of learning the more intricate professional field of educational science. It was said that only about one-third of the total class hours were utilized for the teaching of professional content, which, of course, added to the severe collapse in the quality of teachers.

Most of the teachers were considered bourgeois intellectuals. They were criticized severely by officials in the government and CCP and this attitude descended through the system until the students themselves turned on their educators. Disrupting the classroom was soon considered heroic. For instance, a young girl openly objected to the teachers' regular class assignment and became a heroine. With Jing Qing's support, a new movement was born — to rise against teacher authority. The Gang of Four entered the dispute and roundly criticized "shi-dao-xun-yan" (sanctity of the teachers' doctrine), and no longer offered pedagogical protection or concern for the training of teachers. Those responsible for the cultivation of education were left with their hands tied. The final blow was the discontinuance of, and activity in, the Teacher's Trade Union.

Near the end of the Cultural Revolution, the normal universities, teachers' colleges, and normal schools were reopened, but the unified regulations adopted as guidelines for teacher training before the Cultural Revolution were no longer valid. The academic levels in the various schools for teacher training were not standard. This resulted in a dilemma that was laborious to overcome. Some normal universities recruited students with the equivalent of a junior high school education and some work experience, while some normal schools (formerly equal to high schools) recruited senior high graduates. This unequal and paradoxical recruitment system for replenishing the teaching force lasted until 1978, when at last the unified entrance examination was again restored.

However, in some local provinces the normal schools continued to recruit high school graduates until the 1980s. These contrary methods of recruitment were the determinants in the lack of stabilization of the quality of teachers. For instance, the universities provided higher level teaching professions, but the students enrolled in their classes had but junior high level schooling. In contrast, the normal schools provided instructors who had a lower level of learning than their students of senior high level.

FOUR MODERNIZATIONS PERIOD: 1980-PRESENT

After the Cultural Revolution but during the Four Modernizations Movement a new emphasis was placed on education. As Deng Xiaoping expressed it, "To realize the purpose of the Four Modernizations, education is the fundamental base." The educational process itself began its recovery and teacher education was reborn.

The Fourth Teacher Education Meeting involving the entire country of China was held in June 1980. Among the participants were principal authorities in the Communist Party Central Committee. This meeting proved especially significant for the development of Chinese teacher education inasmuch as the importance of a revised method of training teachers was reaffirmed and climaxed the growth of teacher education over the past 30 years. The authorities stressed that the status of teachers was to be improved, for without teachers the schools could not remain open. Society as a whole was called upon to heed these warnings and was advised to respect teachers and cherish their students, since only through the teacher could education regain priority and mass education — the basis and starting point for fundamental educational enterprises and improvement of scientific and cultural levels — develop. From this point forward, teacher education was to be the focal point when launching the programs for improved education, which, like a machine tool that not only produces the product but also produces the machine that makes the product, educates the qualified personnel and also trains the qualified teachers to educate the qualified personnel. It was noted that such a solid foundation would not only last for generations, but what was needed above all else to implement the programs was to improve teacher training to a superior quality. At the meeting the requirements for the recruitment of students for the different levels of teacher education was reestablished to what had been defined in the early 1950s, the contradictory requirements were corrected, and the teachers assured that henceforth the requirements could not be changed wantonly without permission from governmental authorities.

Also debated was how to improve teacher education and how to solve other current problems that plagued the system. Landmark decisions resulted. Areas deliberated were: improving the social status of teachers, establishing educational standards for teachers, requirements to be defined for teacher certification, strengthening educational research so as to build socialistic educational theories, the main concerns involving current teacher education, and the tendentious problems of the near future requiring identification.

Three basic requirements for teacher education were finally defined. First, a teacher must possess a noble-minded personality and a lofty spirit in order to be a model for students. Second, a teacher must possess a wider range and more concentrated professional and modern scientific knowledge than heretofore. Third, a teacher must master educational theories, and know thoroughly and put into practice the rules of education. Of course, different requirements are specified for the different levels of learning.

THE SYSTEM OF TEACHER EDUCATION, CURRICULUM, AND PEDAGOGICAL GOALS AND OBJECTIVES

In the normal universities and the teachers' colleges, the length of study required was four to five years of education. The objective was to train teachers and researchers in educational science as well as to train administrators in certain professional management competencies for application to the educational administrative bureaus.

Besides the four categories mentioned earlier, the curricula in normal universities and teachers' colleges were to teach students the up-to-date knowledge of their speciality and further enhance their preliminary competence in the field of scientific research. In addition to the curricula of their speciality, educational theories and teaching aptitudes are still emphasized.

In higher teacher education, the teaching program prescribed a probationary period of subject teaching and practice to be a classroom (homeroom) teacher. The probationary period and the courses of educational science were to be scheduled during the first two years of the curriculum. After the courses in educational theories, the student was to participate in six weeks of teaching practice, and, except for observation of the master teacher's methods and classroom activities, the student teacher was required to instruct four to six class periods in a speciality and to organize an activity for the classroom. To implement these activities, of course, requires a detailed teaching plan.

It was pointed out that it was necessary also to raise the level of educational research and teacher education, and to strengthen and enhance the quality of adjunct schools (primary and secondary). This is especially consequential because the adjunct schools are either where the student teacher practices his/her craft or they are the educational research base. Inasmuch as most of the adjunct schools had been sabotaged during the Cultural Revolution, and had not for sometime been involved with the role for which they were originally intended, the budgets, the facilities, and the personnel necessary for their reconstruction and enhancement were at last being given due consideration.

In recent years, the development of teacher education has been rapid. In 1980 there were 161 normal universities and teachers' colleges and 210,000 enrolled students. Comparing this to 1949, students in higher education then numbered only 12,000. You can easily visualize the degree of change. Unfortunately, both the quantity and the quality of higher teacher education is far from reaching the projected goal. For example, although the quality of education is much higher than at any time since the Great Leap Forward, it still does not reach the highest peak of China's educational history. The quantity of teachers also needs to be accelerated. According to the ration of 20:1 — of student:teacher — there are still needed 3 million teachers to replenish the secondary schools.

The Ministry of Education, in order to raise and guarantee the quality of university-level teacher education, has prescribed that in each province the key normal university and teachers' colleges can recruit students from the first level, as also can key nationwide universities. Too, superior young students enrolled in the secondary schools are encouraged to become candidates. In the meantime, it is stipulated that the leadership of the key normal universities provide adequate experiences and proper examples for their graduates, for those graduates from the teachers' colleges, having once acquired the higher level of education, could become the backbone for quality education in high schools.

During the Cultural Revolution, normal schools and preschool normal schools suffered from a period of confusion. Following the Fourth Teacher Education Conference, normal schools returned to a more regular pattern. Student requirements and quality returned to a level similar to that required during the 1950s. The period of study was increased from the three years of the Cultural Revolution to three to four years — an effort to raise standards and quality in line with the new criteria. The goals and objectives of the normal schools were redesigned to be more flexible and diverse, thus preparing graduates to fulfill the varied needs of being a primary teacher. With respect to the curriculum, normal schools included the following three components.

General courses for senior high schools. Included were courses in Chinese language and literature, mathematics, politics, English, physics, chemistry, biology, physiological hygiene, history and geography, and physical education. In this respect, the preschool normal schools and the regular normal schools have almost identical requirements, although preschool normal schools place greater stress on child development. For example, special courses focus on children's literature in both the Chinese language courses and the literature courses. The emphasis is on the history of children's literature, the analysis of children's literature, and methods of compiling and telling children's stories. In national minority normal schools special courses are offered in minority languages. There is also a special section on horticulture and animal husbandry, as related to teaching young children. Finally, preschool hygiene is offered in the preschool normal schools.

Education courses. Included were courses in pedagogy, psychology, and teaching methods for different subjects. In normal schools the pedagogy courses are concerned with education for the general public, while in preschool normal schools special courses have been developed for preschool pedagogy. The psychology course in the normal school is a standard educational psychology course utilizing a unified textbook for all normal schools. In preschool normal schools, a general psychology course is offered, 40 percent of which is focused on child psychology. Teaching methods courses consist of several courses related to those offered at the precollegiate level. In the normal schools, there are usually methodology courses for the teaching of the primary language courses, arithmetic (with teaching materials for the primary mathematics course), physical education, art and music, and teaching materials and methods for the primary general knowledge (natural science) course. In the preschool normal school, the methodology courses are wider ranging and are combined with child development concepts. This includes language development, arithmetic, general knowledge of nature, music, dance, and fine arts. The major difference between three- and four-year curricula is that in the latter more time is allotted for education courses and teaching practice.

Teaching probation and practice. Usually during the first year, students had an opportunity to go to adjunct primary schools to observe master teachers and participate in the classroom (both kindergarten and regular primary grades). In the second year they engaged in practice teaching, either teaching a specific course or observing one particular student. At the kindergarten level, they engaged in nursery school work for about three weeks. In the third year, they either spent about four to six weeks in a kindergarten or six weeks in a primary school. In comparison with university teacher education, normal schools required that the students learn and develop in a more practical and active manner. In addition, two weeks per school year were assigned to physical labor with the eruption of the third year.

IN-SERVICE TRAINING

In-service teachers' education became one of the larger branches of teacher education. The Fourth Teacher Education Meeting indicated that the huge percentage of unqualified teachers was a national disgrace. According to one investigation, one-third of the teachers in primary and secondary schools were unqualified, and it was estimated that even after taking in-service training, 1 million teachers would still fit into this category. In other words, unqualified teachers will occupy 10 percent of the total teaching force. This dilemma is of deep concern to the Ministry of Education, therefore in-service teachers' training is gaining closer attention. One factor in eliminating the problem is to reestablish in each province, city, and autonomous region one educational institute or an institute of teacher in-service training.

There are a variety of methods and means of developing in-service teacher training. The most fundamental would be to reestablish those schools that train teachers in this speciality. A first step was taken in 1977 by the Ministry of Education after holding a forum principally to discuss on-the-job training. From that time forward progress was made throughout the country, and the primary and secondary school system began its slow road to recovery. A nationwide network of teacher in-service training courses branched outward. By the fall of 1980; 30 or so educational institutes were in operation in the provincial areas; practically every province boasted of at least one such school. In addition, 2,000 prefectural (or municipal) educational institutes, institutes of in-service training, or schools for teacher in-service training were established at the county level. There were approximately 50 normal universities and colleges.

It had been decided at the Fourth National Teacher Education Meeting that the institutes mentioned should be placed on an equal basis as that of teachers' colleges and normal schools. These institutes and schools were, indeed, an important component of the teacher educational system in China. On the one hand, in face of the overwhelming percentage of unqualified teachers, it would be necessary to form a specific organization to train students for on-the-job teaching. On the other hand, this would have a strategic impact over the long term since teachers must update their knowledge at frequent intervals.

The institutes of teachers' in-service training are responsible for the various programs. There are some programs lasting approximately one-half to one or two years in which the teachers are released from teaching duties yet still receive their regular pay. Such programs consist of only one special course, or offer basic courses covering rudimentary knowledge. Some of the special programs present various educational theories through either systematic lectures or colloquia. The various lectures or colloquia are usually scheduled once every week, or one every two weeks. For instance, Beijing Teachers Training Institute organized psychology and pedagogy lectures for teachers of all primary and secondary schools in the city. Attendance was required. The lectures were offered through the radio broadcasting stations and the invited lecturers were primarily professors at Beijing Normal University and the Beijing Teachers College. The lecture drafts were available to the participants in advance and some school districts provided tutors and gave examinations on the material covered. The series impressed the educational circles and, as a consequence, many provincial educational institutes used the drafts and reprints of the presentations for their own institutes. The teachers proved eager to participate in the program and began to view the field of education through new eyes.

Besides training in theory, the offerings of different subjects in the institutes of teachers' in-service training initiated improved practical skills. Teachers were instructed in research methodologies of various kinds, activities were organized to instruct in the preparation of lessons, to clarify the teaching materials, and to select the proper teaching methods, provide references, and so on.

Correspondence courses were offered through some of the normal universities and colleges, and advanced courses for teacher training through a so-called TV University. Teachers, then, could obtain instruction in three ways — through organized classrooms, self-instruction via television, or correspondence courses. Many school districts and the school itself provided aid to the younger or inexperienced teacher by means of "model" teacher demonstration classes, or by organization of more experienced teachers into advisory groups.

In general, then, it can be said that various kinds of in-service teacher education programs were offered. At the institute level, three basic types of in-service education can be found. The first is a full-time program, two years in duration, whereby teachers continue to receive full pay and are given a two-year leave of absence. Second, spare-time programs are available, three years in duration, whereby teachers are given leave time during the school year (as well as utilizing vacation time) in order to study and attend classes and experiment in the laboratory. Finally, correspondence courses are available, again for three years, primarily on the teacher's own time. However, at least one month per year is devoted to classroom instruction.

Universities and colleges also offer in-service teacher education. The first type is a regular four-year term of study with teachers being given leave with pay from their previous employers. The second approach is part time for five years, and the third type is a correspondence approach for five years.

Special in-service courses and programs are also offered for school administrators, these lasting for one-half to one year. These courses are offered at the provincial level and focus on educational science and policy formation and analysis. Finally, new programs are being offered for developing a new contingent of university leaders in university administration and management.

In summary, the recent teachers' in-service training program in China has developed in many directions, although the program is hampered by the fact that it is still in the recovery stage. The status of the less qualified teachers has not completely changed, but certainly the outlook seems promising. From 1977 to 1980 more than

1 million high school teachers and 1.3 million primary school teachers participated in the in-service training programs. This means that roughly one-half of the teachers have already received such training, and one-half are yet to participate in the program. This is quite an achievement when one thinks of the original deficiencies in the educational system.

To assure future training for unqualified teachers, the Ministry of Education requires that each teacher be given, before the year 1985, the means and methods of reaching the prescribed qualifying goals. If any teacher remains unqualified after training, he/she will be transferred to another position outside the teaching field.

When a teacher has attained the national goals, he/she may then take the certifying qualification exam. Upon receipt of the certification, the instructor may proceed to further training. Those who have not received formal school education, but have proven their abilities through correspondence, TV courses, or self-instruction are qualified also to receive certification and are promoted to the same level as that granted those graduates from the formal schools. This regulation serves to motivate many teachers to take all means for enhancing their own education.

To improve the quality of teachers, it has become a primary concern of the officials to advance the teachers' social and economical position. Therefore, the Chinese government has recently increased the salaries of teachers to at least a living wage.

CONCLUSION

The development of teacher education in China evolved through a torturous path. Realizing that teacher quality is of profound significance to the enhancement of the country's cultural future, the government has recently taken many measures to ensure improvement in the programs for teacher education and teacher on-the-job training. There is yet a long road to travel before these goals are completely fulfilled and there are problems still to be solved; for example, even though the teachers' social and economic position is fast climbing, their salaries still remain in the low category.

And while a great portion of the teachers have received ample training, it is only the beginning step in the right direction, for the overall quality — when compared to the historical past — still remains low. The recovery process, especially in educational research, must suffer through an arduous maze before it can reach its goal. Even though many institutes of educational research have been established and educational research is emphasized in the programs of normal universities and colleges, the Chinese educators and psychologists do not boast of teaching their own theories of curriculum or educational psychology and pedagogy. But as the system ushers in confidence, this will be introduced. Reform of the secondary educational structure is certainly under way, but since the development of professional teacher education is a new issue, there are many improvements yet to be made.

REFERENCES

The information contained in this chapter comes from a variety of sources including the author's own experience and personal knowledge. For further information on current development in teacher education in China, the following sources are available in Chinese.

1982

"Jiao yu bu zhao kai quan guo jiao yu xue yuan jiao shi jin xiu yuan gong zuo hui yi" (The Ministry of Education Convened the National Working Conference of Educational Colleges and Colleges for Teachers' Advanced Studies). Renmin Jiaoyu, no. 1, January 1981, p. 61.

Tang Ruizhan, "Mian xiang xing xue ban hao zhang shi" (Run Well Secondary Teacher Education to be Geared to the Needs of the Primary Schools). Renmin Jiaoyu, no. 6, June 1982, pp. 11-13.

Shanghai shi jiaoyu xueyuan, "Jian chi jin xiu biao zhun pei yang he ge jian shi" (Insist on the Standards of Advanced Studies, Train Teachers to Become Qualified). Renmin Jiaoyu, no. 6, June 1982, pp. 7-8.

"Bi xu jia qiang jiao yu xuon yuan uiao shi jin xiu yuan xiao de jian she" (The College of Education and Teachers' College of Advanced Studies Must Be Strengthened). Renmin Jiaoyu, no. 6, June 1982, pp. 5-6.

1981

"Zhong deng shi fan jiao yu bi xu mian xing xiao xue" (Secondary Teacher Education Must Be Geared to the Needs of Primary Schools). Renmin Jiaoyu, no. 5, May 1981, pp. 49-51.

1980

"Jiaoyubu zhao kaiquan guoshi fan jiaoyu gongzuo huiyi" (The Ministry of Education Has Convened the National Working Conference on Teacher Education). Guangming Ribao, July 3, 1980.

"Henan 8000 minban jiaoshi jinru shifan xuexiao xuexi" (8000 minban teachers in Henan Province Enter Teacher's Schools To Study). Guangming Ribao, September 25, 1980.

"Quefu shifanxueyuan nuli ban hao hanshou jiaoyu" (The Qufu Teachers College Strives to Run Well Correspondence Education). Guangming Ribao, September 20, 1980.

"Guangzhou Teacher's College for Advanced Studies Issued Graduation Certificates to Secondary School Teachers Who Attained the Bachelor's Level through Self-Study," Guangming Ribao, October 2, 1980.

"Lingling shifan ren zhen ban hao shao shu minzushi fan ban" (Lingling Teachers School Conscientiously Runs Well the Teachers Education Class for National Minorities). Guangming Ribao, October 9, 1980.

"Yueyang xian hen zhuashi zi pei xun gongzui" (Yuenyang Country Vigorously Promotes the Work on Teacher Education). Guangming Ribao, November 30, 1980.

"Shanghai xiang 188 xuejiao shi ban fa ying yu zhuan ye zi xue kao shi bi ye zheng shu" (188 Shanghai School Teachers Were Issued Graduation Certificates on Self-Study Examination of English Language Subjects). Guangming Ribao, November 27, 1980.

"Jiaoyubu pin qing 75 wai ji jiao shi zai quan guo she dian p-i xun gao xiao ying yu shi zi" (The Ministry of Education Has Invited 75 Foreign Teachers To Train English Teachers for Higher Schools). Guangming Ribao, December 25, 1980.

10

REVOLUTION AND REFORM
IN EDUCATION:
PROSPECTS AND PROBLEMS

J.N. Hawkins

During the past two and a half decades, China's educational system has undergone dramatic shifts in both policy and practice at all levels. Each of the preceding chapters demonstrates the dimensions of these changes. The two periods that have served as the focus of this study on one level appear to be diametrically opposed to each other with respect to goals and objectives, theory and practice, and overall implementation strategy. More often than not, the entire 25-year period has been marked by conflict and contention, seen even today when stability is desperately being sought. Yet conflict and change have been an endemic part of China's educational history since 1949. There have been at least four major educational reform efforts that resulted in both political and institutional change. During the period 1950-57, the educational system was transformed from the framework of the 1920s and 1930s to one more conducive to a system of state socialism. In 1958, the Great Leap Forward included a restructuring of the schools, especially in the area of introducing productive labor into the curriculum. As we have seen, the GPCR resulted in an effort to totally restructure the schools, and today a massive reform effort is underway to bring order and stability (as well as quality) back to the arena of education. Over these rather hectic years, much progress has been made. Adult literacy has steadily risen despite periodic setbacks and enrollment ratios for each level of schooling have dramatically improved over time. The number of educational institutions has increased at a geometric rate and much progress has been made in science and technology when compared with other large developing nations.

On another strata, the national economic level, progress has been significant as well. The GNP has grown steadily at about 6 percent since 1952, which compares favorably with both developing and industrialized nations alike. Industrial output has risen each year by about 9 to 10 percent and agricultural production by about 2 to 3 percent. Despite all of the nay-saying about the Great Proletarian Cultural Revolution, Chinese economists and policy-makers will quietly concede that during the tumultuous period a great deal of rural modernization occurred, especially in the area of the introduction and expansion of appropriate technology. One might well ask then why all the conflict, policy shifts, political purges, and casting of blame on previous administrations? At the risk of overgeneralizing, it appears that China's vast population has placed education in the position of being an even more scarce resource than it is in many other developing nations. Although the role of population in determining educational policy does not dominate published policy discussions in the Chinese press, and at times was strictly forbidden, it clearly dominates discussions and interviews I have had with Chinese officials since 1966. China's current census shows slightly over 1 billion people in the nation, half of whom are school age. How best to allocate the scarce resource of education (from teachers to physical plant, textbooks to seats in a classroom) has been a major source of disagreement among China's leaders since 1949, and especially during the two periods we have focused on in this study. Stated in simple terms, the debate has centered on how to achieve both growth and equity within the population and resource context. These two goals often collide, even in nations not facing China's tremendous constraints. The situation appears in even more relief in the case of China because of a national ideology (espoused by both GPCR and Four Modernizations leaders) that stressed both equity and growth and maintains that they can be achieved simultaneously. Regardless of some of the elitist language currently appearing in China's publications, and Deng Xiaoping's "whatever works" mentality, the long-range goals of the modernization movement are focused on improving the quality of life and educational opportunities of China's workers and farmers. The contradiction that has faced China's leaders in attempting to achieve both equity and growth was most evident during the GPCR and since 1976. If one dissects slogans that are still in use in China, it is possible to line up the following emphases under each of the two periods:

GPCR	Four Modernizations
Red	Expert
Practice	Theory
Manual Labor	Mental Labor
Self-Reliance	Interdependence

Both administrations would disagree that these concepts are mutually exclusive and we are cautioned that listing them as such is a device only to see trends and emphases. Yet as the previous chapters have demonstrated, educational policy and practice during the GPCR, as expressed in published documents and witnessed in the schools, placed much more emphasis on political education and activism (Red), learning by doing, and vocational education (practice), combining schooling with productive labor (manual labor), and seeking both national and international independence (self-reliance). By contrast, the Four Modernizations Movement is focusing attention on research and development and higher education (expert), core curriculum and fundamentals (theory), and developing strong links with other nations for cultural, scientific, and technical interchange (interdependence).

Seen in terms of the educational system and its components the two periods might be contrasted as follows:

	GPCR	Four Modernizations
SYSTEM:	one track	multiple tracks
	short cycle K-9	conventional cycle K-12
	mandatory postsecondary moratorium	direct route to university level possible for about 4%
CURRICULUM:	reduced course load	increased course load
	lower standards	emphasis on high standards
	affirmative action policy for workers and peasants	achievement focus — "promote the bright, hold back the dull"
	emphasis on all students moving through the system together ("no fails" policy)	general education focus
		centralized textbook production
	vocational-technical focus	
	decentralized curriculum development policy	
ACCESS:	social class as a major determinent for admission to higher levels of schooling	meritocratic emphasis; focus on examinations for screening; rural-urban gap not a priority
	effort to reduce rural-urban gap	

There are many finer points of distinction between the two periods and these have been discussed in the previous chapters, but the table above serves to highlight major policy areas. With respect to the distinction raised earlier between equity and growth, in some respects it can be said that political and educational leaders during the GPCR were prepared to sacrifice growth for advances in equity, particularly for industrial workers and rural farmers (at least in theory). China's current leaders, on the other hand, readily admit that there are and will continue to be inequities between groups in China; but sustained and dramatic growth policies ("modernization") over time will reduce the resource inequalities such as access to education. One approach was clearly more extensive (labor absorbing, mass line, improving inputs, appropriate technology, and so on) and the current approach more intensive (capital-intensive, high technology, technology transfer, human capital approach). Both approaches entail costs; those incurred during the GPCR are being paraded for all to see; those being incurred during the current period are not yet readily apparent. It remains to be seen how the new administration will handle the costs once they become critical.

Outside observers will continue to be surprised and frustrated with future shifts in China's educational and development policies. In the area of educational policy and practice as linked to broader social change efforts, there are at least four research areas that will in the future warrant scrutiny. They have been touched upon in this study but will continue to raise more questions than have heretofore been answered.

First, regardless of leadership changes and factional disputes over the past three decades, there has been an overall commitment to achieve some fundamental goals of socialism, as defined by China's Marxist theoreticians. Many of these goals are directly related to both formal and nonformal education, and the educational system as a whole has been remarkably successful in discharging the responsibility of transmitting skills, expanding educational access to sectors of the population previously denied, and in providing moral-political education designed to result in a new socialist person. These achievements would not have been possible if educational reform and change had been allowed to develop in an evolutionary manner. The various revolutionary movements launched since the 1911 revolution of Sun Yat-sen have represented a dialectical process in which internal and external contradictions have forced changes in educational priorities. The Red-Expert debate, referred to throughout this book, has been the most visible of these contradictions. Undoubtedly, there have been a variety of influences intermixed with China's changing policies that include differing styles of leadership, international politics, systemic factors such as historical background, culture, and social organization. It is in this area of changing policies that future research is needed to determine more precisely the forces and factors behind the socialist revolution in education in China.

Second, since 1949, a major theme throughout China's educational experience has focused on the issue of educational access. Within the broad confines of Chinese Marxism on the issue, the range of approaches advocated has been substantial. There have been those in the Chinese Communist Party (CCP) that held firm to the belief that having ovethrown landlord and bourgeois rule in 1949, the progression from socialism to communism would be rapid and ridden with conflict. In this scheme, all levels of schooling would be for the exclusive use of China's peasants, workers, and soldiers. Closely related to this concept has been the position that under socialism a strictly egalitarian educational policy should be pursued. Everyone within the ranks of the peasants, soldiers, and workers should move along through the educational track together – or not move at all. Eventually, the society as a whole would become a school, and artificial institutional and intellectual differences would disappear. Finally, the so-called pragmatists, the current leadership, have maintained that individual differences must be recognized and that the schools must respond with a differentiated curriculum. This group optimistically maintains that 30 years of proletarian dictatorship has cleansed Chinese society of the ruling class elements opposed to socialism and, therefore, the concern over the revival of the bourgeoisie is unwarranted. The implication is that a multilayered school system is justified and, in fact, is necessary in order to achieve the egalitarian goals stipulated by competing factions. Of these various approaches, which is correct? Or, as one Chinese educational official queried, does the change in political-economic conditions dictate at any one time different means of achieving the same end?

Scholars interested in the relationship between pedagogical theory and practice will want to study the apparent contradiction between official Chinese interpretations of socialist pedagogy and actual educational practices and outcomes. The central question perhaps is, "how is socialist pedagogy defined?" In pursuit of the answer, a variety of other questions must be posed regarding classical Marxist theory, the contributions of other theorists such as Lenin, Stalin, and Mao, and the relative power of regional and cultural-specific factors associated with nationalism.

Third, although at times China has shown a preference for developing in relative isolation, within educational circles there has been an ongoing debate as to the benefits and dangers of educational transfers of the cross-national type. What, in the modernization effort, will be Chinese and what will be international? Does contact with the differing social, political, cultural, and economic systems infect or somehow pollute the revolutionary innovations that have emerged since 1949? Is it possible to borrow techniques and technologies without also dragging along the unwanted elements of the political-economic system that produced them? Can China really make foreign things serve China? China's leaders have differed on these issues and will more than likely continue to experiment with different forms of educational transfers. China's current quest for education and training has resulted in the sending abroad of hundreds of students, scholars, and practitioners for advanced education and training, or in their terms, to achieve the Four Modernizations by making foreign things serve China. The rationale for such programs is often pragmatic and focuses upon the technical aspects of whatever skill is being pursued. However, a variety of other issues concerning such knowledge transfers are often ignored. In general terms these issues are:

o   What are the social and political norms involved in or affected by the proposed training;
o   What will the impact of the program be upon those norms;
o   Will the sending nation be able to receive and adapt to the newly trained scholar once he/she returns;
o   What areas of conflict might arise once the recipient returns;
o   How can knowledge transfer be carried out so that it will increase the knowledge of both the giver and the receiver?

These are questions of broad generality and will require studies of varying complexity and methods. It is possible that the current exchange program between China and the United States will involve a complex array of institutional change issues falling into at least four major clusters:

Role of the professional educator. What will the exchange program mean for the future roles of research, teaching, and professional service?   Will the definition of an "intellectual" change?

Curricular change. The literature on other nations indicates that following a significant exchange program, the curriculum of the participating institutions is likely to be affected in four areas:

o   structure: role of faculties, schools, departments, programs;
o   administration: central (presidents, chancellors, provosts), local (deans, chairs, directors, and so on);
o   courses and degree programs (degree differentiation, credit system, transfers, and so on);
o   facilities (support services, communications processing, laboratory needs, libraries, and so on).

Personnel. Change in academic personnel policy is another area often influenced by cross-national experiences:

o   use of titles (professional series; research series; administrator series, and so on);

o   reform of the reward structure (salary mechanism, stipend, research grants, travel funds, and so on);
o   promotional criteria (concepts such as tenure, merit review, and so on, are now being discussed in China directly as a result of recent U.S. contacts).

Administration. What changes are likely to occur with respect to the relative role of central (Ministry of Education) and decentralized (university level) authorities in planning, policy formulation, and implementation regarding higher education in general and individual universities in particular?

On the one hand, there are a variety of issues related to institutions receiving foreign scholars. The complexity of the issue here revolves around contradictory perceptions of the costs and benefits of the acceptance of scholars; on the one hand, most U.S. university authorities feel their institutions contribute to the success of foreign scholars, but on the other hand, wonder, in view of the time, energy, and expense involved, whether they are getting anything in return. Some relevant issues and questions are:

o   When is the point of diminishing returns reached in the program; when does the receiving institution have too many foreign scholars?
o   Does the foreign scholar bring something to the university that it would otherwise miss?
o   Does the foreign scholar make an instructional contribution to the receiving institution's own students?
o   Does the foreign scholar make a research contribution relevant to his/her field of study?

Should the current exchange program succeed in allowing China to maintain its political-economic independence and cultural integrity, and at the same time benefit from progressive developments in other countries, China would become a model for other developing nations to emulate.

Finally, the broadest issue of all is what we can learn as a whole about the role of culture and tradition, and historical background as they relate to education and social change. China's bold predilection to experiment with alternative change strategies and educational models has provided us with a rich data source for analyzing this constellation of factors. What is unique about the Chinese experience and what can be generalized or transferred to other settings? Serious questions are raised about the feasibility of adapting elements of a European political-economic theory (Marxism-Leninism) to a society that had recently emerged from semifeudalism. Some Chinese educators have even suggested that it might be necessary for China to pass through a modified stage of capitalism before it can achieve a mature form of socialism, and that in this process the schools will play a major role.

Throughout China's history, formal education has been viewed as a major vehicle for social cohesion on the one hand and social change on the other. Examples of the latter view are those dramatic periods when Chinese society was undergoing social stress and conflict (the May Fourth Movement, the revolution in 1949, the Hundred Flowers Movement, the Great Leap Forward, and the GPCR). Examples of the former are the periods of retrenchment and restoration of discipline (the Soviet influence period of the 1950s), the Liu Shaoqi period of the 1960s, and the current Four Moderniza-tions period). It is difficult to say which view will prevail at any one time in China; the ideology of Chinese Marxism provides ample documentation and logic to support both positions. Although the emphasis now is on stability and harmony (linked to rapid modernization and growth), recent reports of youth unrest and disruption within the People's Liberation Army suggest that all is not well, at least with respect to some interest groups. While no one predicts a return to the kind of mass movement characterized by the GPCR, educational officials are beginning to focus attention on the need for more political and ideological education in the class-room, higher socialist moral standards, and less individualism and competition among and between students. What cannot be doubted is that for the past three decades Chinese society has been charac-terized by both conflict and stability, and the schools have been a staging ground for implementing both models of development. The contradiction between these two approaches has placed in high relief the problems and issues facing revolutionary societies in transition. The future is problematic, but given China's historical longevity, cultural strength, and commitment to change, the prog-nosis is encouraging, and China will likely continue to be an example of a society undergoing planned social change watched carefully by developing and industrialized nations alike.

BIBLIOGRAPHY

Applebaum, R. Theories of Social Change. Chicago: Markham, 1970.

Ayers, William. Chang Chih-tung and Educational Reform in China. Cambridge, Mass.: Harvard University Press, 1971.

Barendsen, Robert D. The Educational Revolution in China. Washington, D.C.: Government Printing Office, 1975.

Barendsen, Robert, ed. The 1978 National College Entrance Examination in the People's Republic of China. Washington, D.C.: Government Printing Office, 1979.

Bennett, Gordon A., and Montaperto, Ronald. Red Guard: The Political Biography of Dai Hsiao-ai. Garden City, N.J.: Doubleday, 1971.

Bernstein, Thomas. Up to the Mountains and Down to the Villages. New Haven: Yale University Press, 1977.

Bettelheim, Charles. Cultural Revolution and Industrial Organization in China - Changes in Management and the Division of Labor. New York: Monthly Review Press, 1974.

Biggerstaff, Knight. The Earliest Modern Government Schools in China. New York: Cornell University Press, 1961.

Brugger, Bill, ed. China Since the Gang of Four. London: Croom Helm, 1980.

_____. China: The Impact of the Cultural Revolution. New York: Harper and Row, 1978.

Buck, Peter. American Science and Modern China: 1876-1936. Cambridge: Cambridge University Press, 1980.

Chen, Theodore Hsi-en. The Maoist Educational Revolution. New York: Praeger, 1974.

Chin, Robert and Ali. Psychological Research in Communist China: 1949-1966. Cambridge, Mass.: M.I.T. Press, 1969.

Chu, Godwin C., and Hsu, Francis L. K. Moving a Mountain: Cultural Change in China. Honolulu: University of Hawaii Press, 1979.

Colletta, Nat J. Worker Peasant Education in the People's Republic of China: Adult Education During the Post-Revolutionary Period. World Bank Staff Working Papers, 527. Washington, D.C., 1982.

de Bary, William Theodore; Chan, Wing-tsit; and Watson, Burton, eds. Sources of Chinese Tradition. New York: Columbia University Press, 1960.

Dennis, Jack. Socialization to Politics: A Reader. New York: Wiley, 1973.

Donnithorne, A. China's Economic System. London: George Allen and Unwin, 1967,

Fraser, Stewart E. Chinese Communist Education: Records of the First Decade. New York: Wiley, 1963.

Gamberg, Ruth. Red and Expert: Education in the People's Republic of China. New York: Schocken Books, 1977.

Greenblatt, Sidney L.; Wilson, Richard W.; and Wilson, Amy Auerbacher, eds. Organizational Behavior in Chinese Society. New York: Praeger, 1981.

Harding, Harry. Organizing China: The Problem of Bureaucracy 1949-1976. Stanford, Calif.: Stanford University Press, 1981.

Harper, Paul. Spare-Time Education for Workers in Communist China. Washington, D.C.: Government Printing Office, 1964.

Hawkins, John N. Mao Tse-tung and Education: His Thoughts and Teachings. Hamden, Conn.: Shoestring Press, 1974.

_____. Shanghai: An Exploratory Report on Human Resource Development and Food for the City. Monograph Series, Resource Systems Institute. Honolulu: East-West Center, 1982.

Howe, Christopher. China's Economy: A Basic Guide. New York: Basic Books, 1978.

Johnson, Chalmers, ed. Ideology and Politics in Contemporary China. Seattle: University of Washington Press, 1973.

Kaplan, Frederic M.; Sobin, Julian M.; and Andors, Stephen, eds. Encyclopedia of China Today. New York: Harper and Row, 1980.

Kessen, William, ed. Childhood in China. New Haven: Yale University Press, 1975.

Kuo, L.T.C. The Technical Transformation of Agriculture in Communist China. New York: Praeger, 1972.

Kwong, Julia. Chinese Education in Transition: Prelude to the Cultural Revolution. Montreal: McGill-Queens University Press, 1979.

Levenson, Joseph R. Modern China and Its Confucian Past. New York: Doubleday, Anchor Books, 1964.

Lindbeck, John. China: Management of a Revolutionary Society. Seattle: University of Washington Press, 1971.

Lofstedt, Jan-Ingar. Chinese Educational Policy. Atlantic Highlands, N.J.: Humanities Press, 1980.

Munro, Donald. The Concept of Man in Contemporary China. Ann Arbor: University of Michigan Press, 1977.

Myers, Ramon H. The Chinese Economy: Past and Present. Belmont, Calif.: Wadsworth, 1980.

1981/82 China Official Annual Report. Hong Kong: Kingsway International, 1981.

Peake, Cyrus H. Nationalism and Education in Modern China. New York: Columbia University Press, 1932.

Price, Ronald F. Education in Communist China. London: Routledge & Kegan Paul, 1979.

Prybla, Jan S. The Chinese Economy: Problems and Policy. Columbia, S.C.: University of South Carolina Press, 1978.

Renshon, Stanley Allen. Handbook of Political Socialization: Theory and Research. Riverside, N.J.: Macmillan, The Free Press, 1977.

Richman, Barry. Industrial Society in Communist China. New York: Random House, 1969.

Ridley, Charles P.; Godwin, Paul H.B.; and Doolin, Dennis J. The Making of a Model Citizen in Communist China. Stanford, Calif.: Hoover Institution Press, 1971.

Rosen, Stanley. Red Guard Factionalism and the Cultural Revolution in Guangzhou. Boulder, Colo.: Westview Press, 1982.

_____. The Role of Sent-Down Youth in the Chinese Cultural Revolution: The Case of Guangzhou. Berkeley: Center for Chinese Studies Publication, University of California, 1981.

Rozman, Gilbert, ed. The Modernization of China. Riverside, N.J.: The Free Press, 1981.

Scalapino, Robert, ed. Elites in the People's Republic of China. Seattle: University of Washington Press, 1972.

Schram, Stuart R., ed. Authority, Participation and Cultural Change in China. Cambridge: Cambridge University Press, 1978.

_____. Mao Tse-tung. Harmondsworth: Penguin Books, 1966.

Seyboldt, Peter J., and Kuei-ke Chiang, Gregory, eds. Language Reform in China. White Plains, N.Y.: M. E. Sharp, 1979.

Shirk, Susan. Competitive Comrades: Career Incentives and Student Strategies in China. Berkeley: University of California Press, 1982.

Solomon, Richard. Mao's Revolution and the Chinese Political Culture. Berkeley: University of California Press, 1971.

Starr, John Bryan. Continuing the Revolution: The Political Thought of Mao. Princeton, N.J.: Princeton University Press, 1979.

Townsend, James R. Politics in China, 2d ed. Boston: Little, Brown, 1980.

Tsang Chiu-sam. Society, Schools and Progress in China. Oxford: Pergamon Press, 1968.

Unger, Jonathan. Education Under Mao: Class and Competition in Canton Schools. New York: Columbia University Press, 1982.

Whyte, Martin King. Small Groups and Political Rituals in China. Berkeley: University of California Press, 1974.

Wolff, Arthur P. Studies in Chinese Society. Stanford, Calif.: Stanford University Press, 1978.

JOURNALS

Baum, Richard. " 'Red and Expert': The Politico-Ideological Foundations of China's Great Leap Forward." Asian Survey (September 1964): 1048-57.

Chambers, David. "Worker's Education in the People's Republic of China." Australian Journal of Adult Education 16 (1976): 51-60.

Chen, Theodore Hsi-en. "Chinese Education After Mao: More Revolutionary or More Academic." Teachers College Record 79 (February 1978): 365-88.

Dittmer, Lowell. "Thought Reform and the Cultural Revolution: An Analysis of the Symbolism of Chinese Politics." American Political Science Review 61 (March 1977): 84-85.

Dow, Marguerite. "The Cultural Revolution and China's Educational System." International Education 3 (1975): 14-23.

Erisman, A. L. "China's Agricultural Development." In People's Republic of China: An Economic Reassessment. Washington, D.C.: Government Printing Office, 1974-1975.

Fan, Wenlan. "Problems of Conflict and Fusion of Nationalities in China." Social Sciences in China 1 (1980): 83-98.

Fei Xiaotong. "Ethnic Identification in China." Social Sciences in China 1 (1980): 71-82.

Fraser, Stewart E., and Hawkins, John N. "Chinese Education: Revolution and Development." Phi Delta Kappan (April 1972): 487-500.

Glassman, Joel. "The Political Experience of the Primary School Teachers in the People's Republic of China." Comparative Education 45, no. 2 (June 1979): 159-74.

Goldman, R. J. "Education in China." Educational Forum 41 (1977): 455-63.

Hawkins, John N. "Deschooling Society Chinese Style: Alternative Forms of Nonformal Education." Educational Studies 4 (1973): 110-21.

_____. "Educational Changes in China: The Post Gang of Four Era." Educational Perspectives 18 (May 1979): 12-25.

_____. "National Minority Education in the People's Republic of China." Comparative Education Review 1 (1978): 150-72.

Hsieh, C. "The Status of Geography in Communist China." Geographical Review 49 (1959): 323-41.

Kent, Ann. "Red and Expert: The Revolution in Education at Shanghai Teachers' University 1975-76." China Quarterly 86 (June 1981): 304-21.

Kong, Shiu. "China Educates the People-Ocean." Convergence 7 (1974): 32-42.

Li Kejing. "Is Education a Superstructure or a Productive Force?" Social Sciences in China 1, no. 3 (September 1980): 17-18.

Liu, W. H. "The Dialectical Materialist Approach to University Administration in Peking's Post Cultural Revolution Era." Journal of Educational Administration and History 8 (1976): 37-44.

Li Yining. "The Role of Education in Economic Growth." Social Sciences in China 2 (1981): 66-84.

Lucas, Christopher. "Academic Work and Productive Labor in Contemporary China." Journal of Career Education 2/4 (1976): 57-65.

_____. "Maoist Pedagogy: In Combining Learning and Labor." Journal of Industrial Teacher Education 11 (1974): 79-84.

Martin, Roberta. "The Socialization of Children in China and Taiwan: An Analysis of the Elementary Textbooks." China Quarterly 62 (June 1975): 242-62.

Ovdiyenko, I. "The New Geography of Industry in China." Soviet Geography 4 (1961): 39-56.

Pepper, Suzanne. "Chinese Education After Mao: Two Steps Forward, Two Steps Backward, and Begin Again." China Quarterly 81 (March 1980): 11-12.

_____. "Education After Mao." China Quarterly 81 (March 1980): 1-65.

_____. "Education and Revolution: The 'Chinese Model' Revisited." Asian Survey 18, no. 9 (September 1978): 847-90.

_____. "Education and Revolution: The 'Chinese Model' Revisited." Asian Survey 18 (1978): 847-90.

Price, R. F. "Chinese Textbooks: Fourteen Years On." China Quarterly 83 (September 1980): 550-62.

Ray, Dennis. " 'Red and Expert' and China's Cultural Revolution." Pacific Affairs (Spring 1970): 22-33.

Reynolds, Bruce L. "Two Models of Agricultural Development: A Context for Current Chinese Policy." China Quarterly 76 (December 1978): 842-72.

Riskin, Carl. "Local Industry and the Choice of Techniques in the Planning of Industrial Development in Mainland China." Planning for Advanced Skills and Technologies 3 (1969): 171-81.

Shirk, Susan. "Educational Reform and Political Backlash: Recent Changes in Chinese Educational Policy." Comparative Education Review 23, no. 2 (June 1979): 183-217.

_____. "Integrating Work and Study in Chinese Education." Liberal Education 63 (1977): 271-83.

Shor, Ira. "Education to the People: Higher Education in China." Social Policy 5 (1974): 30-37.

Swetz, Frank. "Field Survey: An Aid to Geometry Instruction in the PRC." School Sciences and Mathematics 73 (1973): 335-43.

Sigurdson, J. "Rural Industry: A Traveler's View." China Quarterly 50 (1972): 21-69.

Solomon, Richard. "On Activism and Activists: Maoist Conceptions of Motivation and Political Role Linking State to Society." China Quarterly 39 (July-September 1979): 76-114.

Tien, Jocelyen Slade. "Everyone Getting Ahead; Nobody Left Behind: Education in the People's Republic of China." Journal of Educational Thought 9 (1975): 183-91.

Unger, Jonathan. "Bending the School Ladder: The Failure of Chinese Educational Reform in the 1960's." Comparative Education Review 24, no. 2, pt. 1 (June 1980): 221-37.

_____. "The Chinese Controversy Over Higher Education." Pacific Affairs 53, no. 1 (Spring 1980): 29-31.

Vogel, Ezra. "From Friendship to Comradeship: The Change in Personal Relations in Communist China." China Quarterly 21 (January-March 1965): 46-60.

Whyte, Martin King. " 'Red and Expert' Peking's Changing Policy." Problems of Communism (November-December 1972): 18-27.

INDEX

ABOUT THE CONTRIBUTORS

JOHN N. HAWKINS is an associate professor of comparative and international education and director of the Curriculum Inquiry Center at the University of California, Los Angeles. He has conducted research on educational policy and planning in Asia for the past 15 years and is a specialist on education and national development in the People's Republic of China. He is the author of five books on education in China and Asia. He holds degrees from the University of Hawaii, the University of British Columbia, and a Ph.D. from George Peabody College at Vanderbilt University.

CHEN QI is a professor of education at Beijing Normal University, Beijing, People's Republic of China. She specializes in early childhood education, particularly mathematics, and in teacher training.

NAT J. COLLETTA is a research associate and specialist in the Far East for the World Bank, New York. His specialty is in the areas of adult education and education and work. He has published widely in the field and has worked internationally on the relationship between education and work. He is the author of Adult Education in the People's Republic of China (New York: World Bank, 1983).

IRVING EPSTEIN is a doctoral candidate specializing in comparative and international education at the University of California, Los Angeles. He has taught on the secondary and adult school levels in the United States, Australia, Hong Kong, and Taiwan. His previous publications, which concern themselves with various aspects of Chinese education, have appeared in International Education, Peabody Journal of Education, and Comparative Education Review. At this time he is completing his doctoral dissertation on juvenile delinquency and reformatory education in Chinese society.

STANLEY ROSEN is an assistant professor of political science at the University of Southern California, Los Angeles. He is author of Red Guard Factionalism and the Cultural Revolution: Guangzhou (West View Press, 1982) and The Role of Sent-down Youth in the Chinese Cultural Revolution (Center for Chinese Studies, University of California, Berkeley, 1981). Beginning in 1984 he will be the editor of Chinese Education.